The Ruthless Critique of
Everything Existing

T0349275

Andrew Feenberg is the author of *Critical Theory of Technology, Questioning Technology, The Philosophy of Praxis,* and *Technosystem.* He has taught at Simon Fraser University and the Collège International de Philosophie.

The Ruthless Critique of Everything Existing

Nature and Revolution in Marcuse's Philosophy of Praxis

Andrew Feenberg

VERSO

London • New York

First published by Verso 2023
© Andrew Feenberg 2023

1 3 5 7 9 10 8 6 4 2

Verso
UK: 6 Meard Street, London W1F 0EG
US: 388 Atlantic Avenue, Brooklyn, NY 11217
versobooks.com

Verso is the imprint of New Left Books

ISBN-13: 978-1-80429-083-5
ISBN-13: 978-1-80429-084-2 (UK EBK)
ISBN-13: 978-1-80429-085-9 (US EBK)

British Library Cataloguing in Publication Data
A catalogue record for this book is available from the British Library

Library of Congress Cataloging-in-Publication Data

Names: Feenberg, Andrew, author.
Title: The ruthless critique of everything existing : nature and revolution
  in Marcuse's philosophy of Praxis / Andrew Feenberg.
Description: Brooklyn, NY : Verso, 2023. | Includes bibliographical
  references and index.
Identifiers: LCCN 2022040969 (print) | LCCN 2022040970 (ebook) | ISBN
  9781804290835 | ISBN 9781804290859 (US ebk) | ISBN 9781804290842 (UK
  ebk)
Subjects: LCSH: Marcuse, Herbert, 1898-1979. |
  Science—Philosophy—History—20th century. | Critical theory.
Classification: LCC B945.M2984 F44 2023 (print) | LCC B945.M2984 (ebook)
  | DDC 191—dc23/eng/20221024
LC record available at https://lccn.loc.gov/2022040969
LC ebook record available at https://lccn.loc.gov/2022040970

Typeset in Minion by Biblichor Ltd, Scotland
Printed and bound by CPI Group (UK) Ltd, Croydon CR0 4YY

For Felix, Liv, and Flynn

"If we have no business with the construction of the future or with organizing it for all time, there can still be no doubt about the task confronting us at present: the *ruthless critique of everything existing,* ruthless in that it will shrink neither from its own discoveries, nor from conflict with the powers that be."

Karl Marx, 1843

Contents

Acknowledgments ix

Introduction x

1. Remembering Marcuse 1

2. Marcuse's Marx 15

3. The Logos of Life 76

4. The Politics of Eros 109

5. The Critique of Technology 131

6. A New Concept of Reason? 166

Conclusion: A Look Back 216

Index 227

Acknowledgments

Thanks for helpful comments and suggestions are due to Ian Angus, Robert Pippin, Martin Jay, David Ingram, Stefano Giacchetti Ludovisi, Steven Crowell, John Bellamy Foster, Charles Reitz, Thomas Lindemann, Pietro Omodeo, Ivan Domingues, Hans Radder, Frédéric Monferrand, Dana Belu, and Steven Taubeneck. Special thanks are due to Anne-Marie Feenberg for her help, both theoretical and practical, throughout the long process of writing this book.

These chapters contain extensively revised material from the following sources:

"Realizing Philosophy: Marx, Lukács, and the Frankfurt School." In *Critical Theory and the Challenge of Praxis*, edited by Stefano Giacchetti Ludovisi, 117–30. Farnham, UK: Ashgate, 2015.

"Remembering Marcuse." In *Collected Papers of Herbert Marcuse*, vol. 5, *Philosophy, Psychoanalysis and Emancipation*, edited by Douglas Kellner and Clayton Pierce, 234–41. London: Routledge, 2011.

"The *Logos* of Life"; "Afterword: Marcuse's Dialectic." In Herbert Marcuse, *Transvaluation of Values and Radical Social Change*, edited by Peter-Erwin Jansen, Sarah Surak, and Charles Reitz, 117–33. N.p.: Amazon, 2017.

"The Bias of Technology." In *Marcuse: Critical Theory and the Promise of Utopia*, edited by Andrew Feenberg, Robert Pippin, and Charles Webel, 225–54. Granby, MA: Bergin & Garvey Press, 1988.

"Marcuse: Reason, Imagination, and Utopia." *Radical Philosophy Review* 21, no. 2 (2018): 271–98.

"Technoscience and the Dereification of Nature." *Filosofia Unisinos* 21, no. 1 (January–April 2020): 5–13.

Introduction

For several years after 1968, Herbert Marcuse was one of the two most famous philosophers in the world—the other was Jean-Paul Sartre. His fame was due to two remarkable books he wrote while living in the United States, *Eros and Civilization* and *One-Dimensional Man*. These two books represent the utopian aspirations and dystopian fears of the time. Together, they offer an original critique of advanced capitalism focusing on the social construction of subjectivity and technology. In the 1960s and '70s, young people seeking a philosophical basis for their revolution found it here. Marcuse was so closely identified with the New Left that after its decline his theoretical contribution was overlooked. But today, that contribution is more relevant than ever.

Of course, much has changed. Political theorist Raffaele Laudani has called *One-Dimensional Man* an "untimely" book, given the differences between the integrated welfare state Marcuse criticized in 1964 and neoliberal capitalism. Yet Laudani defends Marcuse's many anticipations of current political trends. His understanding of the psychic power of advanced capitalism and the strategic perspective of his late writings resemble much current discussion on the left.[1]

In fact, after a period of eclipse, interest in Marcuse is increasing. His critique of advanced capitalism is more concrete and more obviously political than that of his Frankfurt School colleagues Horkheimer, Adorno, and Benjamin. It has inspired much recent writing concerned with the politics of the media and social movements in the United

---

1 Raffaele Laudani, "The Relevance of an Untimely Book," *Radical Philosophy Review* 19, no. 1 (2016): 63–84.

States and around the world. Indeed, Marcuse arguably offers the most usable version of critical theory.[2]

These political contributions represent an implicit challenge to the trend, deriving from Jürgen Habermas and his successor Axel Honneth, in which critical theorist Michael J. Thompson sees the "domestication of Critical Theory." Thompson argues that the turn toward pragmatism and philosophy of language has blunted the radicalism of the first generation of the Frankfurt School, as exemplified by Marcuse.[3]

This book is primarily concerned with Marcuse's philosophy, especially the most puzzling and difficult aspects of his thought. However, his philosophical views are inseparable from his politics. This is particularly true of his critique of science and technology. He elaborates on the critique of instrumental reason, a central preoccupation of Horkheimer and Adorno that has since been abandoned by their successors in the Frankfurt School. In my view, this is one of his most important political contributions for us today. It will be considered at length here.

Despite Marx's own interest in technology, there are surprisingly few Marxist philosophers who deal with the subject. However, in recent years, the global COVID-19 pandemic, the crisis of the environment, and a growing fear of surveillance have placed technology back on the agenda. In particular, Marcuse's critique of media manipulation, rejected during the heyday of cultural studies, rings true in the new world of corporate-based social networking. His critique of behaviorism and operationalism in *One-Dimensional Man* could hardly be more up

---

2 For examples, see John Abromeit and W. Mark Cobb, eds., *Herbert Marcuse: A Critical Reader* (New York: Routledge, 2003); Andrew Lamas, Todd Wolfson, and Peter Funke, eds., *The Great Refusal: Herbert Marcuse and Contemporary Social Movements* (Philadelphia: Temple University Press, 2017); Terry Maley, ed., *One-Dimensional Man 50 Years On: The Struggle Continues* (Halifax: Fernwood Publishing, 2017); Arnold Farr, *Critical Theory and Democratic Vision: Herbert Marcuse and Recent Liberation Philosophies* (New York: Lexington Books, 2009). The *Radical Philosophy Review* published two special issues on Marcuse, in 2013 (vol. 16, no. 1) and 2016 (vol. 19, no. 1). There is also considerable interest in Marcuse's philosophy and politics in Brazil; see *Artefilosofia: Homem Unidimensional* 10, no. 18 (2015).

3 Michael J. Thompson, *The Domestication of Critical Theory* (London: Rowman & Littlefield, 2016), 41–2. See also Stathis Kouvelakis, *La critique défaite: Emergence et domestication de la théorie critique* (Paris: Éditions Amsterdam, 2019).

to date in the era of big data, with its promise of ever more effective control of human beings. Environmentalism only became an important public issue toward the end of his life, but his advocacy of the protection of nature from the destructive force of technology was deeply rooted in his philosophy. The critique was not, however, unqualified. Marcuse also recognized the constructive uses of science and technology on the basis of which a socialist society could be built.

I was one of Marcuse's last students. Although I was never a disciple, his work inspired my interest in technology, and I have written about him in previous books and articles.[4] I interpret his thought as a contribution to what, in the English-speaking world, is called continental philosophy. This book brings together and completes my ideas on his work. I introduce here new perspectives that help to understand the originality of his interpretation of Marxism. Chapters 2 and 6 contain critical reflections on problems in his ontology and his critique of science. I propose new approaches to these controversial aspects of his thought.

I regret not having had the chance to debate these issues with him while he was alive, but I have been slow to understand all the implications of my own reservations about his thought. I grew up quite literally in the midst of the scientific community and spent most of my childhood and adolescence enthusiastically studying science. I was simply too familiar with the world of natural science to believe that philosophy could foresee its future. This may explain why I could never accept Marcuse's speculations about the future of natural science under socialism. Yet, at the same time, I was impressed by the concepts he derived from his critique of science as they applied to technology. It has taken a long time, but I have finally resolved my ambivalence. Here, I can only offer my side of a missing dialogue.

My goal is not to provide an overview of Marcuse's whole work but to concentrate on several of the most significant episodes in his development. These include his early work on Hegel and on Marx's *Economic and Philosophical Manuscripts* of 1844, as well as his revolutionary interpretations of psychoanalysis, technology, and aesthetics. In each of these episodes, his approach depends on a quasi-phenomenological

---

4 See, for example, Andrew Feenberg, *Heidegger and Marcuse: The Catastrophe and Redemption of History* (New York: Routledge, 2005); Andrew Feenberg, *The Philosophy of Praxis: Lukács, Marx, and the Frankfurt School* (London: Verso, 2016), chapter 8.

concept of experience, a Hegelian theory of potentiality, and, in the later work, a Freudian theory of the imagination.[5]

Marcuse's early Marxist work was written under the influence of Heideggerian phenomenology. However, even while he studied with Heidegger, he frequently delivered Marxist correctives to the excessive abstraction of his teacher's thought—for example, introducing class difference into the concept of "worldhood." Most commentary on his work accepts his own later view that he left phenomenology behind in his review of Marx's *Manuscripts* in 1932.

Marcuse's own late evaluation of his relation to Heidegger's thought seems to me only partially correct. He was neither as loyal a Heideggerian in his youth, nor as free of his influence later, as he claims.[6] It is true that Heidegger's specific doctrine no longer plays a role in Marcuse's work after 1932, but he never gives up important aspects of the underlying conceptual framework of phenomenology, especially the distinction between the lived world of everyday experience and the empirical facts studied by natural science. My argument is thus not that he remained a Heideggerian, with all the dubious political associations that implies, but that his work takes up certain technical achievements of phenomenology and incorporates them into Marxism. His purpose, I contend, was to provide an account of subjectivity that was lacking in the Marxist tradition.

I came to this conclusion reflecting on what Marcuse himself calls the "outrageously unscientific" demand for a "liberation of nature"—a counterintuitive demand that is only the most extraordinary of many other puzzling notions.[7] What are we to make of his claim that science and technology are ideological and that art holds the power to redeem them? Taken seriously, these strange notions open the door to a renewed

---

5 For a broad discussion of all aspects of Marcuse's work, see Douglas Kellner, *Herbert Marcuse and the Crisis of Marxism* (Berkeley: University of California Press, 1984). See also Barry Kātz, *Herbert Marcuse and the Art of Liberation* (London: Verso, 1982); Charles Reitz, *Art, Alienation, and the Humanities* (Albany: State University of New York Press, 2000.)

6 For this, see Frederick Olafson, "Heidegger's Politics: An Interview with Herbert Marcuse," in *The Essential Marcuse*, ed. Andrew Feenberg and William Leiss (Boston: Beacon Press, 2007), 115–27.

7 Herbert Marcuse, "Nature and Revolution," in *Counterrevolution and Revolt* (Boston: Beacon Press, 1972), 65.

interest in phenomenological themes in Marcuse's work. These themes are largely implicit, but I will show that they play an essential role in his thought.

Marcuse's early writings already announce the basic concepts of the work that comes after. Two concepts are especially important: *reason*, the capacity to know the universal and, on that basis, to freely create projects that transcend the given; and *potentiality*, the perpetual dissatisfaction of beings with their current state as they strive for a higher state. These concepts are addressed, over and over, through the many twists and turns of Marcuse's thought. Let me briefly sketch their role.

Reason operates with universal concepts that enable the ordering of the infinite flux of experience in a coherent world. That world can be understood rationally in terms of its nature and the laws that move it. But reason is also a subjective disposition, a mode of being. As such, it empowers the rational individual to hold the world and its own impulses at a distance. Reason thus achieves a free relation to reality. Marcuse is centrally concerned with the *existential meaning of rationality* in this sense. It is the basis of critique and so makes possible revolutionary consciousness. It forms a bridge between the objective knowledge of capitalism represented by Marxist theory and the subjective action that challenges it. The concept of potentiality mediates between the two, on the one hand, as objective social tendencies and, on the other hand, as consciousness of possibilities denied by the system.

Since Plato, philosophers have known that the ordering work of reason is incomplete. Particulars fall short of the perfect realization of the concepts that identify them. No drawing of a triangle is actually a triangle; no white object can be perfectly white. But if that is so, concepts cannot be reduced to particulars. They contain what Marcuse calls a "transcending" content that is available to the experiencing subject as a sense of incompleteness or imperfection. In the case of life, and especially of society, that content takes the form of potentialities awaiting realization. These potentialities are real, not simply as theoretical projections but in a strong sense that implies an ontology to which Marcuse repeatedly referred but never fully elaborated.

Consciousness of social potentialities must be attributed to the imagination because it alone has the power to project beyond the given toward an ideal form. Marcuse argues that the imagination is an essential aspect of rationality since it directs the subject toward a valid, if unrealized, dimension of the experienced world. He understands the tension between real and ideal in Hegelian terms as the truth of the negative. The universal is not merely different from the particular but "negates" it, condemns its imperfection, and implicates the subject in the realization of its potentialities.

The imagination is a psychological faculty as well as a source of insight into reality. In attributing an essential cognitive role to the imagination, Marcuse binds ontology to psychology. *Eros and Civilization* develops that connection on the basis of Freud's instinct theory.

As Marcuse interprets Freud, the imagination is associated with the erotic, in a generalized sense he understands as life affirming. Life is motility, becoming, development. The gap between imagined fulfillment, the universal, and the actual condition of particular beings is the stimulus to development. Life is perpetually engaged in overcoming that gap through transforming the environment and absorbing it into the world of the self. The utopian realization of the universal is not the static resolution of the contradiction between concept and object, but its deployment under social conditions that permit a continuing development of human capacities. The Marxist application of these ideas is obvious. Marxism has always considered socialism to be a potentiality of capitalism, its negation and true significance in the history of humankind.

In *One-Dimensional Man*, Marcuse argues that among the conditions of socialism is a transformation of technology, which now provides a total life environment, a "world" in the phenomenological sense of the term. Marcuse was the only member of the Frankfurt School to address the issue of technology in detail. Adorno and Horkheimer introduced the concept of instrumental reason in *Dialectic of Enlightenment* but never developed its implications for technology beyond their initial critique. Marcuse's concept of technological rationality echoes this critique but concretizes it, suggesting an alternative form of rationality corresponding to the spirit of a socialist society. His concept of technological rationality may seem abstract, but it opens up concrete paths for critique and reform I explore here, as I have in several books on the philosophy of technology.[8]

---

8 See, for example, Andrew Feenberg, *Technosystem: The Social Life of Reason* (Cambridge, MA: Harvard University Press, 2017).

The impulse behind Marcuse's critique of technology goes back to what Habermas derisively called the "secret hope" of the first generation of the Frankfurt School for harmony between human beings and nature.[9] The unity of subject and object promised by idealistic philosophy is a more significant source of harmonistic aspirations than the romantic *Schwärmerei* to which Habermas alludes. Idealism postulated an essential correspondence between thought and things as the guarantor of human reason. The rejection of mystery exposed the objective world to understanding and therefore also to technical control. Marxism demonstrated the futility of this promise under capitalism while renewing it for a socialist future.

Marcuse attempts to bring the idealist concept of subject-object unity down to earth and to reconstruct it as a social category. The affirmation of reason against myth remains valid, but the conception of rationality in earlier philosophy was too narrowly identified with science and technology. Capitalism turned these powers of reason into enemies of life. Technology under capitalism opposes human beings to nature in a struggle fatal for both, whereas under socialism a reformed technology could protect the natural world and favor forces in nature that contribute to human well-being.

These are the basic concepts developed in what follows. I will show how Marcuse employs them at several different levels: in his interpretation of Hegel, Marx, and Freud; in his concepts of society, world, and essence; and in the reformulation of the concepts of sexuality, aesthetics, and reason in a utopian alternative to capitalism.

Let me now briefly review the chapters of this book.

Chapter 1 is a reminiscence of Marcuse as I saw him when I was his student and an activist in various political movements in France and the United States. We shared a week in Paris during the events of May 1968. This chapter raises philosophical issues stemming from the student movement that resonate throughout the book.

---

9 Jürgen Habermas, "Technology and Science as Ideology," in *Toward a Rational Society: Student Protest, Science, and Politics*, trans. Jeremy J. Shapiro (Boston: Beacon Press, 1970), 87–8. For more on Habermas's critique and my view of Marcuse's position, see Andrew Feenberg, *Questioning Technology* (London: Routledge, 1999), chapter 7. See also Ben Agger, "Marcuse and Habermas on New Science," *Polity* 9, no. 2 (Winter 1976): 158–81; C. Fred Alford, *Science and the Revenge of Nature* (Tampa: University of Florida Press, 1985).

The second chapter discusses Marcuse's 1932 essay on Marx's *Economic and Philosophical Manuscripts* of 1844. Marcuse seeks a non-metaphysical interpretation of Marx's concept of world-constitution through labor that does not trivialize it or treat it as a metaphor, and he explains some of Marx's most puzzling propositions, such as his call for a "resurrection of nature" through social revolution. Although this text is said to mark his break with Heidegger, I show that it is still deeply implicated in phenomenology. This chapter is rather technical. While the material in the second section is essential for the following chapters, some may prefer to read this chapter at the end of the book, after its themes have been reprised in concrete contexts.

Chapter 3 addresses Marcuse's interpretation of Hegel. Hegel's dialectic offered a resolution of the dilemma opposing formalistic ethics to conformist adaptation to reality. The idea of potentiality is defined here as a critical "second dimension" of reality, providing Marcuse with a normative standpoint rooted in history. This is the background to his controversial distinction between true and false needs, which has given rise to questions about his commitment to democracy.

Chapter 4 explains Marcuse's interpretation of Freud. Marcuse's ontological categories, imagination, and life, explored in his earlier work, become concrete through psychoanalytic theory. The historicization of Freud's instinct theory adds psychological depth to his Marxism. Marcuse argues for the possibility of a "concrete utopia" that is both technically feasible and compatible with human individuality.

The fifth chapter discusses Marcuse's claim that science and technology are ideological. Here, I identify several different strands of the critique, one of which concerns the legitimating function of technology in advanced capitalism. Another identifies social bias in the concept of rationalization, while a third strand criticizes the bias of scientific-technical rationality itself.

The sixth and final chapter reviews Marcuse's puzzling proposal for an aesthetic reconstruction of scientific-technical rationality. Although this proposal is implausible, it contains unexplored resources for understanding contemporary struggles over technology and the environment.

A brief conclusion reviews the path followed in the book.

Marcuse's late thought evolved in a period of political turmoil that in important respects anticipated the crises we are living today. As calm returned with the end of the Vietnam War and the decline of the New Left, his style of thought and the rhetoric in which he expressed it went out of fashion. My purpose in this book is to reveal the philosophical basis of Marcuse's uncompromising critical stance, which is relevant to a world once again in crisis.

1

Remembering Marcuse

I first met Herbert Marcuse in 1965, shortly after he joined the philosophy department of the new University of California, San Diego (UCSD). The move to the palms and beaches of Southern California seemed to contradict the gloomy pessimism of his writings, but in person, he was not gloomy at all. I recall my own surprise at his ironic humor and rejection of the exaggerated gestures of respect that some students believed appropriate for a German professor.

Marcuse was an outstanding figure at UCSD, both as a political inspiration and as a scholar. His uncompromising criticism of the war in Vietnam made him a hero for the left-wing students on campus. However, his courses were rigorous; in the classroom, he was simply a dedicated teacher of the history of philosophy. My own initial encounter with Marcuse was strictly academic: soon after arriving at UCSD, I asked him to read *Being and Time* with me.[1] Nevertheless, he became a target of conservative criticism and was eventually expelled from the university in a complicated maneuver designed to placate Governor Ronald Reagan while preserving the appearance of academic freedom.[2]

---

1 We disagreed from the very start. I recall arguing that Heidegger's existential analysis presupposed what Husserl called "pure consciousness." I insisted that Heidegger "bracketed" the natural attitude. Marcuse protested, rightly, that Heidegger was opposed to the very idea of consciousness and situated his analysis at the level of reality. But what is meant by "reality" in this context? We never got clear on this. Now, many years later, I propose a resolution of our disagreement in chapter 2.

2 The story is told in Paul A. Juutilainen's documentary *Herbert's Hippopotamus: Marcuse and the Revolution in Paradise* (1996), video, available on YouTube.

Marcuse viewed Hegel, Husserl, and, with serious reservations, Heidegger as great idealist philosophers with whom he was still engaged in dialogue. From Hegel, he took the idea that each stage in history lives in the shadow of a better future, the realization of which it obstructs. Those of us who studied with Marcuse found in his Hegelian vision a validation of our own dissent. Our protests, we now understood, were not merely personal but belonged to History with a capital H.

Marcuse believed, perhaps incorrectly, that he took very little from his teacher Heidegger. While his disappointment over Heidegger's Nazism was never assuaged, he nevertheless acknowledged the importance of Heidegger's false path as an advance to the outer limits of bourgeois philosophy.[3] What did he mean by this backhanded tribute?

Marcuse criticized Heidegger's early phenomenological approach for abandoning the concrete ground of history. But there was something right about a philosophy that resisted the hegemony of the "facts," the uncritical scientistic naturalism then predominant in American philosophy. And Marcuse's own most radical speculations on the "new sensibility" of the New Left implied a phenomenological concept of lived experience, an "aesthetic *Lebenswelt*." Despite his skepticism about phenomenology, he imparted a therapeutic dose of experiential philosophy that immunized some of us against positivism.

Even before he became famous, Marcuse was the star of the UCSD philosophy department. His erudition and charm gained him the respect of many scientists in this science-dominated university. His speeches at rallies against the war in Vietnam were attended by hundreds and eventually thousands of students on our rapidly growing campus. We knew how fortunate we were to have such a teacher, and I think he was truly dedicated to us, despite our clumsiness and naivete.

---

3 For Marcuse's own view of his relation to Heidegger, see Frederick Olafson, "Heidegger's Politics: An Interview with Herbert Marcuse," in *The Essential Marcuse: Selected Writings of Philosopher and Social Critic Herbert Marcuse*, ed. Andrew Feenberg and William Leiss (Boston: Beacon Press, 2007). Marcuse's sharp criticism of Heidegger is confirmed by a rude response to an inquiry from Karel Kosík in which he dismisses Heidegger's thought as worthless or worse. But, as we will see in chapter 2, this is not the whole story. Herbert Marcuse, "Letter to Karel Kosik," in Herbert Marcuse, *Marxism, Revolution and Utopia*, ed. Douglas Kellner (London: Routledge, 2014), 322.

He took his intellectual mission seriously, but he also demonstrated with us for our causes, which were his as well.

When Angela Davis, his student, was accused of murder and placed on the FBI's Ten Most Wanted list, he defended her publicly, attracting undesirable attention on the right. When his life was threatened, his students showed up to patrol his house. When he was fired from the university, we wanted to protest, but he discouraged us; he had worked out a deal allowing him to finish his work with his last graduate students, from which I benefited. His priorities were clear.

Marcuse is remembered today primarily for his remarkable prominence during the late 1960s and '70s. Few philosophers have achieved such fame. After all, he was not just a "public intellectual"; he was a media celebrity—precisely the sort of figure he criticized in his writings.

I was present when he first discovered this paradoxical status. At that time, he was already well known on the left in the United States and Germany, but he had not yet become famous in the world at large. In early May of 1968, he arrived in Paris for a UNESCO conference on Marx, just as the largest protest movement of the '60s broke out a few blocks from his hotel.[4]

The May Events were precipitated by a movement like no other in an advanced industrial country then or since. A nationwide student revolt was relayed by a general strike. Nearly ten million workers joined the movement, and hundreds of factories were occupied by their workers. Soon, schools and government ministries joined in. But the police and military continued to support the government, and that was enough. After several months of violent protests, the movement receded, and "order" reigned again.

Upon entering the UNESCO conference hall, Marcuse was swarmed by journalists with cameras and notebooks. Unbeknownst to him, a press campaign in the preceding week had painted him as the "idol" of the student revolt. (A few weeks later, the newspapers published articles refuting their own inflated estimate of his role.)

Observing Marcuse's discomfort at this unexpected attention, a young reporter whispered in my ear that he would be happy to help "*le*

---

4 For my view of the May Events and translations of documents, see Andrew Feenberg and Jim Freedman, *When Poetry Ruled the Streets: The French May Events of 1968* (Albany: State University of New York Press, 2001).

professeur" escape. When he promised to ask no questions, I agreed to relay his message. We soon found ourselves in a small car fleeing the scene, to Marcuse's great relief. The reporter offered to take us anywhere in Paris. Marcuse asked to meet the North Vietnamese delegation to the Paris peace talks, which had just begun.

At the desk of the Lutetia Hotel, we requested an audience with the Vietnamese. They sent us the delegate responsible for public relations. He was a small, extremely thin, poorly dressed fellow who could not have looked less like a diplomat. He opened the conversation by complimenting Marcuse on his great age. Marcuse was taken aback. He did not think of himself as the "ancient of days"; on the contrary! After a further exchange of compliments, the conversation took a political turn. Marcuse warned the Vietnamese not to count on the American working class to end the war. His interlocutor nodded in agreement. No doubt, the Vietnamese had reached the same conclusion long before.

On the walk to his hotel afterwards, Marcuse was recognized by the students who had just seized the École des Beaux-Arts. They invited him to address their general assembly. He greeted them in the name of the American movement, praising them for rejecting consumer society. This puzzled the Maoists in the audience, who were seeking a Chinese-style "worker-peasant alliance" against French capitalism. Marcuse presented a rather different notion in his UNESCO talk, "Re-Examination of the Concept of Revolution."[5] He argued that the revolution was no longer just a matter of replacing one ruling class with another, but also concerned the technological underpinnings of modern societies. The "continuity of domination" could be broken only by transforming the repressive technological infrastructure.

Marcuse's Marxism was very different from the "orthodoxy" that prevailed among most of the French left at that time. Like his Frankfurt School colleagues Horkheimer and Adorno, he had lost hope in proletarian revolution for the foreseeable future. Advanced capitalism had integrated the working class. Consumer society offered benefits, to be sure, but it blocked progress toward a democratic form of socialism made possible by the very same technological advance that "delivered the goods." The new contradiction of the society, succeeding the

---

5 Herbert Marcuse, "Re-Examination of the Concept of Revolution," in *Marxism, Revolution and Utopia*.

now-muted struggle between capital and labor, consisted in the contrast between its immense wealth, sufficient under socialism to provide everyone with security and leisure, and the unending competitive scramble for an ever-increasing supply of private commodities. To the extent that this contradiction becomes conscious and provokes resistance, the society is threatened.

Marcuse soon identified this threat with the French May Events of 1968. This was the last major outburst of opposition to advanced capitalism. Its famous slogan, "All Power to the Imagination," corresponded exactly with his radical vision. Nineteen sixty-eight was the "messianic moment," in Walter Benjamin's sense, if on a small scale that only prefigured the future. It laid down the horizon of progressive possibility for our time. Marcuse paid tribute to the activists who animated this moment in the preface to his most optimistic book, *An Essay on Liberation*.

Marcuse recognized himself in the students rebelling around the world, who in turn recognized themselves in this figure from a heroic past. Young people rejecting consumer society and the capitalist "rat race" found in him an ally, as they performed the "Great Refusal" of which he wrote in his books. His confidence in the validity of ethical and social ideals and his call to defend them challenged the prevailing cynicism.

What was it about Marcuse that made him a symbol of this moment? He was not flamboyant and did not seek publicity. His writings were considered obscure, and although his books sold widely, it is hard to believe that they were widely read. Two things made him such an attractive symbol: the convergence of certain of his ideas with the sensibility of the movement, and a peculiar kind of personal authority he emanated. He was not only old; he was a German philosopher who had lived through many of the major events of the twentieth century and survived to tell the tale. It is easy to dismiss the enthusiasm of youth, but not so easy to ignore the fidelity of age to the dreams of youth.

This is where Marcuse, like his friend, the Marxist literary critic Lucien Goldmann, differed from many of those who attended the UNESCO conference. In the middle of one tedious panel discussion, Goldmann expressed outrage that we were merely discussing revolution while the real thing unfolded outside the conference hall in the streets. But not all the participants took the movement seriously.

Adorno's notion that the movement was a form of "pseudo-activity" had a certain currency among older left-wing intellectuals who failed to recognize themselves in its slogans, demands, and, crucially, its style.[6] After Marcuse left Paris, I met a well-known Italian Marxist in the courtyard of the Sorbonne, which we students had "liberated" a few days before. I was full of enthusiasm, but he complained that we had created a mess—"*casino, casino!*"—not a revolution. Marcuse did not share our confidence that revolution was around the corner, but he appreciated our spirit and found traces in it of the "negativity" advocated by the Frankfurt School.

As he later explained, it was merely a coincidence that his ideas linked him to a movement he no more than others had foreseen. But what a coincidence! Marcuse called for a less repressive society that valued peace and pleasure over war and sacrifice. He argued for eliminating the competitive pressures and acquisitiveness of rich societies, which have the resources to eliminate poverty and to transform work into a creative activity. He protested inequality and media manipulation, analyzing their causes in the structure of the system. These ideas, developed with philosophical rigor in his books and speeches, were all themes of the movement. Indeed, they quickly became clichés.

Much has been made of Marcuse's ideas on sexuality. He is remembered, mistakenly, as an advocate of the sort of orgiastic excess associated in the public mind with the movement, if not actually enjoyed by many of the participants. In fact, he anticipated some of Foucault's most counterintuitive conclusions about the politics of sexuality in modern societies. To explain the instrumentalization of sex by the capitalist system, he introduced the concept of "repressive desublimation," arguing that the intense focus on sexual attractiveness and sexual activity was not liberating but was part of the larger process of containing libidinal energy within the confines of the existing society.

---

6 For Adorno's rejection of the New Left, see his "Marginalia to Theory and Practice," in *Critical Models: Interventions and Catchwords*, trans. Henry W. Pickford (New York: Columbia University Press, 1998). There is an interesting discussion between Adorno and Marcuse on this subject. See Herbert Marcuse, "Correspondence on the German Student Movement," trans. Esther Leslie, *New Left Review* 1, no. 233 (January–February 1999), 123–36.

Of course, Marcuse opposed the sexual puritanism that still held sway in America, but he also sounded the alarm over exaggerated expectations of sexual liberation.[7]

A shared dystopian vision of American society constituted the most interesting of the coincidental convergences between Marcuse and the movement. The New Left experienced America as a closed system, a "Brave New World" capable of repelling or absorbing opposition. Marcuse's thought belonged to a tradition of dystopian critique that had long expressed such notions. Like Aldous Huxley, he saw a threat to individuality in the rise of modern technological society. Cultural pessimism of this sort was rare on the left, where most Marxists still celebrated technical progress while anxiously awaiting the proletarian revolution. By contrast, Marcuse emphasized the role of science and technology in the organization of a repressive system.

These themes appealed to a generation of young people who had grown up in the America of the 1950s, when the ideology of progress was at its height. After all, we were masters of the atom and had put a man on the moon. No less significant was the integration of the labor unions into consumer society, a shift that demonstrated the obsolescence of socialism. These achievements announced the end of history, the triumph of the existing society over its own utopian potential. To many in the New Left and the counterculture, radical change seemed both necessary and impossible. Paradoxically, however, by the end of the 1960s, the dystopian vision of isolated social critics like Marcuse was echoed by a mass movement. For that movement, the struggle against the war in Vietnam became a surrogate for the struggle against the imperium of technology at home.

Beyond these convergences of ideas, there was a peculiar charisma about his person, evident to those present at the many protest meetings at which he spoke. He did not indulge in the emotional gestures and rhetorical flourishes of a political orator but addressed his audience soberly, as someone authorized by historical experience and philosophical reflection. This stance made a shocking contrast to the content of his discourse. Here was an old and, presumably, wise professor calmly advocating revolution in complacent and self-satisfied America.

---

7 Herbert Marcuse, *One-Dimensional Man: Studies in the Ideology of Advanced Industrial Society* (Boston: Beacon Press, 1964), chapter 3.

But perhaps something more profound was at work in Marcuse's astonishing presence. He participated as a young conscript in the Berlin soldiers' council in the German revolution that followed World War I. He fled the Nazis and worked for their defeat during World War II and, soon afterward, for the denazification of German society. He criticized both postwar American society and Soviet communism as failed realizations of emancipatory ideals. Few of those present at his speeches were aware of the details, but these accumulated experiences were expressed in his person, in the deep and strongly accented voice that spoke with authority of the European disaster and foresaw a similar fate for American imperial ambitions, despite the triumphalist discourse of the politicians and the media.

Marcuse's presence evoked a kind of mentorship: he taught by example the value of a life of political engagement. This impression of his impact can be explained in terms of the theory of experience he shared with his Frankfurt School colleagues. They worried that modern life had damaged the capacity for experience. Presumably, in earlier times, a richer and more complex relation to reality was available. This critical notion of experience stemmed from the thought of Walter Benjamin, who distinguished between *Erfahrung*, experience shaped by a deep relation to reality, and *Erlebnis*, experience as a momentary response to passing sensation. *Erfahrung* registers the real at a subconscious level and changes the person who undergoes it, while *Erlebnis* is a defensive response to the speed and shock of daily life in a modern society. *Erlebnis* has no resonance and quickly slips out of consciousness as new experiences challenge the subject. These characteristic modern experiences leave few traces, in contrast to *Erfahrung*, which has existential depth. Marcuse represented the possibility and the result of a rich and deeply reflected political *Erfahrung*—something not yet available to his young audience.

Marcuse's long political experience and deep knowledge of Marxism made for occasional disagreements with the young revolutionaries who received him with so much enthusiasm. He constantly exhorted them to attend to theory and work on organization. *Anti-intellectualism and ritual anti-authoritarianism are false paths. Spontaneity is good, but organized spontaneity is better. No, rock concerts do not prefigure socialist community. It is foolish to fetishize violence; it has a place in defense of the right to protest, but terrorism under democratic conditions is not a legitimate political weapon*; I could continue. However, these proved to be minor disagreements, and despite them Marcuse remained in solidarity with the movement as "the true historical heirs of the great socialist tradition."[8]

As such, the New Left had something to teach Marcuse. His historical experience was not yet over; rather, his involvement in the New Left represented a final chapter in which his own ideas underwent a further transformation. What did he draw from the movement? We have his own testimony in the form of the many articles and books he wrote from the late '60s until his death in 1979. These texts testify to a revision of his earlier dystopianism. The one-dimensional society was challenged at the level of culture, if not effectively at the political level.

In this context, cultural revolution means politics in the "depth dimension" of the psyche, at the level of needs and identities. Earlier, Marcuse had argued that advanced capitalism reached down into the very instincts with its promised paradise of consumption, and thus that the manipulation of consciousness by the system leads to the internalization of social control. Now, he claimed, this overwhelming force of social integration was answered by a new form of resistance. This was not simply a matter of political opinion or intellectual critique but, more profoundly, an existential revulsion at the destructiveness of the system.

The New Left mobilized new tactics against the new psychic oppression. Instead of a unified socialist party based in the labor movement, it put forward demands emanating from various marginalized sectors of social life, such as minority communities, youth, and students. Their actions were more or less spontaneous and so difficult to prevent. In the absence of access to mass media, they innovated new ways of attracting attention, such as dramatic, even clownish demonstrations of dissent. New forms of sociability flowered, such as collective living spaces known as "communes." New media appeared, the so-called underground press, that carried the message outside the regular channels of information.

Of course, Marcuse never imagined that students could overthrow the system. He always insisted that revolution, were it possible at all,

---

8 Herbert Marcuse, "On the New Left," in *The New Left and the 1960s*, ed. Douglas Kellner (London : Routledge, 2005), 127.

could only be the work of the mass of the population. Rather, what the New Left and the counterculture revealed was a "new sensibility" that, if generalized, would destabilize the society and expose it to revolutionary transformation. This theory, explained in *An Essay on Liberation*, was an implicit response to the pessimistic vision of the decline of experience. It was the new sensibility, rather than the old idea of class consciousness, that constituted the threat to capitalism. Or perhaps it would be more accurate to say that Marcuse reinterpreted the notion of consciousness in this richer form, as revealed by the contemporary movements for radical change.

It was while studying with Heidegger in the late 1920s and early '30s that Marcuse made his earliest contribution to Marxist theory: a new theory of the revolutionary disposition as an existential stance critical of the social world. This was not the traditional notion of class consciousness, nor was it a matter of political opinions or economic interests. Under the influence of Lukács, Heideggerian concepts were given a Marxist interpretation. "Inauthenticity" was understood as reification, overcome by the "radical act." What excited him about the New Left was the return of an existential politics, a politics of global refusal of the existing society and the identities it supported. The individuals' very being rebelled at the conformist pressures of the postwar world, a resistance that was expressed not simply in discourse or strategic calculations but in emotion and action—and that had to be so expressed.

The New Left thus renewed the power of the negative, the driving force behind history. While the simple fact of negativity was not politically significant in itself, it was rendered so on account of its rejection of war and racism, demand for a just society that privileged solidarity over competition, and hope for a "pacified" relation to nature based on a less destructive technological dispensation. Marcuse conceived this as the "determinate negation" of the existing society, the potentialities blocked by the system.

Interpreted in terms of the moral and aesthetic tradition, the "new sensibility" of the New Left represented a new form of individuality and a new mode of experience that challenged capitalism in the pursuit of a more humane society. This new sensibility was informed by the aesthetic imagination, which opened up the aura of possibility surrounding the "facts of life" established by capitalism and the technological system that supports it. Why aesthetics? As Charles Rachlis aptly puts it, "The construction of a free existence is an aesthetic under-taking in that it is guided by criteria which traditionally have characterized works of art."[9] Perception was no longer confined to the given but had become critical in terms of those criteria: beauty, harmony, a focus on the essential. Alternatives to the oppressive structures of the society appeared thinkable once again. The individuals regained the mental independence required to break with the rituals of conformity that bound them to the system. The personal had become political, as participants in the movement liked to say.

For Marcuse, however, it was not enough for the personal to become political; it was also necessary for the political to become technological. Here, his thought joined that of the most radical participants in the movement. After 1968, he amplified his earlier (rather abstract) remarks on technology. At a time when many Marxists were skeptical of environmentalism, which some saw as a diversion from class strug-gle, he argued that the technological domination of both human beings and nature traces back to the same source: the indifference of capital-ism to the essential potentialities of life.[10]

But Marcuse was no technophobe. He did not propose a return to premodern conditions. Rather, he argued that the imagination could inform technological design and realize the values of the movement in the very structure of the machines. A technology respectful of human beings and nature could replace a system adapted to competition and war. This would be a technology of liberation capable of supporting a modern society without reproducing the domination inherited from the past.

These speculations on technology turned out to be prescient: a gene-ration of environmental protest has refuted old deterministic and technocratic notions, and a new spirit of concern for nature has motivated a vast movement to transform technology in response to climate change. Whether the transformation is compatible with capitalism as we know it is very much in question. If capitalism can adapt, environmentalism may

---

9 Charles Rachlis, "Marcuse and the Problem of Happiness," *Canadian Journal of Political and Social Theory* 2, no. 1 (Winter 1978): 71.

10 Herbert Marcuse, "Ecology and Revolution," in *New Left and the 1960s*; Herbert Marcuse, "Ecology and the Critique of Modern Society," in *Philosophy, Psychoanalysis, and Emancipation*, ed. Douglas Kellner and Clayton Pierce (London: Routledge, 2011).

be another scene on which the dystopian logic of the system has the power to absorb all opposition, but that is by no means clear.

What are we to make of these late developments in Marcuse's thought? While his ideas seem remote after the last forty years of increasingly reactionary political and economic developments, the horizon of radical politics has not shifted much since his day.[11] Marcuse argued that, despite its collapse in the mid-1970s, the New Left would leave its mark on the future of radical politics. It differed from earlier socialist movements in its "insistence on the subversion of experience and individual consciousness, on a radical revolution of the system of needs and gratifications, in short, the persistent demand for a new subjectivity." It called for "rebellion and change in human existence" and it "redefined the concept of revolution"—consequences of the break with the old left that persist.[12]

For the most part, left political activity no longer takes the form of party militancy but consists in the sort of punctual protests against the dominant way of life that characterized the New Left. We still hope for many of the changes it struggled to achieve. Indeed, feminism, racial equality, environmentalism, various democratic alternatives to capitalism all survive as ideals, despite what Marcuse called the "preventive counter-revolution" that reacted to the rise of this new form of radicalism.[13]

Marcuse's philosophical contribution to the early Frankfurt School is now overshadowed by Benjamin and Adorno. Nevertheless, while their ideas influenced him, his political thought goes far beyond theirs. Benjamin's politics are revolutionary, but sketched only in brilliant aphorisms.[14] Adorno's polemic against "identity" embraced not merely

---

11 Michael Thompson points out the surprising actuality of much of what Marcuse wrote in the 1960s, despite the changes. Michael Thompson, "The Work of Violence in the Age of Repressive Desublimation," in *The Great Refusal: Herbert Marcuse and Contemporary Social Movements*, ed. Andrew T. Lamas, Todd Wolfson, and Peter N. Funke (Philadelphia: Temple University Press, 2017), 163–4.

12 Herbert Marcuse, "The Failure of the New Left?," in *New Left and the 1960s*, 183–6.

13 See Herbert Marcuse, *Counterrevolution and Revolt* (Boston: Beacon Press, 1972). Pages 24 to 29 of this text contain a prescient discussion of reactionary trends in advanced capitalism that seemed exaggerated at the time, but no longer.

14 For an example of what can be built on the basis of Benjamin's aphorisms, see Michael Löwy, *Fire Alarm: Reading Walter Benjamin's "On the Concept of History,"* trans. Chris Turner (London: Verso, 2016).

the repressive capitalist version of social unity, but any harmony not confined to the ideal sphere of art. As a result, it is difficult to relate his thought to politics. Marcuse, in contrast, retained and transformed the classical philosophical project of reconciliation of individual with society, human beings with nature, and subject with object. His fidelity to that project explains why he is the only member of the Frankfurt School to have elaborated a revolutionary political theory.

The eclipse of Marcuse's thought represents a startling reversal of fortune. Hundreds of thousands of copies of his books were sold, and he was, for a time, the public face of the Frankfurt School. These books were not mere popularizations but difficult and innovative philosophical works. Yet, with the passing of the historical moment in which the Frankfurt School reached a wide public through his work, he is too often dismissed.[15] An academic culture that values difficulty and dismisses utopian thinking finds him hard to appreciate for lack of these dubious qualities, and as the left declined the academy became the main audience for radical philosophy.

Was Marcuse the naive romantic he is often taken for today? A romantic, yes, but not naive. Indeed, he was well aware of the danger of underestimating the obstacles to a radical transformation of the human condition. A print of Brueghel's famous painting of the Fall of Icarus hung on the wall of his dining room. It shows the barely visible legs of the fallen hero as he plunges into the ocean, a punishment for flying too close to the sun with his artificial wings. Perhaps the painting reminded Marcuse of the warning implied in W. H. Auden's poem: "In Breughel's Icarus, for instance: how everything turns away / Quite leisurely from the disaster."[16] Idealists, beware!

The self-irony of Marcuse's position bears emphasis: in spite of suffering terrible disappointment, he did not give up hope. Why, after

---

15 The dismissal of Marcuse started early. W. Mark Cobb, "Diatribes and Distortions: Marcuse's Academic Reception," in *Herbert Marcuse: A Critical Reader*, ed. John Abromeit and W. Mark Cobb (New York: Routledge, 2003). For a recent survey, see Maroje Višic, "Renaissance of Herbert Marcuse: A Study on Present Interest in Marcuse's Interdisciplinary Critical Theory," *Interdisciplinary Description of Complex Systems: INDECS* 17, no. 3-B (2019).

16 W. H. Auden, "Musée des Beaux Arts," in *Another Time: Poems* (New York: Random House, 1940).

all the tragic catastrophes of the twentieth century, did he not lose heart? Two motives stand out: a belief that life and nature itself contain active forces working toward survival and fulfillment, and a belief that these forces are echoed by universal reason. Thus, to give up would have been an unjustifiable betrayal, paid for in intellectual complacency and abject conformism.

Marcuse once wrote, "Critical theory preserves obstinacy as a genuine quality of philosophical thought."[17] The obstinate refusal of intellectual compromise characterizes his whole life and work, despite so many unfavorable circumstances. Samuel Beckett detected this essential aspect of Marcuse's existential stance, commemorated in a poem for his eightieth birthday:

> Pas à pas
> Nulle part
> Nul seul
> Ne sait comment
> Petits pas
> Nulle part
> Obstinément[18]

On Marcuse's gravestone is inscribed *Weitermachen*—"Keep on going."

Marcuse had a unique stance within the Frankfurt School, drawing productively on the whole tradition of Western philosophy to chart a direction for the future. That stance is relevant to today's new period of political activism, much of it posing questions around issues involving technology. While it remains to be seen whether it will take on the existential depth he identified with revolutionary possibilities, it is clear that philosophical understanding can—and must—contribute to this movement. Indeed, it is high time for a fresh look at Marcuse.

---

17 Herbert Marcuse, "Philosophy and Critical Theory," in *Negations: Essays in Critical Theory*, trans. Jeremy J. Shapiro (Boston: Beacon Press, 1968), 143.

18 Edith Fourier has translated the poem: "step by step / nowhere / not a single one / knows how / tiny steps / nowhere / stubbornly." In *Herbert Marcuse: Art and Liberation*, ed. Douglas Kellner (London: Routledge, 2007), 200.

2

Marcuse's Marx

Introduction: Existentialism or Marxism

During my junior year in college, my teachers in the United States sent me to Paris with a long list of recommended scholars. Among them were several aligned with either existentialism and phenomenology or Marxism—two of the main trends contending for hegemony at a time when Paris seemed the center of the intellectual world. Even as Europe struggled with the trauma of World War II and decolonization, it was already becoming the principal scene of the new Cold War. Large Communist parties in France and Italy represented a challenge to American hegemony. Intellectuals seeking a "third way" between Soviet communism and capitalism were drawn to existentialism and phenomenology or to heterodox interpretations of Marxism. The argument between them was one of the major theoretical controversies of the 1950s and '60s in Europe.

I was introduced to one such version of Marxism by Lucien Goldmann, whose course on Lukács I followed that year. I also attended Paul Ricoeur's course and an informal seminar at the home of the Gabriel Marcel, a Christian existentialist whom I had met during his visit to the United States the year before. This was my personal version of the great contest between Marxism and existentialism that roiled French intellectual life.

The fundamental issue was the relation of experience to objectivity. Existentialist thinkers as different as Camus, Sartre, and Marcel focused on concrete experience. Whether analyzing the experience of revolt, sex, or religious faith, they agreed that the subject of philosophy was to be found in what Bergson had called "the immediate data of consciousness." Marxists, in contrast, emphasized the objective facts of class oppression and struggle, drawing on *Capital*'s explanation of the logic of the social world that determined individual experience. The so-called "immediate," they observed, was mediated through and through. Yet Marxists were engaged with experience too. After all, they had to believe that there was something in the experience of labor under capitalism that made possible a critical attitude toward society. As the early Lukács and the late Sartre argued, experience and objectivity were destined to meet in the proletariat. Fanon applied a similar argument to the colonized.

Upon my return to the United States to study with Marcuse, I was confronted with his version of the Marxist critique of experience. He writes in *One-Dimensional Man*:

> Dialectical logic . . . denies the concreteness of immediate experience. To the extent to which this experience comes to rest with the things as they appear and happen to be, it is a limited and even false experience. It attains its truth if it has freed itself from the deceptive objectivity which conceals the factors behind the facts—that is, if it understands its world as a historical universe, in which the established facts are the work of the historical practice of man. This practice (intellectual and material) is the reality in the data of experience; it is also the reality which dialectical logic comprehends.[1]

This passage is emblematic of the puzzling ambiguity of Marcuse's whole intellectual career. He asserts, on the one hand, that immediate experience is false; that is the lesson of Marx's objective analysis of capitalism. On the other hand, another kind of experience is possible that "attains its truth" through historical understanding. What is that other experience? Qua experience, it too must have the quality of immediacy; yet it somehow incorporates a rational mediation, that is, knowledge of the historical basis of every immediacy.

The dilemma stems from what Marx calls the "fetishism of commodities"—the necessary form of appearance of objects under

---

1 Herbert Marcuse, *One-Dimensional Man: Studies in the Ideology of Advanced Industrial Society* (Boston: Beacon Press, 1964), 145.

capitalism. In Marx's explanation, the value form takes on a life of its own. Commodities act independently of the human beings who make them; indeed, they determine the thoughts and actions of those human beings. The fetishism of commodities mediates consciousness, which is plunged into an illusory world of self-acting things. The conundrum Marxism repeatedly fails to resolve is the passage from fetishistic immediacy to that other form of experience Marcuse invokes: that which penetrates the fetishistic veil and reveals the truth of the society.

Marcuse wavers between the two sides of this dilemma from one period to another. He is divided between phenomenology and the Marxist analysis of capitalism, sometimes emphasizing experience, sometimes objective knowledge. Therein lies the challenge: How can experience be coordinated with knowledge? Marcuse's response to this challenge will take us back to the strange world of early twentieth-century German philosophy.

The Philosophical Background

Marcuse first addressed the challenge during his study with Heidegger. His principal loyalty was always to Marxism, but his early essays substituted the existential concept of authenticity for class consciousness. Although he later dropped that approach, the phenomenological concept of lifeworld stays with him to the end, providing him with theoretical resources he continued to employ after he abandoned Heidegger and joined the Frankfurt School.

I contend that it is impossible to understand his work without reference to this phenomenological background. This is the most controversial aspect of my interpretation of Marcuse's thought. As such, it needs a preliminary explanation, which will occupy the first sections of this chapter. I will then show how this background influenced his unusual interpretation of Marx's *Economic and Philosophical Manuscripts*. The concluding sections will explain in greater depth the quasi-phenomenological ontology implied by that interpretation.

Phenomenology presents itself as an alternative to naturalism, the belief that natural science explains ultimate reality. In the early twentieth century, in a context of rapid scientific and technological advance, naturalism was on the rise. Much mainstream liberal thought accepted it, as did what became known as "orthodox" Marxism. The very legitimacy of philosophy was in question: What was to be its role, now that the realm of objective knowledge had been handed over to the natural sciences? Now only facts were considered real, and philosophy had no facts of its own to study. Familiar philosophical categories such as "essence," "ideal forms," "substance," "monads," and the Cartesian cogito lost their footing in the objective world. This is also the significance of the critique of the suprasensible entities posited by metaphysics, such as the soul and God—a critique which began with Kant and continues down to the present in various forms.

At the end of the nineteenth century, Wilhelm Dilthey and the neo-Kantians identified the realm of meaning as the specific domain of philosophy, a notion Marcuse develops in an early essay on the German philosopher and historian. Dilthey contrasts lived meaning with a causal account of the relations of human beings to their environment:

> Life is an "interaction complex" [*Wirkungszusammenhang*] which is essentially determined by the category of "meaning" [*Bedeutung*] . . . With the concept of interaction complex not only can the ensemble of relations which governs historico-social reality be distinguished from mere causal relations, but at the same time the real mode of being of this reality can be characterized as *becoming*.[2]

For Dilthey, the individual and the milieu stand in essential relations. A world of meaningful objects and practices corresponds to individuals' cultural dispositions and understandings. Dilthey distinguishes

---

2 Herbert Marcuse, "Das Problem der geschichtlichen Wirklichkeit," in *Herbert Marcuse: Der deutsche Künstlerroman, Frühe Aufsätze* (Frankfurt: Suhrkamp Verlag, 1978), 480, my translation. A partial French translation is available in Gérard Raulet, *Herbert Marcuse: Philosophie de l'Emancipation* (Paris: PUF, 1992), 99–102. For the influence of Dilthey on Marcuse, see Seyla Benhabib, "Introduction: The Problem of Historicity as the Starting Point and Goal of This Work. The Purpose of the Present Interpretation," in Herbert Marcuse, *Hegel's Ontology and the Theory of Historicity*, trans. Seyla Benhabib (Cambridge, MA: MIT Press, 1987); Charles Reitz, *Art, Alienation, and the Humanities: A Critical Engagement with Herbert Marcuse* (Albany: State University of New York Press, 2000), 42–6. Reitz writes, "Dilthey's neo-Kantian philosophy permeates Marcuse's effort, from his first to his last works" (ibid., 50).

the lived experience of such essential relations from contingent causal interactions, a distinction whose ramifications play out in Marcuse's interpretation of the early Marx. Responding to Marx's argument that human faculties are "objectified" in nature through labor, Marcuse interprets objectification as a positing of meaning in the built environment.

The neo-Kantians applied a related conception of meaning to the study of science, arguing that scientific facts are not simply there for the taking but must be granted meaning to become objects of study. On this view, each discipline defines the kind of objects it recognizes in nature. The philosopher of science Hans Reichenbach, who studied with Ernst Cassirer, explains the neo-Kantian concept of object construction in his early book on the theory of relativity: "The conceptual schema, the category, creates the object; the object of science is therefore not a 'thing-in-itself' but a reference structure based on intuition and constituted by categories."[3]

We are familiar today with similar ideas from Bruno Latour's ethnographic study of laboratory life, in which he detailed the practical procedures through which natural scientific objects are constructed. Similarly, Foucault explained the construction of the objects of social sciences such as psychiatry (the insane) and criminology (the criminal) in terms of discursive and social arrangements. Foucault acknowledged the neo-Kantian influence, saying, "Nous sommes tous néokantiens."[4] By this he meant that philosophers and social scientists recognize that the cross section of reality they study is selected in terms of various social determinations. In the language of neo-Kantianism, it is "posited." Chapter 6 of this book will take up the concept of object construction in the context of contemporary social struggles over science and technology.

On neo-Kantian terms, philosophy was to be pursued as a "transcendental" enterprise engaged in the study of the meaning-positing function. Roughly defined, the "transcendental" refers to prior conditions of knowledge. In Kant, those conditions are the most general

---

3 Hans Reichenbach, *The Theory of Relativity and A Priori Knowledge*, trans. and ed. Maria Reichenbach (Berkeley: University of California Press, 1965), 49.

4 "We are all neo-Kantians." Michel Foucault, "Une histoire restée muette," *Dits et ecrits: 1954–1988*, vol. 1 (Paris: Gallimard, 1994), 545–9.

categories and forms of intuition (perception) that are imposed by the mind on the material of experience. The study of conceptuality in this sense was called "logic" in this period.

One neo-Kantian in particular had a considerable influence on Lukács and Heidegger, two thinkers who influenced Marcuse. Emil Lask observed that Kant's critique of reason left a puzzling gap: what is the status of the transcendental categories and forms of intuition that order experience? According to Kant, these categories and forms grant meaning to what would otherwise be a chaos of incomprehensible sensations. They are not suprasensible entities such as God or the soul, nor are they factual constituents of the world.

To account for them, Lask elaborated an existing distinction between factual existence and validity [*Geltung*]. Things *are*, but meanings *are not*; they are *valid*—that is, they "hold" of the things of which they are the meaning. In sum, meanings are attributed to things but are not things themselves, at least not in the usual sense, and their connection to the things they name is not a material property of those things. Lask thereby opened up a third form of being, in addition to the *sensible* and the *suprasensible*: the *valid*, the realm of meaning, the subject of philosophical logic.[5] According to Lask, the study of the sensible belongs to the sciences and the study of the suprasensible to metaphysics. He called the study of the valid "alethiology," from the Greek word for truth.

Husserl radicalized a similar approach by exploring the role of subjectivity in the construction of meaning in experience. His "transcendental phenomenology" explained experience from the first-person standpoint. By contrast, natural science constructs a third-person standpoint through procedures that strip the data of perception of anything personal. Science treats the purified residue that remains as objective facts. The ideal subject of such knowledge is

---

5 Emil Lask, *Die Logik der Philosophie und die Kategorienlehre* (Tübingen: Verlag von J. C. B. Mohr, 1911). In his rather sketchy text on German philosophy of 1934, Marcuse briefly mentions Lask, for whom it is necessary "to jettison the categories of traditional logic, because these categories correspond only to the existence of reality; they are incapable of understanding the existence of values." See Herbert Marcuse, "German Philosophy: 1871–1933," in *Heideggerian Marxism*, ed. Richard Wolin and John Abromeit (Lincoln: University of Nebraska Press, 2005), 155.

the "one," as in "one observes," (*on* in French, *man* in German); an "it," not an "I."[6]

Lost in such constructions are the intentional structures of perception and certain deictic or indexical properties of experience such as "I," "this," and "now." The qualities of lived spatial and temporal experience disappear in objective representations. For example, lived space is characterized by "near" and "far," and by a "horizon" that hides further spatial experiences that are in principle available. These features of spatial experience are not found in Euclid. They are only available to a subject that is itself located in space, and they are constitutive of the spatial experience of all such subjects.

In addition, meanings implicate a subject able to recognize them. Subjectivity is thus involved both in the individual recognition of meanings, and in their cultural contingency. The point is not to dissolve existing things into subjectivity but to account for the dependence of their meanings on consciousness. For example, this dependence is intuitively obvious in the case of the many mysterious objects to be found in hardware stores. There, we confront a thing of unknown nature and use. Its existence is not in question, but its meaning is obscure. We have no idea what it "is"—that is, what it *means* to a competent subject, namely a carpenter or electrician who can recognize it. In the absence of the proper subject, it is literally meaningless.

Phenomenology is not a subjective idealism. In phenomenological language, human existence "discloses" or "reveals" a world. The structures and meanings it reveals are not imposed on the facts but illuminate them. It is perhaps easiest to understand this in terms of the concept of perspective. The various perspectives on an object—for example, a table—come together in consciousness in a virtuality we signify as a thing with the meaning "table." A perspective does not create what is disclosed; rather, it enables an aspect of reality to be perceived. But, of course, a perspective as such necessarily involves a subject.

As phenomenology conceives it, first-person experience claims a different kind of objectivity from that of natural science. Husserl's method in the study of this form of objectivity consisted in the analysis of intentional acts such as seeing, hearing, remembering, imagining,

---

6 The history of those procedures has been explained by Lorraine Daston and Peter Galison. See their *Objectivity* (Cambridge, MA: Zone Books, 2007.)

and so on. Each act correlates with a corresponding object: the seen, the heard, the remembered, the imagined. Husserl argued that the sphere of intentional acts must be investigated on its own terms, without naturalistic assumptions. He "suspended" the "natural attitude" in which we take objects to be real existents in a world independent of consciousness, not to deny existence but in order to focus on the experience in which it presents itself.

For Marcuse's generation of European thinkers, phenomenology offered the most persuasive critique of naturalism. Steven Crowell explains:

> The difference between entities and validities, the difference between what is and what holds, implies a difference between the thing and its meaning. This in turn is no empirical or "ontic" distinction, but rather a difference in the way one and the same thing is "taken"— first in straightforward experience, and then again in the reflective inquiry that grasps the conditions of possibility for the first. Meaning *is* the thing as it presents itself to phenomenological reflection.[7]

Heidegger continued the phenomenological study of meaning under the name "being." In so doing, he followed Lask's approach in distinguishing between what he called the "ontic," the realm of entities, and the "ontological," the realm of meaning. In *Being and Time*, he focused on the most general categories of meaning in human experience, which he called "existentials." The ontic realm is available to objectivistic common sense and properly studied by science. It is "founded" ontologically, in the sense that its mode of being—the kind of being it is—is determining for its nature and possibilities. There is no corresponding dependence of the ontological on the ontic.[8]

---

7 Steven Crowell, *Husserl, Heidegger, and the Space of Meaning* (Evanston, IL: Northwestern University Press, 2001), 89.

8 In Heidegger's *Being and Time*, the relation between the ontic and the ontological is complicated by the fact that Dasein, an ontic being, has an ontological role insofar as meaning can only be revealed through it. This complication does not change the independence of ontology from ontic action. Marcuse, in any case, considered Heidegger's categories static and rigid, which I assume means that, in *Being and Time*, ontological categories are not influenced by the variety of their ontic instances. This seems plausible, but Kurt Mertel has a different interpretation. See his "Toward a Social Paradigm of

Here are two examples that clarify this distinction. The nature of language, its "ontological constitution," is not altered by the addition of new words to the vocabulary. These "ontic" changes do not change the nature of language as such, but, on the contrary, are only possible because language is what it is. Similarly, human technical interventions into nature do not change nature's ontological constitution, its essence, but are only possible because nature is what it is: the sort of thing subject to technical interventions. No particular technical intervention can change *that*. As Mallarmé put it, "Un coup de dés jamais n'abolira le hazard."[9]

Heidegger applied this ontological approach to a concept of "world-hood," understood as the basis of meaning in general (a concept to which I shall return later in this chapter). He emphasized the unity of the subject, *Dasein*, with the meaningful objects associated with its practice. His use of the term "metaphysics" in a critical sense varied from one period to another, but in *Being and Time* it corresponds in important respects to Lask's.[10] Metaphysics, as traditionally understood, confounds the problem of validity with the identification of a particular being that grounds beings. This terminology was shared by Marcuse in his early writing, and, even in his later work, "ontology" retains a conceptual background from that period. I will use the terms "ontology" and "metaphysics" in this sense.

Of course, other definitions of these terms are possible, but these are noteworthy for imposing a clear division of labor between philosophy and natural science: philosophy will not posit real entities, and science will not pretend to explain being. A certain austere reserve was required on both sides. Although Marcuse's postwar writings appear to violate that reserve, I will show that his most provocative claims apply within the lifeworld. In other words, what looks like metaphysics is

Left-Heideggerianism," in *Marxism and Phenomenology*, ed. Bryan Smyth and Richard Westerman (Lanham, MD: Lexington Books, 2020), 180–1.

9 Stéphane Mallarmé, *Un coup de dés jamais n'abolira le hasard* (Paris: Gallimard, 1993). "Never will a throw of the dice abolish chance."

10 Steven Crowell, "Transcendental Logic and Minimal Empiricism," in *Neo-Kantianism in Contemporary Philosophy*, ed. Rudolf A. Makkreel and Sebastian Luft (Bloomington: Indiana University Press, 2010), 172n27. For more on Heidegger's concept of metaphysics, see Iain Thomson, *Heidegger on Ontotheology: Technology and the Politics of Education* (Cambridge, UK: Cambridge University Press, 2005).

actually still within the boundaries separating science from everyday experience.

There was another influence on Marcuse and the other young Marxists who created the Frankfurt School: a remarkable book published by Lukács in 1923 entitled *History and Class Consciousness*.[11] Responding to Marxism's unfinished theories of ideology and consciousness, Lukács introduced a new theory based on a quasi-transcendental concept of meaning. This is the significance of his notion of reification, which was foundational for later Western Marxism. Indeed, Marcuse acknowledges *History and Class Consciousness* as "a contribution to the development of Marxism that is essential and whose importance cannot be overestimated."[12] Although Lukács is hardly mentioned, his theories of reification, totality, and revolution underlie Marcuse's interpretation of the *Economic and Philosophical Manuscripts*.

Lukács rejects the notion that social change can be understood simply through causal interactions. Like Gramsci, he understands the revolutionary process as the collapse of bourgeois hegemony, the advent of a new structure of meaning—a change in what he calls the "form of objectivity" (*Gegenständlichkeitsform*) of social objects. This concept derives from neo-Kantianism, where it occupies the place of Kant's transcendental categories. The form of objectivity defines the basic characteristics of thinghood, which may be different in different epochs and different domains. For example, artistic works have qualities as objects that differ from the qualities of everyday utilitarian objects, and this difference varies from one epoch to another. In Lukács's theory, the form of objectivity signifies the way objects are generally conceived in society and the corresponding practices and institutional realities.

Reification is the ultimate form of objectivity under capitalism. It defines the objectivity of social objects—that is, their intelligibility—and implicates their existence in processes that appear to have a deterministic logic. As such, the reified objects appear as isolated things

---

11 See Douglas Kellner, *Herbert Marcuse and the Crisis of Marxism* (Berkeley: University of California Press, 1984), 40, 381n27.

12 Herbert Marcuse, "On the Problem of the Dialectic," in *Heideggerian Marxism*, 67. There are relatively few references to Lukács in Marcuse's early writings, but his insistent use of Lukács's terminology testifies to a profound influence.

in causal relations. This meaning structure prevails as a consequence of the generalization of commodity exchange.

Lukács attributes this version of his quasi-transcendental approach to Marx himself. In his reading, the capitalist system constitutes society in terms of economic categories:

> Marx has formulated this idea in countless places. I shall cite only one of the best-known passages: "A negro is a negro. He only becomes a slave in certain circumstances. A cotton-spinning jenny is a machine for spinning cotton. Only in certain circumstances does it become capital. Torn from those circumstances it is no more capital than gold is money or sugar the price of sugar." Thus the forms of objectivity of all social phenomena change constantly in the course of their ceaseless dialectical interactions with each other. The intelligibility of objects develops in proportion as we grasp their function in the *specific* totality to which they belong.[13]

With these notions, Lukács brought Marxist philosophy into the general philosophical consensus of the time, with its focus on meaning and rejection of both metaphysics and naturalism. However, in Lukács's Marxist version, the meaning-granting function is no longer identified with individual consciousness or some variant of consciousness such as Heidegger's Dasein but with the unconscious collective practice of capitalism. Importantly, this is not a regression to naive materialism. Meaning is still "posited"; it is not a "fact" in the scientific sense. But now, the positing is performed by a system of interlocking human relations—an economic system that, when viewed as the source of meaning, Lukács calls the "totality." The totality encompasses not only

---

13 Georg Lukács, *History and Class Consciousness*, trans. Rodney Livingstone (Cambridge, MA: MIT Press, 1971), 14, translation modified. The quoted passage is from "Wage Labor and Capital," in Karl Marx and Friedrich Engels, *The Marx-Engels Reader*, ed. Robert C. Tucker (New York: Norton, 1978), 207. For further discussion of the relation between Lukács's theory of reification and contemporary neo-Kantianism and phenomenology, see Andrew Feenberg, *The Philosophy of Praxis: Lukács, Marx, and the Frankfurt School* (London: Verso, 2014); Konstantinos Kavoulakos, *Georg Lukács's Philosophy of Praxis: From Neo-Kantianism to Marxism* (London: Bloomsbury, 2018); Richard Westerman, *Lukács's Phenomenology of Capitalism: Reification Revalued* (New York: Palgrave Macmillan, 2019).

the reified categories of the economy but also the human activity operating within the framework of those categories. The revolutionary subject emerges within that totality and bursts the framework, initiating a process of dereification that alters the form of objectivity of the social world.

In his interpretation of Marx's *Manuscripts*, Marcuse relies implicitly on Lukács's theory. He writes that "one of the crucial aspects of Marx's theory" is

> the breakthrough from economic fact to human factors, from fact [*Tat-"sache"*] to act [*Tat-"handlung"*], and the comprehension of fixed "situations" and their lawfulness and thing-like character, which are beyond human power, as in motion in the course of their historical development, out of which they have fallen and become fixed.[14]

One could hardly find a better brief summary of *History and Class Consciousness*.

This radically historical social theory was no longer really transcendental in the proper sense of the term, but it retained the essential distinction between meaning and factual existence. It was thus a bridge between Marxism and contemporary philosophy. In his *Considerations on Western Marxism*, Perry Anderson criticized those who crossed this bridge for abandoning Marx's supposed materialism for idealism.[15] But in reality, Marx was much closer in spirit to these later thinkers than to the crude materialist doctrine attributed to him by "orthodox Marxism." This was verified, at least for so-called Western Marxists, with the 1932 publication of Marx's *Manuscripts*.

---

14 Herbert Marcuse, "New Sources on the Foundation of Historical Materialism," in *Heideggerian Marxism*, 93.

15 Perry Anderson, *Considerations on Western Marxism* (London: New Left Books, 1976).

Marcuse's Phenomenology

Marcuse's earliest Marxist essays, written while he was a student of Heidegger, are explicitly phenomenological. However, the synthesis with Marxism made possible by Lukács's work became untenable once Heidegger, the leading German phenomenologist, came out as a Nazi. The concept of authenticity, which offered Marcuse an existential basis for revolutionary action, appeared bankrupt. At this point, he had to choose. The choice was made easier by the discovery of Marx's *Manuscripts*. Shortly after their publication, Marcuse wrote one of the earliest reviews of the previously unknown text.[16] He dated his break with Heidegger from this encounter.

It is true that Marcuse abandoned Heidegger for a Marxism colored by the *Manuscripts*, but it was the similarity of Marx's early ideas to phenomenology that attracted him. Insights he gained through his study of phenomenology show up clearly in his interpretation of the early Marx. As Habermas writes, "Marcuse appropriated young Marx from the viewpoint of existential phenomenology, taking the very notions of *Praxis* and *Lebenswelt* as guidelines for the liberation from alienated labor."[17] With Lukács's quasi-transcendental approach in the background, he was able to retain much of his phenomenological baggage without reference to phenomenology. Thereafter, a phenomenological shadow follows him as he elaborates his own version of Marxist philosophy—a shadow that is rarely acknowledged but always present.

How important is this survival of phenomenology in Marcuse's later writings? Many commentators would agree with John Abromeit that phenomenology played a small role in his critique of technology in *One-Dimensional Man*, but that "Marcuse's affinity with Husserlian and Heideggerian phenomenology ends here."[18] In other words,

---

16 Marcuse, "New Sources," 1–33.

17 Jürgen Habermas, "Psychic Thermidor and the Rebirth of Rebellious Subjectivity," *Berkeley Journal of Sociology* 24–25 (1980): 6.

18 John Abromeit, "Left Heideggerianism or Phenomenological Marxism? Reconsidering Herbert Marcuse's Critical Theory of Technology," *Constellations* 17, no. 1 (2010): 93.

Marcuse was a Marxist, full stop, who, with one small exception, left phenomenology behind in 1932 when he discovered Marx's *Manuscripts*.

Marcuse himself wished to leave this impression. In an interview with Frederick Olafson, he dismisses attempts to combine phenomenology and Marxism and condemns Heidegger's "false or fake concreteness."[19] Yet that is not his last word. In an interview in 1979, he responded to the question, "Who do you consider the last significant philosophers?" by naming Heidegger among others. When the interviewer reminds him that he has criticized Heidegger's ontology as abstract, he replies, "On the contrary. After a long vacuum in philosophy he presented a concrete ontology even if without the immediacy of concreteness."[20]

The many changes Marcuse made in the text of his review of the *Manuscripts* for its republication in 1978 are an indication of his desire to distance himself from Heidegger. The original version drops most Heideggerian terminology but emphasizes the ontological character of the *Manuscripts* to a degree that seems to have made him uncomfortable later.

First, in the new version expressions employing the word *Wesen* (being or essence) are systematically removed. In many passages, "human being" is replaced by "man," which may have been intended to make the text more readable but also suggests a desire to simplify a more complex argument in which the *Wesen* of man plays an ontological role. The *Wesensbestimmung* ("essential determination") and the *Wesensgeschichte* of man ("essential history") become merely "determination" and "history."

Second, although the 1978 version occasionally references the ontological character of Marx's argument, Marcuse deletes many passages in which it is emphasized, for example, one that reads: "Here we would be moving in the domain of questions concerning the being and essence

---

19 Frederick Olafson, "Heidegger's Politics: An Interview with Herbert Marcuse," in *The Essential Marcuse: Selected Writings of Philosopher and Social Critic Herbert Marcuse*, ed. Andrew Feenberg and William Leiss (Boston: Beacon Press, 2007), 118, 119.

20 Herbert Marcuse interviewed by a Hungarian scholar, "A Conversation with Herbert Marcuse: On Pluralism, Future, and Philosophy," in Herbert Marcuse, *Marxism, Revolution and Utopia*, ed. Douglas Kellner (London: Routledge, 2014), 420–1.

of man, in the domain of 'ontological' questions, and 'labor' and its related determinations would be ontological categories."

Third, the one survival of the Heideggerian term "Dasein" disappears: "With his own Dasein man lets all encountered beings happen."[21]

These changes tend to hide, perhaps unintentionally, the continuity between Marcuse's interpretation of the *Manuscripts* and his early phenomenological Marxism.

The connection is more tenuous in the later work. Ian Angus explains Marcuse's rejection of Heidegger's phenomenology on grounds of principle: the phenomenological critique of objective representation is fundamentally different from the Marxian critique of alienation. The concept of alienation promises the return of what has been lost in a progressive development. Thus, the alienation of labor under capitalism generates both capital and a working class capable of recovering its powers and subordinating capital to its will. In Angus's view, Heideggerian phenomenology offers not a return of the alienated content of objective representation to the lived world of the subject, but a simple juxtaposition of personal authenticity and inauthenticity.[22] Accordingly, there can be no Hegelian *Aufhebung* transforming society as a whole.

These are reasonable arguments, but consider Marcuse's 1966 inaugural lecture, delivered on his appointment to the new University of California, San Diego. His audience consisted primarily of scientists. The university was their creation, and he was among the early appointments in the humanities. He owed them an explanation for his presence on their campus, and one so basic, so transparent that it would communicate across the gap between disciplines. His lecture drew on an essential phenomenological concept to show these scientists the validity of a different, nonscientific kind of thinking.

---

21 The republished text is Herbert Marcuse, "Neue Quellen zur Grundlegung des Historischen Materialismus," in *Der deutsche Künstlerroman, Frühe Aufsätze*. The original is available at Die Gesellschaft – Online-Edition der Bibliothek der Friedrich-Ebert-Stiftung, vol. 2, no. 8, 136–74, fes.de. Marcuse misstates the volume number in the Suhrkamp edition. The quoted passages are on pages 144 and 154 of the original. The second passage on page 154 reads, "Mit seinem eigenen Dasein läßt der Mensch zugleich alles begegnende Seiende geschehen."

22 Ian Angus, "Walking on Two Legs: On the Very Possibility of a Heideggerian Marxism: *Heidegger and Marcuse: The Catastrophe and Redemption of History* by Andrew Feenberg," in *Human Studies* 28, no. 3 (November 2005): 335–52.

Marcuse argues that philosophy arises from the problems and contradictions of the philosopher's *Lebenswelt*, a German word whose literal meaning is the "world of life." Marcuse encountered the term in the lectures and writings of his teachers Husserl and Heidegger. The *Lebenswelt* is the world of what Marcuse calls "unpurged, unmutilated experience," in contrast with the restricted notion of experience that underlies the natural sciences.[23] This "unpurged" experience is fraught with potentialities that are sensed along with the given. Value and fact coexist in everyday perception; they are not sharply separated as in the scientific reconstruction of experience for the purpose of research. There is, as he would later write, "a mathematical but also . . . an existential sense" of truth.[24] This is the basis of the possibility of critical reason. I think this is part of what Marcuse meant when he told Olafson that despite his rejection of Heidegger's doctrine, there was "at least a certain type and kind of thinking I learned from him."[25]

Shortly before moving to San Diego, Marcuse published a paper on the *Lebenswelt* that contains his most explicit discussion of phenomenology. He summarizes approvingly Husserl's *The Crisis of the European Sciences*, especially its critique of naturalism. In this final work, Husserl argues that modern science is based on idealizations of concrete experiences belonging to the *Lebenswelt*, the everyday world as it is encountered in the first person. Geometry, for example, works

---

23 Herbert Marcuse, "The Rationality of Philosophy," in *Transvaluation of Values and Radical Social Change*, ed. Peter-Erwin Jansen, Sarah Surak, and Charles Reitz (International Herbert Marcuse Society, 2017), 2, 15. Heidegger uses the term *Welt* to signify something similar to Husserl's *Lebenswelt*. Although Husserl's concept is associated with his late work, he employed it earlier when Marcuse was studying with him. See Antonio Pieretti, "The '*Lebenswelt*' and the Meaning of Philosophy," in *Husserlian Phenomenology in a New Key, Analecta Husserliana* (*The Yearbook of Phenomenological Research*), vol. 35, ed. Anna-Teresa Tymieniecka (Dordrecht: Springer, 1991).

24 Herbert Marcuse, "Nature and Revolution," in *Counterrevolution and Revolt* (Boston: Beacon Press, 1972), 69. By "mathematical truth" Marcuse intends scientific truth. Is this passage a gloss on section 42 of the preface to Hegel's *Phenomenology of Spirit*? It seems likely, as Hegel distinguishes "*mathematical* truths" from philosophy, which offers "a different kind of knowledge." The relation between philosophy and experience is different from what Marcuse envisages, but experience is also central for Hegel. G. W. F. Hegel, *Hegel's Phenomenology of Spirit*, trans. A. V. Miller (Oxford: Oxford University Press, 1979), 24, 26, 55.

25 Olafson, "Heidegger's Politics," 127.

with mathematically precise measures and objects that refine the imprecise everyday phenomena of lived spatial experience. Galileo instituted modern science by conceiving a physics based on such ideal-izations and substituting a naturalist ontology for the world of everyday experience. The original *Lebenswelt*, according to Husserl, was then relegated to the realm of psychology and lost its ontological status.

Marcuse cites Husserl: "The *Ideenkleid* (the ideational veil) of math-ematics and mathematical physics represents and [at the same time] disguises the empirical reality and leads us to take for True Being that which is only a method."[26] Phenomenology dereifies science by show-ing that experience is "objectification of subjectivity." Husserl claims to have found the "constituent subjectivity" underlying experience, but his subject is purely cognitive. Marcuse objects that "empirical reality is constituted by the subject of thought *and* of *action*, theory and prac-tice."[27] The constituent subjectivity of modern capitalist society is not transcendental but all too material; it is human labor as structured by capitalism.

The question remains of how a material principle can play the role of constituent subjectivity. The idealized cogito of a Kant or a Fichte constitutes reality from a transcendental beyond, but human labor is self-evidently part of the reality it is supposed to constitute. The worker finds reality already there as the condition and presupposition of the work. How then can labor constitute reality? Like Münchhausen, it would have to lift itself by its own bootstraps. This would become a central problem in Marcuse's interpretation of the *Manuscripts*.

As we will see throughout this book, the phenomenological concept of "lifeworld" and its related concept of experience are essential to every aspect of Marcuse's thought. Phenomenology enables him to think about experience in an ontological vein, as a domain of reality, rather than as

---

26 Herbert Marcuse, "On Science and Phenomenology," in *Boston Colloquium for the Philosophy of Science (1962–1964): Proceedings, Boston Studies in the Philosophy of Science*, vol. 2, ed. Robert S. Cohen and Marx W. Wartofsky (New York: Humanities Press, 1965), 279–90 (with comment by Aron Gurwitsch, 291–305), 286. The passage is found in the English translation of Edmund Husserl, *The Crisis of European Sciences and Transcendental Phenomenology*, trans. David Carr (Evanston, IL: Northwestern University, 1970), 51.

27 Marcuse, "On Science and Phenomenology," 288–9.

a subjective overlay on the nature of natural science. Claims that remain obscure in his formulations, and are often ignored or treated as mere rhetoric by interpreters, become understandable when related to this unacknowledged background. The point of this interpretive approach is not to reduce Marcuse's thought to phenomenology—and Angus is certainly right to point out the insuperable difference with Heidegger—but to get at the real meaning of his own Marxist version of ideas first developed in his encounter with phenomenology.

That encounter is central to two important themes discussed in this book. First, Husserl's derivation of science from the lifeworld inspired Marcuse's own critique of science and naturalism (explored in chapters 5 and 6). Second, Heidegger's version of the lifeworld underlies Marcuse's interpretation of Marx's *Manuscripts*, as I will show later in this chapter. Drawing on the many parallels between Marcuse's text and similar passages in the writings of his predecessors, the discussion that follows reveals connections to a conceptual heritage significant for his thought.

Excursus: The Lifeworld in Habermas and Marcuse

The role played by the lifeworld in Marcuse's thought can be clarified by comparison with Habermas's late turn to a related understanding of the concept. Both reject Husserl's "pure consciousness" that is revealed by the suspension of the natural attitude, but they retain his concept of the lifeworld as a realm of first-person experience. That experience relates to objective realities, but it does so as those realities are lived by the subject. In one early essay, Marcuse distinguishes between Husserl's theory of consciousness and what he calls "existence," that is, lived experience in all its complexity. He gives the example of a factory that can be viewed in three different modes: as an object of consciousness, as a sum of objective facts, or as facts that are "entwined" with "historical human existence."[28]

This last mode, obscured by the prevalent scientism, is the concern of philosophy. It describes Marcuse's approach and to a certain extent that of Habermas as well. The facts are not simply what is known to an

---

28 Herbert Marcuse, "On Concrete Philosophy," in *Heideggerian Marxism*, 38–9.

observer or researcher but are also given meaning in the experience of the existing individuals. That meaning implicates the subject as a whole person, engaged with reality not only cognitively but also practically. Valuations of various sorts are therefore essential aspects of existence in this sense.

Habermas's "postmetaphysical thinking" also attempts to validate philosophy in the face of the cognitive imperialism of the sciences. According to his argument, the differentiation of knowledge into separate spheres in modern society has divided facts from values. Ethical relativism appears as a reflex of a scientistic worldview. But the lifeworld, understood as the domain of first-person experience, nevertheless retains a claim as the repository of an undifferentiated magma of fact and value that offers a basis for norms that science has failed to provide.

Throughout his career, Habermas was interested in the formal structure of communicative practice. That structure is implied in the "performative" engagement in communication, that is to say, in the first-person encounter with the other through language. "Communicative reason" consists in formal pragmatic principles assumed by communicating subjects, such as truthfulness and sincerity. Exceptions occur, but one would not bother to communicate at all if these principles were not assumed to prevail most of the time. Communication thus transcends relativism while avoiding a dogmatic commitment to particularistic ideological or cultural values.

In later years, Habermas came to regard this solution to the problem of relativism as insufficient, observing that the culturally inflected content of communication contains a richer store of values than these formal principles. As he writes,

> Marx's saying about the realization of philosophy can also be understood in this way: what has, following the disintegration of metaphysical and religious worldviews, been divided up on the level of cultural systems under various aspects of validity, can now be put together—and also put right—only in the experiential context of lifeworld practices.[29]

---

29 Jürgen Habermas, "Themes in Postmetaphysical Thinking," in *Postmetaphysical Thinking: Philosophical Essays*, trans. W. M. Hohengarten (Cambridge, MA: MIT Press, 1992), 51.

The later Habermas believed that aesthetics and religion offered access to that context in a form capable of universalization through philosophical reflection.

Habermas's turn to art and religion is a search for semantic content to supplement the formal-pragmatic structures of communication. It implies recognition of the inadequacy of the structures to specify concrete actions by themselves.[30] But are art and religion the right place to look for the necessary supplement? Marcuse would at least agree that art can play a role, but their purposes in returning to the lifeworld are quite different, and religion held no interest for him.

Marcuse also attributes a certain validity to the communicative contents of the lifeworld. However, his version includes also the sensuous interaction with other people and nature. This richer lifeworld consists in practical relations to a society fraught with contradictions. Outbursts of protest bring society's unfulfilled potentialities to the surface where they can be measured in terms of basic moral and aesthetic intuitions, such as the value of reason, compassion, and the flourishing of life. Marcuse considered these criteria to be obvious to any "healthy" individual, but they are also elaborated in a rational form in philosophy and art. Thus, he did not abandon the critical stance to just any social protest. "Adhering to the abstractness of philosophy is more appropriate to circumstances and closer to the truth than is the pseudo-philosophical concreteness that condescends to social struggles."[31] Where a coincidence between rational and public demands can be established, there he found what Habermas was looking for in religion: a path to the normative content of the undifferentiated lifeworld.

But, as we saw in chapter 1, despite the "obstinacy" with which Marcuse stuck to his philosophical standards, he was surprisingly open to movements that he judged progressive.[32] He believed such movements have a revelatory power from which philosophy can learn the concrete significance of its categories. As he wrote in a letter to Adorno,

---

30 The problem is discussed in David Ingram, *Habermas: Introduction and Analysis* (Ithaca: Cornell University Press, 2010), 324. For a critique of several aspects of Habermas's formalism, see also 175–91, 253–65.

31 Herbert Marcuse, "Philosophy and Critical Theory," in *Negations: Essays in Critical Theory*, trans. Jeremy J. Shapiro (Boston: Beacon Press, 1968), 147.

32 Ibid., 143.

"there are situations, moments, in which theory is pushed on further by praxis—situations and moments in which theory that is kept separate from praxis becomes untrue to itself."[33] This aptly describes Marcuse's relation to the New Left and the "aesthetic *Lebenswelt*" emerging in the counterculture of the 1960s.

In a modern secular society, neither religious authorities nor ancient texts can claim epistemic validity. Only experience can validate knowledge. The postmetaphysical standpoint of Habermas and Marcuse responds to this restriction. However, experience takes two different forms: the everyday lifeworld, revealed in the first-person standpoint of the participant; and a purified residue of its contents on which the sciences rely, revealed to an ideal third-person observer. Philosophy turns to the lifeworld as the only viable alternative to a dogmatic scientism. While Habermas sought ethical principles in its undifferentiated multiplicity of values, Marcuse's interest was ontological: he argued that the realization of reason in reality requires a revolution. This was the inspired notion Marcuse found in Marx's *Manuscripts*.

Marx's Philosophy of Praxis

The *Manuscripts* present an incomplete sketch of what, in my book of the same title, I call the philosophy of praxis.[34] In this early work, Marx seems to hesitate between idealism and materialism, only to adopt a version of naturalism as he turned, in his later thought, to concrete social and economic studies. Nevertheless, ideas from the *Manuscripts* show up later in modified form. The sudden appearance of this text in 1932 therefore had a considerable impact and posed a challenge to Marxists. In this section and the next, I will briefly summarize its argument and show how Marcuse resolves the dilemma it poses with contemporary philosophical means. The three moments of my summary are as follows.

First, Marx undertakes the sociological desublimation of the philosophical concept of the subject as a transcendental cogito. The subject so

---

33 Herbert Marcuse, "Correspondence on the German Student Movement," trans. Esther Leslie, *New Left Review* 1, no. 233 (January–February 1999), 123–36.

34 Feenberg, *Philosophy of Praxis*, chapter 2.

conceived is a version of the soul and as such falls before Feuerbach's critique of the alienation of reason: "What lies in the other world for religion, lies in this world for philosophy."[35] To disalienate philosophical reason, the real subject must be discovered behind the theological veil. What is discovered is a living human being dependent on nature. Since that subject is defined by need rather than knowledge, being cannot be derived from thought as idealist philosophy claims. Need now occupies the place of cognition in the architecture of the theory.

Second, Marx reconceptualizes the relation of the desublimated subject to the objective world in accordance with the cognitive subject-object relation in idealist philosophy. That relation is not causal as in the commonsense understanding of light rays, sound waves, and other natural phenomena impinging on the senses. Instead, for idealism, the logical structure of the mind—that is, reason—correlates with a corresponding structure in the real world. The *Manuscripts* redefine this ontologically fundamental relation to reality as a social happening.[36] The relation between subject and object is lived out in work, no longer in thought. Marx calls this "objectification." By this, he means not the reduction of a human being to an object, as in the current usage of the term, but rather the incorporation of human faculties and needs in artifacts. Objectification, in this sense, takes the place of the cognitive unity of subject and object in idealism. Nature is reduced to a human product through labor and, where labor cannot do the job, through sensation, understood as meaning bearing and thus constitutive of a specifically human dimension of the objective world. "It is only when objective reality everywhere becomes for man in society the reality of human faculties, human reality, and thus the reality of his own faculties, that all *objects* become for him the *objectification of himself.*" Marx concludes, "Man himself becomes the object."[37]

Third, Marx shows that the unity of subject and object in this new sense is obstructed by the alienation of labor that divides subject from object, worker from the means of satisfaction. Only liberation

---

35 Ludwig Feuerbach, *Principles of the Philosophy of the Future*, trans. Manfred Vogel (New York: Bobbs-Merrill, 1966), 70.

36 Feenberg, *Philosophy of Praxis*, 35–6.

37 Karl Marx, "Economic and Philosophical Manuscripts," in *Karl Marx: Early Writings*, trans. and ed. T. B. Bottomore (London: C. A. Watts, 1963), 160–1.

from alienation can satisfy the "demands of reason." The ontological split between subject and object arises in history and is overcome in history. Human being and nature, united in need and satisfaction through labor, are now the concrete form of the "true" unity of subject and object. Marx calls this the "realization" of philosophy in social reality. Revolution appears as a *philosophical method* in place of the speculative methods of modern philosophy since Descartes. Marcuse argues that it is "*only on this foundation* that an economic fact is capable of becoming the real basis of a revolution that will genuinely transform the essence of man and his world."[38]

Marcuse's interpretation of the *Manuscripts* follows Marx in emphasizing the world-constituting power of human labor. For Marx, objectification not only yields products corresponding to human needs; it does more than that, transforming "reality" itself. Labor is not merely ontic, but also ontological. On the face of it, this is the purest metaphysical speculation, as is Marx's claims that "nature is the inorganic body of man." This proposition could be taken to mean that nature mediates itself, creating human consciousness as its own self-consciousness. Alfred Schmidt calls this throwback to pre-Kantian philosophy a "hidden nature speculation."[39] It derives from idealism, not the materialism implied in Marx's frequent references to the "objectivity" of man and nature. Those references seem to conform with the standard materialist view: humans are no more than things among things. There is thus a fundamental ambiguity in the *Manuscripts*. The "nature" belonging to this second description is incompatible with the first description, yet Marx claims to transcend the opposition of idealism and materialism.

Despite the ontological references in the *Manuscripts*, the temptation to reconcile Marx's argument with common sense is very strong. The difficulty is how to understand the nature of the objects presupposed by labor. Are these objects simply there, independent of human being, or are they posited by human being even before they are transformed by labor? It seems there is a dilemma: either independent or posited, either traditional materialism or some sort of idealism.

---

38 Marcuse, "New Sources," 90.

39 Alfred Schmidt, *The Concept of Nature in Marx*, trans., Ben Fowkes (London: New Left Books, 1971), 79–80. Marx, "Economic and Philosophical Manuscripts," 126–7.

Each horn of the dilemma is problematic. Materialism responds to our sense that our causal relation to natural objects is contingent, accidental. The objects have no need of us, and there is no ontological necessity in our relation to them. But lost in this materialist position is the equally signifi-cant fact that without a knowing subject, nature has no more reality than Kant's thing-in-itself, a pure abstraction (as Hegel pointed out). The ideal-ist would argue, therefore, that nature is necessarily dependent on human beings—a logical conclusion from this post-Kantian argument.

It seems that one must choose one's Marx. Marxists commonly resolve the dilemma by selecting one of its horns: the materialist one. Although Marx's early concept of labor certainly sounds like meta-physics, commentators who wish to include the *Manuscripts* in the Marxist corpus do not take it literally. They emphasize his affirmation that the human being is a natural being associated with real, natural objects. They confine Marx's ontological talk to society, while insisting that humans interact only causally with "external nature." On this account, labor merely alters features of the wholly independent nature on which it works. These features reflect human needs and faculties, but they have no general ontological significance. They contribute to a humanly built world that would be a merely contingent offshoot of nature as such. But if this is all Marx had in mind, why did he introduce the elaborate conceptual apparatus of the *Manuscripts*? Why not just say that human beings create useful artifacts without dressing it up in an ambitious philosophical program?

That program is very radical. Throughout Marx's text, the distinc-tion between history and nature is obliterated, as in his remarkable claim that "*society* is the accomplished union of man with nature, the veritable resurrection of nature, the realized naturalism of man and the realized humanism of nature."[40] The collapse of these distinctions supports the rejection of the existing natural sciences, which depend on a nonsocial concept of nature. "Natural science will have to abandon its abstract materialist, or rather idealist, orientation."[41] In its place, Marx promises a new science that will unite nature and history.

The materialist interpretation contradicts the early Marx's goal of grounding a critique of capitalism in a revolutionary *ontology*. Whether

---

40 Marx, "Economic and Philosophical Manuscripts," 157.
41 Ibid., 164.

that goal is worth pursuing is another matter. It seemed necessary to Marx, and later to Lukács, Gramsci, and Marcuse, in order to affirm the ultimate agency of human beings in the face of the deterministic universe of the sciences, both natural and social. To the extent that determinism reflects the actual structure of capitalist society—Lukács's "reification"—it must be challenged at its roots. Marcuse's historicist interpretation thus grounds a concept of revolution based on human agency extending from society to nature as the essential object of human labor.

Marx's Dilemma

Marcuse emphasizes the most philosophically radical aspects of Marx's argument, and in so doing seems to expose its absurdity. The goal of idealist philosophy is to demonstrate the unity of subject and object by showing the *constitution* of the object by the subject. What happens to this ambition if subject and object are redefined as natural beings? This gives rise to an antinomy of society and nature: How can a living social subject constitute nature when it is itself natural?

After Kant and Hegel, the field of possible alternatives to scientific naturalism narrows. A traditional metaphysics is no longer plausible. Who can still believe in entities incompatible with natural science such as spirits, entelechies, or Marx's resurrected nature? But mechanical materialism is also excluded by the consensus of early twentieth-century German philosophy. How then to avoid idealism?

Neither Feuerbach nor Hegel provided Marx with the concepts he required to transcend the opposition of materialism and idealism. He made several attempts to overcome the dilemma in his early work. In the *Manuscripts*, he claims that the standpoint of human existence cannot be transcended, explaining this limitation in a remarkable paragraph that reads like a Zen koan.

> If you ask a question about the creation of nature and man you abstract from nature and man. You suppose them non-existent and you want me to demonstrate that they exist. I reply: give up your abstraction and at the same time you abandon your question. Or

else, if you want to maintain your abstraction, be consistent, and if you think of man and nature as non-existent, think of yourself too as non-existent, for you are also man and nature. Do not think, do not ask me any questions, for as soon as you think and ask questions your abstraction from the existence of nature and man becomes meaningless.[42]

Marx did not work out the implications of this argument, which would have led him in the direction of phenomenology rather than the social philosophy he aspired to create. Without phenomenological resources, he continually equivocates between a discourse of factual thinghood and a discourse of meaning. His frequent invocation of the "real" and the "natural" refers to the one, while his ontological refrain—an affirmation of the unity of subject and object through labor, sensation, and need—evokes the other.

When he tries to unite them in materialist fashion in *The German Ideology*, the result shows how far he was from grasping the problem. There, he repeats the claim that subject and object are united in the sensuous appropriation of nature, but he undercuts his own argument by saying that "of course the priority of external nature remains, and all this has no application to the original men produced by *generatio aequivoca*."[43] Instead of referring the unity of subject and object to the practical first-person encounter with meaning, and distinguishing it from the third-person cognition of an "external" world, he conflates the two in an unsuccessful mixture of idealism and materialism.

Only later were the conceptual resources available to "save" Marx's original insight from the ambiguous and confusing language in which he expressed it. Indeed, it is in terms of the distinction between meaning and factual existence found in Dilthey, neo-Kantianism, and phenomenology that Marcuse resolves Marx's dilemma. This distinction plays out in the claim that there are actually two concepts of nature relevant to the argument of the *Manuscripts*.

---

42 Ibid., 166. For an analysis of this enigmatic passage, see Feenberg, *Philosophy of Praxis*, 52–4.

43 Karl Marx and Friedrich Engels, "The German Ideology," in *Writings of the Young Marx on Philosophy and Society*, trans. and ed. Loyd D. Easton and Kurt H. Guddat (New York: Doubleday & Co., 1967), 418.

Marcuse distinguishes the nature of natural science from what he calls the concept of "'nature' in the wider sense given to this concept by Marx [in the *Manuscripts*], as also by Hegel."[44] It is not entirely clear what Marcuse means by the "wider sense" of nature. He seems to refer to nature insofar as it is implicated in human activity. In one early essay, he attributes this distinction to Lukács, writing, "Lukács did indeed clearly recognize the duality of the being of nature—completely ahistorical as an object of physics, historical as the life-space of human Dasein."[45] This captures at least part of Marx's meaning in the *Manuscripts*.

By distinguishing two senses of nature, Marcuse avoids coming into direct conflict with the claims of common sense and natural science. There is an independent, external "nature," presumably "in the narrower sense," that has no need of human beings, but that nature is ultimately grounded in the social-historical world in which human consciousness and action play an essential role. Marcuse can thus echo the *Manuscripts*' thesis of the unity of history and nature, subject and object while finessing the contradiction between Marx's early critique of the "abstract" natural sciences and his later acceptance of their validity. The "wider" nature, meanwhile, is essential for Marcuse as it is for the early Marx, but he quietly ignores Marx's own call for a new science until, surprisingly, it returns in *One-Dimensional Man*. There, he addresses the question of the relation between the narrower, so-called "external nature," and the wider, social-historical nature. That relation is the theme of the concluding chapters of this book.

We only get hints of a theory of nature from Marcuse's interpretation of the *Manuscripts,* but those hints can be supplemented by explicit reference to his early phenomenological Marxism. The remainder of this chapter will trace out these phenomenological themes in Marcuse's interpretation of Marx's text.

---

44 Marcuse, "New Sources," 97. See also Herbert Marcuse, "Contributions to a Phenomenology of Historical Materialism," in *Heideggerian Marxism*, 21; Herbert Marcuse, "On the Concept of Labor in Economics," in *Heideggerian Marxism*, 139.

45 Herbert Marcuse, "On the Problem of the Dialectic," in *Heideggerian Marxism*, 67; Andrew Feenberg, "Two Concepts of Nature: The Lived and the Reified," *Metodo* 9, no. 2 (2022): 157–70.

Marcuse's Interpretation of Marx's *Manuscripts* of 1844

The *Manuscripts* are a controversial text among Marxists, frequently accused of metaphysical humanism. Marx is said to argue in this early text that capitalism violates a fixed human essence. This interpretation stems from Henri de Man, whose review of the *Manuscripts* was also published in 1932.[46] De Man claimed that there are two Marxes; a humanist Marx who explained the ethical basis of socialism in the *Manuscripts*, and the scientific Marx of the later works, who explained capitalism objectively as subject to economic laws. While de Man preferred the ethical Marx, critics of the *Manuscripts* argue for the superiority of Marx's science. These self-proclaimed "orthodox" Marxists exclude the *Manuscripts* as incompatible with materialism and the "scientific worldview."[47]

It is true that the central argument of the *Manuscripts* concerns human nature, but Marcuse argues that Marx does not define this term in the usual sense. As Hauke Brunkhorst and Gertrud Koch write, Marcuse "insists on an 'ontological' reading of the young Marx which he prefers to the usual anthropological one."[48] Human being is essentially historical; Marcuse observes, "We are no longer dealing with an abstract human essence, which remains equally valid at every stage of concrete history, but with an essence which can be defined in *history* and *only* in history."[49] This historically inflected essence consists in three main modes of being (*Zu-Seins*): *species-being*, *sensuousness*, and *objectification*. Together, these modes motivate the revolution and explain world-constitution through labor. In this section, I will describe Marcuse's unusual interpretation of these concepts.[50]

---

46 Henri de Man, "Der neu entdeckte Marx," *Der Kampf* 25, nos. 5–6 (1932): 224.

47 Louis Althusser, *For Marx* (New York: Penguin, 1969), chapter 2.

48 Hauke Brunkhorst and Gertrud Koch, *Herbert Marcuse: Zur Einführung* (Hamburg: Junius, 2000), 28, my translation. See also Stephan Bundschuh, *"Und weil der Mensch ein Mensch ist . . .": Anthropologische Aspekte der Sozialphilosophie Herbert Marcuses* (Lüneburg: zu Klampen, 1998), 42.

49 Marcuse, "New Sources," 105–6.

50 For a broader treatments of the themes of Marcuse's interpretation of the *Manuscripts*, see Kellner, *Herbert Marcuse and the Crisis of Marxism*, 77–87; Peter Lind, *Marcuse and Freedom* (London: Croom Helm, 1985), chapter 3.

Species-being: Objectivity encountered through meaning

As "species-beings," human beings are fundamentally social. In the *Manuscripts*, Marx argues that the human individual incorporates a wealth of social achievements and possesses a unique capacity for self-consciousness.[51] However, these aspects of species-being are not the main focus of Marcuse's peculiar interpretation. Rather, the human as species-being is characterized by what Marcuse calls, in the original German, "das Sich-verhalten-Können zum 'Allgemeinen' der Gegenstände."[52] The English translation states that the human being has the ability to "relate" to beings through their "species," their meaning. Access to the universal is the specificity of human being, revealing possibilities that go beyond the immediate state of things.[53]

Human freedom is based on this ability, which the German text identifies as a mode of comportment, an essential power. That power is realized in labor, which presupposes a "negative" relation to the given. As I will show in later chapters, this notion of access to the universal plays a central role throughout Marcuse's work. He references it in his 1966 inaugural lecture at the University of California: "'Free' is firstly the being which can form concepts of things and consequently project and define their possibilities."[54]

Sensuousness: Correlation of need and satisfaction

In contrast with the idealist concept of man as essentially mind, the *Manuscripts* emphasize the "sensuousness" of the human being. Marcuse follows Marx in expanding the concept of sensuousness to include needs. The fact of need signifies its object as belonging to the being of the subject. Marx writes, "Man's feelings, passions, etc., are not merely anthropological characteristics in the narrower sense, but are true ontological affirmations of being (nature)."[55] Although Marcuse

---

51 Marx, "Economic and Philosophical Manuscripts," 158, 208. Bertell Ollman, *Alienation: Marx's Conception of Man in Capitalist Society* (Cambridge, UK: Cambridge University Press, 1971), 84–6.

52 Herbert Marcuse, "Neue Quellen zur Grundlegung des historischen Materialismus," in *Der deutsche Künstlerroman, Frühe Aufsätze*, 522; Marcuse, "On the Concept of Labor," 96.

53 Marcuse, "New Sources," 96.

54 Marcuse, "Rationality of Philosophy," 7.

55 Marx, "Economic and Philosophical Manuscripts," 189. This passage is cited by

repeats Marx's insistence that "man" is an "objective natural being," he is at pains to distinguish the concept of "sensuousness" from common-sense materialism. Rejecting the notion that human beings are mere things in the world in a causal relation to matter through the sense organs, he argues that the sensuous relation to objects is not causal but rather should be understood in terms of the concept of receptivity in Kant's *Critique of Pure Reason*. This implies a necessary relation between sensuousness and its objects, a claim whose significance will become clear later in this chapter.

Objectification: Becoming human through labor

The category of objectification is another ambiguous concept that, like species-being and sensuousness, Marcuse interprets in an unusual way. According to him, labor joins the power to construct general concepts with the receptive relation to being in need. They come together in the active transformation of nature in accordance with its potentialities. "*Labor*," Marcuse writes, "as the specifically human 'life activity,' has its roots in this 'species being' of man; it presupposes man's ability to relate to the 'general' aspects of objects and to the possibilities contained therein."[56]

Those possibilities are tailored to human being. Chairs and tables correspond to our height, knives and forks suit the hands that will use them, stairs are designed to be convenient for our feet and legs, and so on. Interpreting Marx's critique of Hegel, Marcuse writes, "The history of man thus occurs and fulfills itself as objectification. The reality of man consists in 'bringing out' [*Herausschaffen*] all his 'species powers' in real objects, 'the positing [*Setzung*] of a real . . . objective world.'"[57]

Marcuse and translated in *Heideggerian Marxism* as "man's feelings, passions, etc., are not merely anthropological characteristics . . . but truly ontological affirmations of his essence (nature)." The word "his" does not appear in the German: "die Empfindungen, Leidenschaften usw. des Menschen nicht nur anthropologische Bestimmungen . . . sondern wahrhaft ontologistche Wesens-(Natur-) bejaungend sind." Furthermore, Marcuse's associated footnote refers to Feuerbach's similar claim that human feelings have an ontological and metaphysical significance. Yet, to confuse matters further, later on the page Marcuse does introduce the word "he" into his description. See Marcuse, "New Sources," 94; Marcuse, "Neue Quellen," in *Der deutsche Künstlerroman*, 519.

56 Marcuse, "New Sources," 96.

57 Ibid., 118, translation modified.

Marcuse goes on to argue that all the various spheres of existence addressed in Hegel's *Phenomenology*—morality, the state, science, the economy—belong to the "objective world." The narrow boundaries usually ascribed to labor are transcended. The next section of this chapter will discuss the relation of Heidegger's concept of world to the notion of world Marcuse introduces here and in many other passages.

Alienation and Revolution

The *Manuscripts* distinguish "alienation" from "objectification." Objectification is the more general term, signifying the ontologically fundamental relation to the world through which the human subject appropriates objects. Alienation is the perverted form of objectification characteristic of class society. Marx attributes private property to alienation rather than the reverse. By this he means that the alienated relation of workers to their objects, to themselves, and to each other makes possible the appropriation of the products of labor by an alien power.

Marcuse interprets the particular form of alienation characteristic of capitalist society in Lukácsian terms, as reification.[58] As we have seen, reification is the "form of objectivity" of capitalist society. Reified objects of perception and action are constructed as facts governed by laws to which the individuals can only relate through technical or strategic practices. The pursuit of personal advantage involves knowing those laws and using them skillfully. But this is precisely the form of practice that reproduces the laws. Reification, Lukács writes, is "an abstraction of the human labor objectified in commodities . . . its historical possibility . . . determined by the real performance [*Vollzug*] of this process of abstraction."[59] Reification is the basis for the false

---

58 Marcuse uses the term "reification" frequently throughout his text but never mentions Lukács, who introduced it into Marxist discourse. Two footnotes elaborate on the concept: Marcuse, "New Sources," 207n30, and 211n101.

59 Lukács, *History and Class Consciousness*, 87, translation modified. I have followed Konstantinos Kavoulakos in translating *Vollzug* by "performance," in preference to Livingstone's "completion." See Kavoulakos, *Georg Lukács's Philosophy of Praxis*, 118. The original text is at Georg Lukács, *Geschichte und Klassenbewusstsein* (Neuwied: Luchterhand, 1968), 176. "Completion" suggests an objective process, but it is more plausible, given the active denotation of *Vollzug*, to translate it in this context with an active word such as "accomplishment" or "performance." The point is the role of practice in instituting and reproducing reification, albeit unconsciously.

consciousness that obscures the role of human practices in producing and reproducing a reified society.

The appropriation of the objects of practice under these conditions takes the form of private ownership. Capitalism is not simply an economic system but is also an ontological condition. As such, it contradicts the basic ontological structure of the human relation to the world. That structure consists in a much wider form of appropriation through which human being and nature complement each other and mutually actualize their potentialities. Marcuse glosses Marx's demand that objects must become "human" and thus "social" by reference to this ontology: reification is overcome where it is consciously dissolved into the social relations that ground it. The revolution is the process of dereifying capitalist reality.

This brief account of Marcuse's interpretation of the *Manuscripts* shows how he intends to resolve Marx's dilemma. Marx's early work could then supply an ontological rather than an ethical foundation for Marxism. Revolution would be necessary not just to bring society into conformity with the human essence, but to establish the appropriate relation of that essence to reality—in short, to achieve "the true resolution of the strife between existence and essence."[60] This explains why his "naturalism" was also a "humanism," affirming the *mutual dependence* of humanity and nature. Feuerbach was helpful for going down this path without regressing to idealism, but Marx introduced socioeconomic considerations in order to incorporate nature into the human world concretely, not just conceptually.

This is a form of absolute historicism pursued later by Lukács and Gramsci on the basis of the same idealist theoretical background that influences Marcuse's interpretation of the *Manuscripts*. They have in common the distinction between the nature of natural science and the lived nature encountered in labor, Marcuse's "nature in the wider sense." The nature of natural science is a conceptual object with an infinite number of properties, most of which are of no human concern, whereas the nature of labor is physically present and is apprehended by the laborer in terms of the few properties relevant to the work. In Marcuse's reading, this latter nature is disclosed as a "world of

---

60 Marx, "Economic and Philosophical Manuscripts," 157.

meaning" ("essence") which prevails ontologically over the facts of natural science ("existence").[61] Once charged with economic content, this world is essentially historical while transforming the very idea of history by revealing its dependence on nature.

"World," in this sense, is the subject of one of Heidegger's most important conceptual innovations, namely his distinction between the third-person standpoint of the cognitive subject and the first-person standpoint of the practical subject. The concept of "world" in *Being and Time* joins the sphere of "validity"—meaning—with materiality as it is manifest to the practical subject. This concept of world, with significant modifications, appears to have served Marcuse in this interpretation of the *Manuscripts*. In the next sections, I will show its relevance to Marcuse's interpretation of Marx.

Heidegger's Concept of World

In his early writings, Marcuse relied explicitly on Heidegger's phenomenological concept of "world." That concept does not refer to the sum of existent things, as common sense would have it, but rather signifies the system of objects correlated with human thoughts, needs, and actions. For example, Marcuse writes:

> The human being always exists in a specific with- and surrounding world [*Mit- und Umwelt*], as a human being with human beings and things, in such a manner that this with- and surrounding world, although it is more and more disclosed in the development of experience, from the very beginning is essentially open as belonging to him.[62]

Such expressions abound in the early essays. However, Marcuse was not uncritical. As a Marxist, he rejected the dependence of Heidegger's theory on a universalized individual, Dasein, and its abstract care for

---

61 Herbert Marcuse, "Contributions to a Phenomenology," in *Heideggerian Marxism*, 30.

62 Herbert Marcuse, "Transzendentaler Marxismus?," in *Der deutsche Künstlerroman, Frühe Aufsätze*, 463.

its own identity. Indeed, Marcuse saw individualism as vitiating Heidegger's concept of historicity. In one early essay, Marcuse argued that worlds are differentiated by the class status of their human subjects.[63] Moreover, he found a more concrete version of Heidegger's "care" in Marx's concept of need. "Care," he argued, concerns the identity of Dasein, while "need" relates to its condition and its survival; both are relevant to Marcuse's interpretation of the idea of "worldhood," the essential relation between the practical subject and its surroundings.

I contend that Marcuse's idiosyncratic version of Heidegger's concept of "world" persists in his interpretation of the *Manuscripts*. This contention cannot be verified by proper citations, which in any case were not always customary in that period. Nevertheless, I am not alone in claiming a connection. For example, Gérard Raulet writes, "It is undeniable that Marcuse treats the Marxian ontology of labor along the lines of an existential ontology of 'being-in-the-world.'"[64]

Marcuse's deployment of the concept of world raises the contentious issue of his relations with Heidegger. According to many commentators, Marcuse was either a covert Heideggerian or a Marxist. However, this dichotomy confuses the real issue, which has to do with his appropriation of certain phenomenological concepts *within* his version of Marxism.

Marcuse's explicit statements on this issue are contradictory. As we have seen, he at first lauded Heidegger for having renewed philosophy, only later to reject his thought as complicit with Nazism.[65] Marcuse's ambiguous stance leaves us with two difficult questions: how thoroughly was *Being and Time* implicated in Heidegger's later Nazism, and how significant was Heidegger's influence on Marcuse's later work, despite his explicit denial?

I want to make two modest points with respect to these questions. Heidegger's philosophy has been treated as a coded version of Nazi ideology, but it would be more accurate to reverse the equation: Heidegger's political interpretation of his early work is only one possible

---

63 Marcuse, "Contributions to a Phenomenology," 16.

64 Raulet, *Philosophie de l'Emancipation*, 79, my translation. For an analysis of the relation between the phenomenological concept of world and Marxism, see Franck Fischbach, *La privation de monde: Temps, espace et capital* (Paris: Vrin, 2011).

65 Olafson, "Heidegger's Politics," 115–27.

reading. Marcuse, for one, associated Heidegger's grim account of death and conscience in *Being and Time* with his later Nazism. In the given historical context, the emphasis on these concepts may indeed have adumbrated Heidegger's later politics, but his students had no idea he was politically engaged, and they were shocked when he declared his Nazi allegiance. Moreover, much of Heidegger's own heroic interpretation after 1933 of concepts formulated in 1927 is quite arbitrary.[66] For example, his later claim, in his *Black Notebooks*, that the Jews are *weltlos* makes no sense in terms of the category of "world" presented in *Being and Time*.

Presumably, then, other readings, and other misinterpretations, are possible and no less plausible—including Marcuse's Marxist appropriation. Whether this is a satisfactory answer to the larger issue of Heidegger's relation to Nazism, it seems adequate for the specific technical innovation in phenomenology that had the most lasting influence on Marcuse's thought. That innovation—Heidegger's version of the phenomenological concept of world—is subject to multiple interpretations, among which there is Marcuse's implicit application to the *Manuscripts*.

Heidegger's initial exposition of his concept of world in *Being and Time* is deceptively mundane. "World" is exemplified in a workshop consisting of tools that are related to each other and, ultimately, to a Dasein, in this case a carpenter. World, in this sense, is a scene of practical activity understood through the meaning-in-use of its constituents. The work addresses each tool in its relation to other tools and to the workshop as a whole. Hammers, nails, boards, all belong together. Heidegger calls this the system of "references."

Dasein's "care," its concern for its future being, gives the system a purpose. Dasein enters its own future and establishes its identity not alone but with all the "equipment" (*Zeug*) it requires in its forward movement through time. This apparently subjective concept of world is the ontologically fundamental "opening" or revelation of meaning.

---

66 See, for example, Samuel Elias Sokolsky-Tifft, "Heidegger and Marcuse: A History of Disenchantment," *Journal of European Studies* 50, no. 2 (2020): 8. See also Steven Crowell, "The Middle Heidegger's Phenomenological Metaphysics," in *The Oxford Handbook of the History of Phenomenology*, ed. Dan Zahavi (Oxford: Oxford University Press, 2018), esp. 242 for further references.

Heidegger's concept of meaning is phenomenological; that is, it depends on a first-person viewpoint on experience to reveal relations obscured by commonsense objectivism and natural science.[67] Heidegger's innovation, anticipated by Marx, is to treat the subject of meaning as primarily practical. Meanings are not just in the mind but inhabit human action and define the objects of action as well. Practice does not depend on theoretical knowledge for access to meaning but has its own kind of "sight."[68] I suggest the term "enaction" in one of its several senses for Heidegger's concept of practical meaning.[69]

Enacted meanings are *lived* "subjectively," rather than formulated explicitly. For example, when one sits in a chair, one enacts the meaning "chair," although it is unnecessary to formulate that meaning explicitly to perform the operation. Sitting *in* a chair involves tacit recognition of a meaning: chairs are *for* sitting. Books stacked on a chair cannot experience this "in" and "for" but are simply impeded in their downward movement under the force of gravity. Nothing about this distinction implies either the unreality of chairs or the merely mental status of the meaning "chair." Subject and object are united in the practical relation of meaning, and because meanings are enacted, real "sensuous" objects are implicated in human practices. The connection is not merely ideal, in the mind, but is played out in concrete relations to objects as they are experienced.

This notion of enacted meaning explains why the Heideggerian world is organized through references. Objects of practice are not isolated facts but are linked together to form a unified whole within a form of life. The unity is not explained by causal relations among the objects. Consider, for example, the miniature world represented by a

---

67 Crowell, *Husserl, Heidegger, and the Space of Meaning*, 81–9. See also Theodore Kisiel, "Why Students of Heidegger Will Have to Read Emil Lask," in Theodore Kisiel, *Heidegger's Way of Thought* (New York: Continuum, 2002).

68 Martin Heidegger, *Being and Time*, trans. John Macquarrie and Edward Robinson(New York: Harper & Row, 1962), 98; Martin Heidegger, *Die Grundprobleme der Phänomenologie* (Frankfurt am Main: Klosterman, 1975), 163.

69 Robert Brandom defines it as follows: "The most fundamental kind of intentionality (in the sense of directedness towards objects) is the practical involvement with objects exhibited by a sentient creature dealing skillfully with its world." Robert Brandom, *Between Saying and Doing: Towards an Analytic Pragmatism* (Oxford: Oxford University Press, 2008), 178.

game such as chess. The pieces may have the same origin in a factory and shop, they may bump against each other in their case, and they may be dropped or broken, but such objective properties and causal interactions are not what unifies them. Rather, they are held together by the rules that prescribe their meaning and their powers, the moves they are authorized to make in the game. Just so, the environment in which human beings "move" is no mere concatenation of isolated facts but is organized and ordered by the meanings of its constituents—the references that tie them to each other and to the projects in which they play a role.

Objective knowledge results from de-worlding entities in order to reveal aspects not specifically engaged by Dasein's care. Outside a context of use, the individual tools in the workshop can be considered as "things" independent of each other, but this is not the way they are originally "disclosed" to the carpenter who engages with them practically at work in terms of their referenced meanings. The hammer and nails of the earlier example need not be conceived exclusively as belonging to the world of the workshop but can also be taken out of context and considered in terms of their properties as things with a specific weight, color, origin, and so on. This distinction allows Heidegger to avoid contradicting the existing natural sciences that study "de-worlded" things, while denying that science grounds worlds, the original scene on which "being" is "revealed."

The Marcuse Archive in Frankfurt contains a transcript of a course on "world" Heidegger gave in 1929 and 1930 that offers a broader view of the concept, relating it to organic life.[70] This course seems to have made an impression on Marcuse. Biology indicated the necessity of overcoming the Cartesian substantialization of a purely cognitive subject separate from its environment. Their unity is signified by the combined word *In-der-Welt-sein*, "being-in-the-world." Implicit in Marcuse's interpretation of the *Manuscripts* is a Marxist version of

---

70 The course is entitled *Grundbegriffe der Metaphysik (Welt, Endlichkeit, Vereinzelung)*. See Thomas Regehly, "Übersicht über die 'Heideggeriana' in Herbert Marcuse-Archiv der Stadt- und Universitätsbibliothek in Frankfurt am Main," in *Heidegger Studies* 7 (1991): 193. The journal editors add a peculiar footnote in which they "stress that the publication of this report *is not* an endorsement of Herbert Marcuse's position on Heidegger." Good to know . . .

Heidegger's substitution of the concept of being-in-the-world for the Cartesian cogito and the reduction of nature to extension.

In this course, Heidegger relies on Jakob von Uexküll's contemporary distinction between *Umwelt* and *Umgebung*.[71] Uexküll argued that organisms select a niche through a process of interpretation in terms of their needs, isolating a species-specific milieu, or *Umwelt*, from the objectively given environment, the *Umgebung*. Each such world is carved out of objective nature in terms of specific attributions of meaning: "This is food," "That is danger," and so on. The organism does not adapt to the natural environment in general but selects its milieu, its world, from the infinite stuff of nature. Life thus exists as a unity of organism and world, constructed around the organism.

Heidegger's course distinguishes three different relations to world. He argues that things are worldless, animals are "poor in world," and humans alone have a fully experienced world. Worldless things have no intentional relation to their surrounding, but interact with it only causally. Animals and humans also relate to the meaning of their surroundings, but Heidegger ends up questioning the attribution of worldhood to animals on the grounds that they are moved by instinct rather than a normatively informed care for identity.[72] He distinguishes the animal's limited reactions to its milieu, its *Umwelt*, from the fuller "openness" of Dasein through which the world becomes a window on reality. Nevertheless, it seems plausible to consider Uexküll's concept of *Umwelt* as background to Heidegger's own concept of worldhood.[73]

Heidegger's ontological version of the concept of world is based on "the relational structure between the animal and its environment."[74] This structure is no merely contingent encounter between self-subsistent

---

71 Jacob von Uexküll, *Theoretical Biology* (New York: Harcourt, Brace & Co., 1926).

72 For an account of Heidegger's distinction between human beings and animals, see Steven Crowell, "We Have Never Been Animals: Heidegger's Posthumanism," *Études phénoménologiques–Phenomenological Studies* 1 (2017): 217–40.

73 Theodore Kisiel, *The Genesis of Heidegger's Being and Time* (Berkeley: University of California Press, 1995), 506.

74 Martin Heidegger, *The Fundamental Concepts of Metaphysics: World, Finitude, Solitude*, trans. William A. McNeill and Nicholas Walker (Bloomington: Indiana University Press, 1995), 263. For the discussion of Uexküll, see 241–52. For further discussion of vitalism in this period, see Anne Harrington, *Reenchanted Science* (Princeton: Princeton University Press, 1996), 53–4.

things, as we usually conceive the relation between physical objects, but internal, implicating the existence of the related terms in each other. Heidegger argues that

> the organism is not something independent in its own right which then adapts itself. On the contrary, the organism adapts a particular environment *into* it[self] in each case, so to speak. The organism can adapt a particular environment into itself only insofar as openness for . . . belongs to its essence.[75]

The living thing cannot be adequately understood without reference to its world and vice versa.

In his first book on Hegel, Marcuse argues that the living subject and its objects are not things in the usual sense—substances—but are "bifurcations" in a larger whole that encompasses them both. "It is the tree *itself* (what we want to designate as its substantiality) which moves itself across the range of its conditions and not the conditions which move themselves *around* the tree."[76] In sum, life is not in the world passively as one object among many, but actively as a central reference point. The unity of living organism and environment is a deeper reality than their separate existences. In Heideggerian terms, they form a world, a way in which a specific range of things pertains to a practical subject.

Marcuse concludes that life is the "original unity [that] first makes this world into the world, and . . . allows it to happen as the world."[77] The "happening" of the world is an ontological act. "Life as self-consciousness is necessarily action; action necessarily treats the world as an immediately available, self-contained 'existent' (*Dasein*) 'from which the fact that it is brought forth by its *action* has disappeared.'"[78] It is not that the separate existence of the object is an illusion, but rather that its objectivity is conditioned on "Life" that constitutes it as both external and essential. Action not only has a direct effect on *the* world; it constitutes *a* world by identifying relevant objects and their relations. Marcuse writes:

---

75 Heidegger, *Fundamental Concepts of Metaphysics*, 264.
76 Marcuse, *Hegel's Ontology and the Theory of Historicity*, 99.
77 Ibid., 13.
78 Ibid., 298.

This is a process of infusing with Life the external world that opposes Life. Worldly objects are made to "correspond" thereby to Life (habitability, enjoyability, usefulness, applicability are not simply present as aspects of Life but are posited with Life itself and find completion in its movement).[79]

These categories are not personal to an individual but belong to the species and realize the truth of its objects in cognition. Thus, universality is implicit in the relation of the human being to its world.[80]

While Marcuse does not invoke Heideggerian categories in his interpretation of the *Manuscripts,* many of the ideas developed in his early essays continue to shape his approach. There is thus considerable continuity between his *Heidegger-Marxismus* and what appears to be the straight Marxism of his essay on the *Manuscripts.*

Heidegger's distinction between animals and humans is echoed in a passage deleted from the republished version of Marcuse's essay on the *Manuscripts.* He writes that, unlike animals, man "has objects not only as milieu [*Umwelt*] of his immediate life activity, and 'works' on them not only as the objects of his immediate needs, but he is open to all beings."[81] The concept of openness with which Heidegger specifies the human relation to its world is similar to Marcuse's account of Marx's concept of species-being as a free relation to the essence of things. Marx's claim that labor objectifies human faculties in nature gains a phenomenological sense: not only does labor make useful things, but labor is the mode in which reality is encountered as meaningful, as a world in the phenomenological sense of the term.

Marcuse develops this notion in many passages in his essay on the *Manuscripts*:

If the objective world is thus understood in its totality as a "social" world, as the objective reality of human society and thus as human objectification, then through this it is also already defined as a historical reality . . . Not only man but also nature "comes to be" in history, insofar as it is not something external to and separated

---

79 Ibid., 158.
80 Ibid., 168, 273.
81 Marcuse, "Neue Quellen," *Die Gesellschaft,* 148.

from the human essence but belongs to the transcended and appropriated objectivity of man.[82]

Statements such as this reflect the ambiguity of the *Manuscripts*.
Marcuse appears at first to assume an external reality, an "objective
world," but he quickly resolves it into the "human essence": "In his
labor man sublates the mere objectivity of objects and makes them into
'the means of life.' He impresses on them the form of his being [*Wesen*]
and makes them into 'his work and his reality.'"[83]

What is new here with respect to Heidegger is the role of labor in
constructing the "world," but Marcuse's version still has the form of
"worldhood" as a system of meaningful objects contingent on the practical subject. It is as though Marcuse had enlarged the context of the
phenomenological world to embrace the material conditions of its
possibility. But those conditions are not exactly what one would expect.
There is no reference to any actual work or raw materials. Labor in this
speculative sense consists in the projection of the human "essence," the
construction of the meanings that make a world. "Objectification:
the determination of man as an 'objective being,' as a natural being, is
not simply a further point appended to the determination of the unity
of man and nature, but is the closer and deeper foundation of this
unity."[84]

This is a rather confusing sentence since it is not clear, at least to an
English speaker, what work the word "objectification" is doing, but it
is plausible to substitute the word "as" for the colon. Then Marcuse is
saying that the human being is not an objective being simply because it
is a natural being, and the unity of the human being with nature is not
due to the natural quality they share. Rather, the human being is properly called "objective" because it objectifies. Objectification is the
specific determination that qualifies the human being as objective,

---

82 Marcuse, "New Sources," 102.

83 Ibid., 101.

84 Ibid., 97, translation modified. Marcuse, "Neue Quellen," *Die Gesselschaft*,
148–9. "Die Vergegenständlichung: die Bestimmung des Menschen als eines 'gegen-
ständlichen Wesens,' kommt nicht zu der Bestimmung der Einheit von Mensch and
Nature: des Menschen als eines 'natürlichen Wesens,' wie etwas anderes hinzu, sondern
sie ist nur die nähere und tiefere Begründung dieser Einheit."

and, furthermore, it is objectification that establishes the unity of human being and nature. In sum, the argument of the *Manuscripts* is not the simpleminded notion that humans are natural things, have a body, and engage in causal interactions with other natural things, but rather that humans have a special role as the beings that bring meaning to nature through the capacity to objectify their own qualities and faculties. Moreover, this special role is not "added on" to the objectivity of the human, but is what it means for humans to be "objective beings." In sum the human being is natural because it objectifies, rather than the reverse. Thus, despite all the talk of man and nature as objective, the interactions of which would presumably be external and causal, there is a "deeper foundation," the objectification that binds them in an essential unity.

How close is this to a Heideggerian "being-in-the-world"? There is a definite asymmetry between Dasein and the things that surround it, an asymmetry resembling that between the objectifying human and nature in Marcuse's interpretation of Marx. Dasein is the *um . . . zu*, the "in order to" of the Heideggerian world, which establishes the referential system of meaningful objects. In Marcuse's interpretation, Marx's "human" has a similar function, establishing the meanings and purposes of the surrounding world. Furthermore, the relation of both Dasein and the human is essential; they cannot be separated as in the Cartesian scheme where soul and things are independent substances. Heidegger's being-in-the-world resembles Marx's "unity of man and nature." Of course, there are important differences between Heidegger's theory and Marcuse's interpretations of Marx, but the determination of human being as objective *because* objectifying suggests a Heideggerian origin.

The Priority of Practice

There is an intriguing mention of Marcuse in Heidegger's conversations in Le Thor. Heidegger notes that production is defining for the "world" in Marx and, further, that production is a type of praxis:

> Reversing Hegel's idealism in his own way, Marx requires that being be given precedence over consciousness. Since there is no consciousness in *Being and Time*, one could believe that there is something

> Heideggerian to be read here [in Marx]! At least Marcuse had under-
> stood *Being and Time* in this way.[85]

Heidegger implies that this is an error, but in fact, *Being and Time*
repeats in phenomenological guise two Marxian innovations: that the
human relation to its world is *essential* and fundamentally *practical*.
Moreover, Marx's concept of practice resembles Heidegger's by poss-
essing its own form of "sight," an inherent cognitive power. Lucien
Sebag concludes:

> Marx breaks with every limitation of signifying activity to the
> understanding alone, the true subject no longer being the subject of
> knowledge alone . . . but the real human being inserted into the
> concrete life of the society of which he is a member.[86]

Perhaps Marcuse was not wrong to find a deep connection between
aspects of Heidegger's early work and Marx. In this section and the
next, I will review and test Marcuse's quasi-phenomenological reading
of Marx.

There is, of course, nothing like phenomenological analysis in
Marx's work, but he adopted some sort of anti-Cartesian ontology. His
first thesis on Feuerbach is the strongest evidence that phenomenology
is relevant to his thought. Marx writes, "The chief defect of all previous
materialism . . . is that the object, actuality, sensuousness is conceived
only in the form of the *object or perception* [*Anschauung*], but not as
sensuous human activity, practice [*Praxis*], not subjectively."[87]

The reference to subjectivity must surely have something to do with
the first-person standpoint. However, to affirm that standpoint without
returning to idealism requires the concepts of intentionality and lifeworld first developed at the turn of the twentieth century in phenomenology. The intentional subject is bound to its object, its world, and so
cannot float off into the transcendental beyond of idealism. Lacking
those concepts, Marx nevertheless finds a way of signifying the connection

---

85 Martin Heidegger, *Four Seminars*, trans. Andrew J. Mitchell and François
Raffoul (Bloomington: Indiana University Press, 2003), 52.

86 Lucien Sebag, *Marxisme et structuralisme* (Paris: Payot, 1964), 88, my translation.

87 Karl Marx, "Theses on Feuerbach," in *Writings of the Young Marx*, 400.

of subjectivity to a world through the idea of practice. For instance, *The German Ideology* argues that "the sensuous world [is] the total living sensuous activity of the individuals composing it."[88]

Marx's emphasis on sensuousness as practice suggests a relation to meaning, without which practice is mere mechanical performance. Sensuousness, understood "subjectively," reveals possibilities, meanings. Indeed, Marx writes, "The meaning of an object for me extends only as far as the sense extends."[89] As Konstantinos Rantis writes, "The senses do not simply copy things in their given form, but discover in them possibilities, facilities, forms, qualities, and press them toward their realization."[90] Sense thus enacts a "world," a way of life and its associated objects. A correlation between sense and object is here established through the meaning of the object to which corresponds a developed sensory capacity. That capacity is itself a function of labor through which the senses are humanized and disclose the meaning labor has posited in their objects. The objectified meanings, realized in artifacts, react back on sensation and enrich its powers.

In the essay on the *Manuscripts*, Marcuse understands the merging of the concepts of sensation and practice in terms of the relation of theory and practice. He writes that "what seems to him [the subject] 'theoretically' objective (*Gegenständliche*) must be taken up into his practice in order that it be made into the object of his '*life's activity*'— that is, adapted (*bearbeiten*)."[91] The world appears to sensuousness

---

88 Marx and Engels, "The German Ideology," 419. Like Althusser, Michael Löwy proposes that there is a sharp "epistemological" break between the *Manuscripts* and the *Theses on Feuerbach* and the *German Ideology*. I see no evidence that Marcuse would have agreed at the time he was writing on the *Manuscripts*. Be that as it may, the problem of understanding the "concrete sensuous world" of these later texts is adumbrated in the *Manuscripts*. Michael Löwy, *La théorie de la révolution chez le jeune Marx* (Paris: Editions Sociales, 1977), 38n1, 166.

89 Marx, "Economic and Philosophical Manuscripts," 161.

90 Konstantinos Rantis, "Kants Kritik der Urteilskraft und Marcuse's Befreiung der Natur," in *Zeitschrift für kritische Theorie* 48–49 (2019): 115, my translation. This article contains an account of Marcuse's interpretation and use of Kant's third critique.

91 "Und das ihm so 'theoretisch' Gegenständliche muß er in seine Praxis aufnehmen, zum Gegenstand seiner 'Lebenstätigkeit' machen–bearbeiten." Marcuse, "Neue Quellen," in *Der deutsche Künstlerroman*, 522, my translation. In the English version:

already endowed with universality, meaning. It presents itself "theoretically," as though independent of the subject, but it is not indifferent to human being. The theoretical object is destined to become the practical object adapted to human nature. It is thus ready, in principle, to enter the human world even before it is worked on by labor.

Another passage repeats and develops this notion further. Marcuse argues that the priority of practice separates Marx from Feuerbach, for whom perception remains purely contemplative: "For Marx, to put it briefly, labor replaces this [Feuerbachian] perception, although the central importance of the theoretical relation does not disappear; as we will see, it turns toward [*tritt . . . zur*] labor in a founding relation."[92] Marcuse interprets the persistence of "theory" in the practical relation to objectivity in terms of the meaning-bearing practice of labor. Practice is not simply a causal interaction with things but is also a relation of meaning. In this context, meaning is not an alternative to praxis but arises from it. Practical activity structures a world articulated by thought.[93]

The ontological priority of the practical relation to reality suggests a nondeterministic way of understanding the relationship of consciousness to being. Marxists usually argue that material circumstances determine thought causally—a claim Marx himself makes on occasion. But a dialectical relation seems to be implied by the priority of practice in the *Manuscripts*. That priority is reflected in later texts such as *The German Ideology*, where Marx writes: "Conceiving, thinking, and the intellectual relationships of men appear here as the direct result of their material behavior . . . Consciousness can never be anything else except conscious existence, and the existence of men is their actual life-process."[94] Note that it is not the material circumstances that are

---

"He has to include these 'theoretical' objective things in his praxis. He must make them the object of his 'life activity' and work on them." Marcuse, "New Sources," 96.

92 Marcuse, "New Sources," 101, translation modified. The last phrase in the original is "es tritt, wie wir noch sehen werden, zur Arbeit in ein Fundierungsverhältnis." Marcuse, "Neue Quellen," in *Der deutsche Künstlerroman*, 529.

93 The mature Marx offers a version of this early theory of meaning that is compatible with commonsense realism, yet the reference to praxis persists and harks back to the early view. See Karl Marx, "Notes on Adolph Wagner," in *Texts on Method*, ed. Terrell Carver (London: Basil Blackwell, 1975), 190–1.

94 Marx and Engels, "The German Ideology," 414.

decisive but "material *behavior*." In the *Manuscripts* the "world" is posited by material behavior understood as objectifying practice.[95]

This shows up later in one of Marx's canonical definitions of historical materialism, where he writes,

> This mode of production must not be considered simply as being the reproduction of the physical existence of the individuals. Rather, it is a definite form of activity of these individuals, a definite form of expressing their life, a definite *mode of life* on their part.[96]

Marcuse interprets this passage on contemporary philosophical terms. Where Marx contrasts physical reproduction taken "simply," presumably as a causal relation, and the "mode of life" as a form of expression and a practice, Marcuse sees the philosophical distinction between existence and meaning. He writes,

> The simple fact that one of the main tendencies of Marxian economy is to divest the objectivity of the economic world of its reified character (*Dingcharakter*) by grasping its origin in concretely historical human behavior is already proof that the ontological (*seinsmäßige*) union of human and world, taken in full concretion, is the premise and foundation of Marx's pure economy.[97]

In other words, human being and world are one *in action*, in "historical human behavior."

Once this conflation is admitted, the whole quasi-phenomenological reconstruction of Marxism follows. Where Marxism traditionally distinguished the economy as material reality from the ideal beliefs of individuals, separating object from subject, Marcuse imposes a different distinction between the "with- and surrounding world" "exactly as it is lived" in contrast with the realm of objective facts. The first is an

---

95 Marcuse, "New Sources," 102.

96 Marx and Engels, "The German Ideology," 409.

97 Herbert Marcuse, "On the Critique of Sociology," trans. Annette Kuhlmann and David Smith, *Mid-American Review of Sociology* 16, no. 2 (1992): 23, translation modified. First published as "Zur Kritik der Soziologie," *Die Gesellschaft: Internationale Revue fur Sozialismus und Politik* 2, no. 9 (1931): 270–80.

order of meaning, a "world," the second a causal order known to a disincarnated subject, a cogito. The lived reality of social life includes both the economy *and* individual beliefs as they unfold in practical experience. Those same material and ideal aspects have another existence as objects of knowledge. Marcuse considers the former to be ontologically fundamental.[98]

This is not subjective idealism. Marcuse, and Marx in his interpretation, conceive meaning as access to the real. The real, in this context, is not what the early Marx calls the "abstract" nature of natural science but the "wider" nature as it is experienced and transformed. This lived nature is objective, but it belongs to human history, as do human needs and the labor that satisfies them. According to Marcuse, "What happens to objects worked on and obtained through labor does not take place in the dimension of 'nature,' 'materiality,' etc., but in the dimension of human history."[99]

World-Constitution

The concept of world introduces necessity into the relation to things insofar as everything worked on is adapted to the being of the subject. But how, precisely, are things implicated in a world in this sense? And what makes the correlation of subject and object operative in each particular case? Missing is a fuller explanation for the ontological necessity of the practical subject-object relation. In this section, I will show how the concepts of need, world, sense, and practice Marcuse deploys in his interpretation of the *Manuscripts* could have been further developed in a consistent philosophy of praxis.

---

98 This unusual interpretation of historical materialism is developed in Marcuse's early essay on Dilthey. Marcuse, "Das Problem der geschichtlichen Wirklichkeit," 480n7, 483–5.

99 Marcuse, "On the Concept of Labor," 139. Although published after the essay on the *Manuscripts*, Marcuse's essay on labor appears to have been written earlier, when Heidegger's influence was more pronounced. That influence is clear in propositions such as this: "Human praxis is labor on and in the present through the transformative 'sublation' of the past with anticipatory care for the future." Ibid., 141. See also Alberto Toscano, "Liberation Technology: Marcuse's Communist Individualism," *Institute for the Radical Imagination* 3, no, 1 (2009): 10.

Marx, as Marcuse understands him, affirms the implication of human being in being as such. The entry of objects into history through labor is no mere accident of their being but realizes them most fully, enables them to "become real objects." The meaning of what it is to be an object now includes a quasi-teleology in accordance with which objects become "real" through incorporation into a human world.[100] Marcuse writes:

> In this freedom man reproduces "the whole of nature," and through transformation and appropriation furthers it, along with his own life, even when this production does not satisfy an immediate need. Thus the history of human life is at the same time essentially the history of man's objective world and of "the whole of nature" ("nature" in the wider sense given to this concept by Marx, as also by Hegel). Man is not in nature; nature is not the external world into which he first has to come out of his own inwardness. Man is nature. Nature is his "expression," "his work and his reality."[101]

In his first book on Hegel, Marcuse explains that life incorporates nature into history. Life is a process of appropriation and transformation of nature and self through work. "Self-consciousness had recognized that the world constituted only the cycle of its activity . . . It recognized that actuality is in essence an object of work."[102] This is work as world constituting. But this seems a regression to pre-Kantian metaphysics. How can work, an intraworldly phenomenon, constitute "reality"?

Objectification, on these terms, is not merely a contingent causal relation between separate substances but rather actualizes the object, grants it its appropriate form. This is the sense of Marcuse's reference to Hegel, for whom the "actual" is not immediate existence but results from the labor of the concept, here reinterpreted as labor *tout court*. Implied in objectification is thus the notion that raw materials are not indifferent to labor but suffer a kind of ontological privation until labor

---

100 Marcuse, "New Sources," 112; Marcuse, "Neue Quellen," in *Der deutsche Künstlerroman*, 544.

101 Marcuse, "New Sources," 97.

102 Marcuse, *Hegel's Ontology and the Theory of Historicity*, 276.

grants them full reality, "actuality" in Hegel's sense. The human power to identify the universal in things, that is, their potentialities, makes possible their incorporation into a world where they can become what they "truly" are.

Of course, this leaves the question of the independence of nature in suspense. Marx treats it under the category of "estrangement." As such, Marcuse argues, it is a necessary aspect of the "true" unity of human being and nature: "It is man's 'neediness' . . . for objects alien to him, 'overpowering, and 'not part of his being,' to which he must relate *as* to external objects, although they only become real objects through and for him."[103] Thus "external nature" is only apparently independent. The word "as" here reduces nature to a condition of need which it is destined to fulfill. But in what sense are need and nature so correlated?

The Greeks answered a similar question with the notion that technē brought tendencies in nature to fulfillment. In his discussion of Greek technē, Heidegger offers the work of the potter as an example. The *pathein* (tolerance) of the clay allows it to achieve its potentialities under the hands of the craftsman:

> With the transformation of the clay into a bowl, the lump also loses its form, but fundamentally it loses its formlessness; it gives up a lack, and hence the tolerating here is at once a positive contribution to the development of something higher.[104]

This answer presupposes a teleological metaphysics that is no longer believable in modern times. Marx needed a different account of the subject-object relation. He only hints at the basis of such an account with his claim that needs are ontologically significant. Presumably, this means that the relation of need to satisfaction is *necessary*. Thus

---

103 Marcuse, "New Sources," 112; Marcuse, "Neue Quellen," in *Der deutsche Künstlerroman*, 544, my italics.

104 Martin Heidegger, *Aristotle's Metaphysics 1–3: On the Essence and Actuality of Force*, trans. Walter Brogan and Peter Warnek (Bloomington: Indiana University Press, 1995), 74; see also 116–18. I discuss this aspect of Heidegger's thought in Andrew Feenberg, *Heidegger and Marcuse: The Catastrophe and Redemption of History* (London: Routledge, 2005), chapter 2. See also Steven Crowell, "Günter Figal's *Objectivity*: From Transcendental to Hermeneutic Phenomenology (and Back)," *Research in Phenomenology* 44 (2014): 121–34, esp. 132.

he writes, "The sun is an *object*, a necessary and life-assuring object, for the plant, just as the plant is an object for the sun, an *expression* of the sun's life-giving power and *objective* essential powers."[105] And, since labor mediates the satisfaction of needs, it too has ontological significance. Marcuse's interpretation of the *Manuscripts* does not work out the implications of this alternative to traditional teleological metaphysics, but there are indications that he was tending in this direction. I will develop those indications here in more detail.

The starting point for this exercise in completing Marcuse's argument is a question he would later formulate as follows: "How can the human sensibility, which is *principium individuationis*, also generate a universalizing principle?"[106] Marcuse claims that Kant's theory of sensibility is the basis of Marx's concept of sensuousness. He registers only the passive side of the Kantian formulation, but there is an active aspect as well: sense experience is structured by the categories. Could Marcuse have intended that side also to play a role in his interpretation of sensuousness? On these quasi-Kantian terms, sensuousness is not mere immediacy, nor is it a simple causal interaction with stimuli in the environment. Rather, sensuousness is informed by concepts as an encounter with meaning. This is in fact the conclusion Marcuse reaches in his late essay "Nature and Revolution."

> The senses are not merely passive, receptive: they have their own "syntheses" to which they subject the primary data of experience. And these syntheses are not only the pure "forms of intuition" (space and time) which Kant recognized as an inexorable a priori ordering of sense data. There are perhaps also other syntheses, far more concrete, far more "material," which may constitute an empirical (i.e., historical) a priori of experience.[107]

Pursuing this connection, we arrive at a solution to the enigma of world-constitution. The notion of enacted meaning discussed in the previous sections emphasizes the cognitive content of sensation.

---

105 Marx, *Economic and Philosophical Manuscripts,* 207.
106 Marcuse, "Nature and Revolution," 72.
107 Ibid., 63.

Marcuse writes that sensuousness is a "mediating concept [that] designates the senses as organs of cognition."[108] This relates the senses to his interpretation of species-being as a relation to the universal. There is a hint of this in Marx, who claims that the universal as well as the particular, the given as well as the possible, is revealed to sensation. "The senses have, therefore, become directly theoreticians in practice."[109]

In Kant, experience is formed by a specific type of meaning, which he designates as transcendental "categories." Causality, for example, is such a category. The mind will always find cause-effect relations a priori in the experience of empirical objects. Every event has a cause in principle, and this is a necessary relation, whatever that cause might be, whether known or unknown. According to Kant, such categories are both in the mind and in experience as a result of the formative operations that constitute objects.

As usually understood, Kant's theory of sensory experience belongs to epistemology, since it explains the conditions of possibility of objects of knowledge. Marx and Marcuse presuppose something like Kant's notion of the constitution of objectivity, but they interpret it in terms of the concept of sensuousness, which includes both sensation and need. The reference to an ontology of need suggests a necessary correlation between needs and the means of satisfaction, with labor operating the formative work Kant attributes to the transcendental subject. Just as in Kant, the categories of the mind are also found in experience, so needs and satisfactions must be the empirical form of correlated meanings. The ontological interpretation of needs binds them to their objects in an essential unity.

For example, consider hunger and food. How are they *essentially* related as Marx claims? Certainly not as ordinary things in the world; indeed, neither science nor common sense find an essential relation there. But food, as a category under which certain objects are understood, is essentially related to hunger as the corresponding category under which human beings relate to what is understood as food. The two categories thus stand in essential relations *conceptually*.[110] This is what it

---

108 Herbert Marcuse, *Eros and Civilization: A Philosophical Inquiry into Freud* (Boston: Beacon Press, 1966), 183.

109 Marx, "Economic and Philosophical Manuscripts," 160.

110 This seems to be the import of J. M. Bernstein's interpretation of the

means to say that the object, food, "is brought forth by its [human] *action.*"[111] From a "logical" standpoint in Marcuse's sense, hunger and food are mutually necessary: there is no concept of hunger without a concept of food, but, from an objective standpoint, the relation between any particular hunger and the food that satisfies it is merely accidental.

That distinction, in itself, is not remarkable, but the emphasis on practice shared by Marx and Marcuse suggests a third standpoint: *the practical enactment of the conceptual relations* as they are manifest to the acting subject, that is, "subjectively," as Marx says in his first thesis. Perhaps this is the "founding relation" to which Marcuse alludes in his remark on the theoretical character of labor in the *Manuscripts.* The correlated concepts reflect a way of being in the world in accordance with which objects of action take on specific meanings. The acting subject lives the logical necessity of the correlation in a particular instance. Its objects are real objects, as Marx continually insists, and not merely representations or thoughts, but they are encountered through their enacted meaning. The necessity of this encounter stems from the logic of the *lived relation* of the meanings engaged in the lifeworld.

In that case, meaning and "reality" cannot be distinguished. Of course, any given meal is only accidentally related to the person who eats it. The unity at the level of enacted meaning does not cancel the contingency of any particular encounter of the human being with an object, nor does the role of meaning cancel material existence. And, to be sure, hunger and food are two separate things in the ordinary sense of the word "thing." But "subjectively" considered, they are not things in that sense. Rather, in their lived practical relation, they are enacted meanings that require each other to be intelligible. As enacted, they are less than a cognitive subject and more than an objective thing; they are moments in a praxis, "sensuous human activity," *implicated materially in each other's being.*[112]

---

concept of material inference. J. M. Bernstein, "Mimetic Rationality and Material Inference: Adorno and Brandom," *Revue internationale de philosophie* 58, no. 227 (2004): 7–23.

111 Marcuse, *Hegel's Ontology and the Theory of Historicity,* 298.

112 Merleau-Ponty writes that "praxis [is] . . . less than a subject and more than an object." Maurice Merleau-Ponty, *Les Aventures de la dialectique* (Paris: Gallimard, 1955), 66, my translation.

Meaning is now conceived as the medium in which material exist-ence is first encountered. The practical object is not in the mind but is there to see and touch. Meaning is not a mental projection but the aspect of that object revealed by the practice that engages it. We are in what Adorno calls a "somatic" relation to it.[113] As such, it has all the features we associate with "reality": it has weight and depth, appears different from different angles, and can be lost and found. It is against the background of an enacted meaning that such particularities of objects appear. This may be what Gramsci meant when he said of philosophy of praxis that after "perfecting . . . the old materialism there remains only philosophical realism."[114]

Without explicitly stating these phenomenological premises, Marcuse seems to have transposed them to the level of a historical "constituent subjectivity." That subject, the laboring community of the *Manuscripts*, encounters the world through its practice and "produces" it as its essential object. Interpreted "subjectively," the unity of subject and object in practice is a disclosure of meaning. It does not, or in any case need not, challenge the independent existence of nature for an objective observer, because it operates from the first-person standpoint of a collective actor.[115] From that standpoint, the independence of nature is tied up with its entry into the world of the subject of practice as the prior condition of its facticity.[116]

---

113 Theodor Adorno, *Negative Dialectics*, trans. E. B. Ashton (London: Routledge, 1973), 203.

114 Antonio Gramsci, *Selections from the Prison Notebooks*, ed. and trans. Quintin Hoare and Geoffrey N. Smith (New York: International Publishers, 1971), 371.

115 That Marcuse entertains something like this account of collective practice is confirmed in *One-Dimensional Man* by his reliance on the phenomenological concepts of "project" and *Lebenswelt*, applied to capitalism qua collective subject. Chapter 5 will take up this aspect of Marcuse's thought. Marcuse, *One-Dimensional Man*, chapter 6. See also Marcuse's apparent acceptance of Husserl's notion of the *sinngebende Leistung* of the historical subject which he contrasts favorably to the individualized transcenden-tal subject. Marcuse, "On Science and Phenomenology," 289.

116 Here is Heidegger's explanation for this paradoxical dependence/independence: "The independence of things at hand from humans is not altered by the fact that this very independence as such is possible only if humans exist. The being in themselves of things not only becomes unexplainable without the existence of humans, it becomes utterly meaningless; but this does not mean that the things themselves are dependent upon humans." Heidegger, *Aristotle's Metaphysics*, 173–4.

This is a non-metaphysical ontological claim. It establishes the mutual necessity of subject and object without intruding on the domain of the natural sciences. It might be called a *first-person materialism*, in contrast with the usual third-person materialism of common sense and naturalism—or, more precisely, a first-person *plural* materialism, because the subject of practice is the class and ultimately the human species. Moreover, since human beings are historical beings, this is a *historical* materialism where history is understood not as a collection of facts but as the lived experience of a community.[117] This is the sense in which we could agree with Marx that the *Manuscripts* overcome the opposition of materialism and idealism.

As the constitutive subject of its world, the proletariat has remarkable powers manifested in labor, but labor cannot transform itself. That requires another kind of action—revolutionary action—but Marx did not explain in what that action would consist. Marcuse goes well beyond the *Manuscripts* in this respect, as I will show in the next section.

Revolution in Lukács and Marcuse

The human being is essentially a "universal and free" being that objectifies itself in the world through its practice. In so doing, it establishes the unity of subject and object that is implied in the essential sociality of both human being and its objects. That unity is broken by alienation. Alienation is only possible because the object of practice appears as "external," although in reality, as we have seen, it is always already social. Marcuse writes:

> The objective world . . . *is* real objectivity only for self-realizing man, it is the "self-objectification" of man or human objectification. But

---

117 Although there is no clear formulation of such a theory in Marcuse, he was certainly familiar with something similar from Lukács's *History and Class Consciousness*. For an account of Lukács's argument, see Richard Westerman, *Lukács's Phenomenology of Capitalism*, 98–100, 119. In *One-Dimensional Man*, Marcuse calls consciousness "a general disposition which is common, in various degrees, to the individual members of one group, class, society." Marcuse, *One-Dimensional Man*, 208.

this same objective world, since it is real objectivity, can appear as a precondition of his being that does *not* belong to his being, that is beyond his control, and that is "overpowering." This conflict in the human essence—that it is in itself objective—is the root of the fact that objectification can become reification and that externalization . . . *can become alienation.*[118]

The contingency of the practical relations between human beings and particular things seems to exclude any essential relation between them. That is the common sense that gives plausibility to naturalism. However, for Marx and Marcuse, contingency does not prove the ultimate independence of the object from the subject, as naturalism would have it. How contingency is possible without independence, they do not explain, but it is vital to the theory as it accounts for the "conflict" between the ontologically *essential* relation of subject and object and the ontic independence which gives rise to alienation.

Under capitalism, this conflict is manifested in the division of labor and private property. Where alienation blocks the identity of essence and factual existence, a total revolution is necessary.[119] Liberation from private property will resolve the antinomy of subject and object and end the alienation of human beings from nature.[120]

The demand for revolution emerges not from a merely political or economic crisis but from "a catastrophe of the human essence" that "becomes the inexorable impulse for the initiation of radical revolution."[121] That impulse is mediated by knowledge. In a passage omitted in the later version of his essay on the *Manuscripts*, Marcuse argues that "knowledge of the historical-social situation is in itself knowledge of an obligatory and compulsory task: the practical realization of 'truly human' reality required of and in this situation."[122] There is thus no

---

118 Marcuse, "New Sources," 98.

119 Marcuse, "Contributions to a Phenomenology," 106.

120 While the *Manuscripts* do not touch explicitly on ecological themes, the connection has been made. See John Bellamy Foster, Brett Clark, and Richard York, *The Ecological Rift* (New York: Monthly Review Press, 2010), 236–7.

121 Marcuse, "Neue Quellen," *Die Gesellschaft*, 106, my translation.

122 Ibid., 162–3, my translation.

need for a separate normative theory to justify revolution. Rather, the ontologically informed understanding of society imperatively requires human action to institute a new world.

These passages from Marcuse's interpretation of the *Manuscripts* suggest an unusual concept of revolution. For Marcuse, the role of knowledge in revolution is neither strategic nor normative, but effective qua *knowledge*. There is a precedent for this approach: Marcuse follows Lukács in identifying revolutionary action with a dereification of consciousness. For Lukács, revolutionary consciousness transforms its objects precisely in knowing them. The proletariat becomes the agent of revolution through its "self-knowledge" as exploited class, through the immediate practical consequences of the meaning it attaches to its situation under capitalism.[123] Dereification of that situation in consciousness breaks the grip of the laws of the market.

Thought is not just a mental process that might yield practical applications, but rather, Lukács claims, "a form of reality." As such, "the act of consciousness overthrows the form of objectivity of its object."[124] Marcuse concurs: consciousness is no reflection or spectator on reality but an effective aspect of reality with the power to effect fundamental transformation.[125]

Marcuse echoes Lukács: "To what extent can knowledge, the knowledge of objectification as something social, become the real impulse for the abolition of all reification?" And he replies that "the 'conscious' behavior of man, insofar as it discloses his true essence and his true reality, is no merely theoretical knowledge, no uncommitted passive

---

123 "Only if the subject (consciousness, thought) were both producer and product of the dialectical process, only if, as a result the subject moved in a self-created world of which it is the conscious form and only if the world imposed itself upon it in full objectivity, only then can the problem of dialectics, and with it the abolition of the antitheses of subject and object, thought and existence, freedom and necessity, be held to be solved." Lukács, *History and Class Consciousness*, 142. The similarity between this concept of consciousness and the Kantian "intuitive understanding" is discussed in Feenberg, *Philosophy of Praxis*, 105, 112.

124 Lukács, *History and Class Consciousness*, 203, 178, translation modified.

125 Marcuse, "Das Problem der geschichtlichen Wirklichkeit," 470. Marcuse is critical of Lukács's notion of imputed class consciousness but seems to have adopted other more important aspects of his theory wholesale.

assessment, but, in a deep and many-sided sense, praxis."[126] Such revolutionary consciousness is only available to the proletariat, given its class position in capitalist society.[127] Its knowledge, Marcuse writes, "achieves the *practical force and concrete form* through which it can become the lever of the revolution."[128]

This is the unity of theory and practice that is the central theme of Lukács's *History and Class Consciousness*, and that Marcuse, in one early essay, calls "the noblest desideratum of all philosophizing."[129] Revolution is a fundamental ideological transformation that takes place not just in thought but in social reality; in other words, the collective "thought" of the proletariat *is* social reality.

Lukács's concept of consciousness thus departs from the standard Marxist distinctions between subjective and objective factors, superstructure and base. Those distinctions usually imply causal interaction between ideal and real entities. But the revolution, as Lukács conceives it, strikes deeper than causality, to the ontological level, the level of the form of objectivity. And, because forms of objectivity are rooted in practice—that is, are enacted and not simply thought—change in meaning has material consequences.

At the ontological level, social objects take on meaning and function through their relation to the total system to which they belong. Recall Lukács's gloss on Marx's claim that the "negro" and the "cotton-spinning jenny" become slaves and capital through their relation to the totality. What is true of capitalism as a system of meanings imposed on society is also true of the forces that overthrow it. When revolutionary workers claim the factory in which they are employed as social property, its objective reality is altered, as is their behavior toward it. Lukács concludes, "Every substantial change that is of concern to knowledge manifests itself as a change in relation to the whole and through this as a change in the form of objectivity itself."[130] Following

---

126 Marcuse, "Neue Quellen," *Die Gesellschaft*, 163, my translation. The corresponding passage, with some omissions, is found in the English text at page 110 and in the republished version at 541.

127 Marcuse, "New Sources," 114.

128 Ibid., 110–11.

129 Marcuse, "On Concrete Philosophy," 44.

130 Lukács, *History and Class Consciousness*, 13.

Lukács, Marcuse argues that the moving forces of major historical change modify the very meaning of the facts in both theory and practice. He writes, "Every authentic historical movement proves itself to be a 'change of *meaning*.'"[131]

The proletariat, as collective subject, has a world, a proper domain of objects enacted in the collective practice of the class. Lukács signified something similar with his notion that classes have "immediate" objects relative to their class position, which determine their perspective on society. In Marcuse's interpretation, this becomes an implicit phenomenological supplement to the usual notion of proletarian subjectivity that fails to register the specificity of its objects but simply treats them as "objective factors."[132] For both Marcuse and Lukács, the proletariat as subject correlates with the meaningful objects that make up its lifeworld—the central realities of a capitalist society. Those objects develop in an objective sequence of events, but that sequence plays out in the first-person encounter of the collective subject with its world.

The revolutionary transformation of the lived meaning of the social world by the proletariat is not arbitrary, but it must correspond to actual potentialities to be an effective force. Those potentialities are known by Marxist theory and encountered practically in the revolution. That coincidence is historically conditioned; it corresponds to what Lukács calls "the actuality of the revolution," a historical period in which the movement of the revolutionary class aims at realistic targets because revolution is objectively on the agenda.

In such a situation, theory and practice can engage in fruitful encounters, for example, through the interaction of theoreticians, party, and class. Lukács writes,

> This assumes that the forms of mediation in and through which it becomes possible to go beyond the immediate existence of objects as they are given, can be shown to be the structural principles and the real tendencies of the objects themselves.[133]

---

131 Marcuse, "Contributions to a Phenomenology," 30.
132 Lukács, *History and Class Consciousness*, 52, 165–6.
133 Ibid., 155.

In sum, the new meanings (mediations) imposed by the revolutionary movement correspond to causal forces (structures and tendencies) theory identifies in social reality.

In the proletariat, social life as a system of lived meanings and the actual historical development of society as a causal sequence become one and the same. As Marcuse writes in an early essay, "As soon as logical and social being are merged in a *single knowledge system* [*Erkenntniszusammenhang*], the meaning of the distinction between logical and realist conceptualization necessarily disappears."[134] The revolution cancels the distinction between meaning ("logical being") and existence ("social being"), transforming the cultural foundations of social life through action on the totality. The separation of meaning and existence is overcome in this transformation of existence by meaning. Total revolution is a revolution of meaning *and* existence; it is *ontological* revolution.[135]

Conclusion

Marcuse's interpretation of the *Manuscripts* should be read in the light of attempts by a whole generation of thinkers such as Bloch, Benjamin, Adorno, Horkheimer, Korsch, Lukács, and Gramsci to locate Marxist philosophy within the contemporary philosophical debates of the early twentieth century. No longer was philosophy to compete with natural science on the terrain of facts. Neo-Kantianism and phenomenology situated philosophy on a new terrain. The major academic thinkers of the day worked to define the transcendental conditions of scientific knowledge, or explored the subtle structures of everyday experience from which science abstracts in constructing its objects.

The Marxists who entered these debates focused on history as the proper domain of philosophical study. The science they attempted to

---

134 Marcuse, "Transzendentaler Marxismus?," 462, my translation.

135 Lukács applies this concept of transforming consciousness only to society. Nature, he says, will remain reified even under socialism. Marcuse interprets the *Manuscripts* to argue that the revolution will transform not only society but being as such. In a late essay he writes, "Nature, too, awaits the revolution!" Marcuse, "Nature and Revolution," 74.

found was invented by Marx in *Capital*, and the everyday experience they analyzed was life under capitalism, and especially resistance to capitalism. Read in this context, the *Manuscripts* had a lot to say if only one could understand Marx's paradoxical formulations.

Marcuse's interpretation preserves Marx's most daring and difficult claims without metaphysical assumptions and so belongs to this trend in Marxist philosophy. It does so through a quasi-phenomenological approach to the role of meaning in praxis. As we have seen, Marcuse's particular philosophical background provides him with subtle resources for understanding Marx's puzzling argument.

In my conjectural formulation of his argument, Marcuse escapes the dilemma of materialism and idealism by affirming the independence of nature *in the context of human experience*. On this view, the natural presupposition of labor is always already part of the human world through its meaning, and that meaning is enacted by labor.

"Nature" now plays two roles in the argument. On the one hand, natural objects and labor are contingently related at the causal level. No necessity attaches to causal action on the objects of labor. On the other hand, natural objects are essentially related to human being as meaningful, as inscribed in the culture and alive in human experience. In enacting those meanings in labor, the human being is engaged in essential relations with nature. The things of nature are both independent of human being at the causal level and dependent at the level of enacted meaning.

Marx and Marcuse presuppose an ontology that affirms the priority of human experience over every abstract conception of reality. Naturalism is excluded, and modern science is deprived of the ontological halo that has surrounded it since Galileo. In turn, the distinction between primary and secondary qualities, between the objective realm of scientific facts and the subjective realm of human experience, is now treated as a methodological requirement of scientific investigation rather than as an ontological foundation. Science gives insight into causality, but it does not establish the ontological independence of nature. Rather, that independence is now understood in terms of the contingency of the actual causal interactions of human beings and nature. Independence in that sense is not incompatible with dependence at the level of meaning.

Marcuse does not explain himself so clearly but merely implies some such solution to the *Manuscripts*' conundrum. Whether he would have agreed with my interpretation we cannot know, and it is even less certain that Marx would have recognized himself in it. Nevertheless, I think this is the most plausible way of making sense of Marcuse's interpretation of the *Manuscripts*.

This account shows that Marcuse's connection to Heidegger was only partially broken by the discovery of this early text of Marx. While he gave up the individualistic conception of Dasein and the dangerously ambiguous concept of authenticity, he retained a version of Heidegger's concept of world. This enabled him to overcome the dilemma of metaphysics and naturalism that still haunts most interpretations of the *Manuscripts*. The usual objectivistic interpretations dismiss Marx's concept of world-constitution as idealistic or reduce it to a commonsense metaphor, while their emphasis on the ethical implications of Marx's concept of man obscures his more fundamental ontological concerns. Marx's originality is better understood through Marcuse's approach, which, while imposing anachronistic concepts on Marx's argument, successfully articulates the intention behind his complex and ambiguous text.

3

The Logos of Life

Marcuse's Hegel

In 1930, Marcuse published his habilitation thesis, entitled *Hegel's Ontology and the Theory of Historicity*. The thesis was submitted to Heidegger but never accepted. In any case, Marcuse's academic career in Germany was doomed by the rise of Nazism. The thesis was written before the publication of the *Economic and Philosophical Manuscripts*. It still showed a strong influence of phenomenology, but after Marcuse's break with Heidegger, Hegel became his principal philosophical reference—a change in emphasis that is clear from the title of his 1941 book, *Reason and Revolution: Hegel and the Rise of Social Theory*.

Why the turn to Hegel? Marxism is usually interpreted as a deterministic theory predicting socialist revolution. As such, it suffers a huge normative deficit: Why would anyone struggle to bring about the inevitable? The mainstream Marxism of the Second International exemplified the problem. Tainted by determinism and economism, "orthodoxy" failed to mobilize the proletariat in the German Revolution of 1918–19. The "revisionists," who rejected the supposed inevitability of revolution, interpreted the socialist goal in Kantian ethical terms: ethics occupied the place of the disappearing concept of historical determinism on which Marxists had relied. They at least could justify the demand for change, although they preferred reform to revolution.

Lukács's 1923 *History and Class Consciousness* argued that orthodoxy and revisionism were two sides of the same coin: ethics correlated with a fatalistic concept of history. In other words, values must appear as impractical ideals in a world of crass economic realities. "For precisely in the pure, classical expression it received in the philosophy of Kant it remains true that the 'ought' presupposes an existing reality to which the category of 'ought' remains inapplicable in principle."[1] If the good appears as an "ought," that is because entirely different motivations actually prevail in reality. Those motivations, selfish as they are, stem directly from the organization of capitalist society. The solution is not an upsurge of altruism but a reality that does not require an "ought" to motivate normatively valid action. Socialism was to be that alternative reality in which "the free development of each is the condition for the free development of all." This argument was decisive for a whole generation of Western Marxists who rejected both determinism and Kantianism.

A skeptical view of ethics was confirmed by the consequences of the sinister patriotic rhetoric of World War I. As became evident also in France after World War II, the aftermath of war has a tendency to discredit ethical idealism. Appeals to duty and sacrifice ring hollow amid the rubble. In both Germany and France, existentialism responded to the debasement of morality in both its heroic and conventional forms.[2]

Official Marxism was discredited by the blatant jingoism of the socialist movement during World War I. Social critique could not stand on such discredited foundations but required a different basis. At first, Marcuse sought an alternative in Heidegger's concept of authenticity, which seemed to resolve the dilemma opposing ethical principles to practical accommodation of a bad reality. As Heidegger explains it, authentic decision is "precisely the disclosive projection and determination of what is factually possible at the time," that is, the response called for by the situation.[3] Authenticity promised a normatively valid

---

1 Georg Lukács, *History and Class Consciousness*, trans. Rodney Livingstone (Cambridge, MA: MIT Press, 1971), 160. See also 182.

2 See Marcuse's discussion of the origins of existentialism in Herbert Marcuse, "Sartre's Existentialism," in *The Essential Marcuse: Selected Writings of Philosopher and Social Critic Herbert Marcuse*, ed. Andrew Feenberg and William Leiss (Boston: Beacon Press, 2007), 129–30.

3 Martin Heidegger, *Being and Time*, trans. John Macquarrie and Edward Robinson (New York: Harper & Row, 1962), 345.

response emerging directly from concrete circumstances. The basis of revolt would not be an abstract principle but rather the refusal of conformist passivity in the face of oppression. However, this solution did not survive Heidegger's Nazi interpretation of its demands. It was in this context that Hegel supplied Marcuse with a new way of thinking about the normative grounds of revolution.

What Marcuse sought in Hegel was not a *justification* of values à la Kant or Habermas, but *proof of their relevance* in a world that repels them as utopian, unrealistic, or ideological. Hegel rejected Kant's attempt to base ethics on formal-rational principles, independent of human nature and material circumstances. A critique of Kantian ethical formalism was also implicit in Marx's skeptical view of bourgeois right. Instead of abstract proofs of the validity of ethical principles, both Hegel and Marx looked to history for the actually operative principles. Hegel found those principles in the prevailing institutions and Marx in the struggles generated by the contradictions of capitalism.

Marx interpreted Hegel's anti-utopianism to mean that social critique requires a basis in reality. This explains his rejection of the rationalism of Enlightenment thinkers such as Rousseau and Kant and the utopian schemes of contemporary socialists. The existence of the proletarian struggle provided the historical rationale of a critical stance toward reality grounded in reality itself. The first volume of Marx's *Capital* culminates in a chapter that proclaims the coming expropriation of the expropriators, the negation of the negation. This was no mere "fancy" but a reality fraught with normative significance.

Dialectics of Liberation

Hegel's *Philosophy of Right* begins with a particularly ferocious attack on utopian thinking. He dismisses "the pettifoggery of caprice" that "has usurped the name of philosophy," concluding his diatribe with the claim that the ideal world of the critical philosopher "exists indeed, but only in his opinions, an unsubstantial element where anything you please may, in fancy, be built."[4] This attack aims to place philosophy on

---

4 Georg Wilhelm Friedrich Hegel, *The Philosophy of Right*, trans. T. M. Knox (Oxford: Clarendon Press, 1952), 7, 11.

a solid footing as the discovery of the rational in the real. By this is meant concretely: the rationale of the institutional arrangements of a modern society of citizens.

Hegel attacks not only the utopians, but also formalists like Kant. The categorical imperative is useless, he argues, too abstract to actually determine any particular action. What is more, the attempt to distinguish rational from empirical motivations is hopeless. Customs and institutions, "ethical substance" (*Sittlichkeit*), must form the background to individual judgments of conscience (*Moralität*).[5]

Marx and Engels managed to extract a revolutionary doctrine from Hegel's rejection of utopianism. Engels argues that, where Hegel had claimed that "all that is real is rational; and all that is rational is real," for Marxism, "in accordance with all the rules of the Hegelian method of thought, the proposition of the rationality of everything which is real resolves itself into the other proposition: All that exists deserves to perish."[6]

This statement of the case implied a normative understanding of social change Marx and Engels never elaborated. Following Hegel's strictures, they rejected utopian speculation and never justified socialism formally. Perhaps it seemed unnecessary, given Engels's raw description of the condition of the working class in his book of that title. In any case, the early socialist movement expanded rapidly with Marx's *Capital* guaranteeing ultimate success, but favorable conditions had disappeared by the time Marcuse took up the defense of the dialectical theory of history. An explicit normative approach was needed, and, as usual, he did not hesitate to put forward the most radical claims.

This is how he began his lecture at the famous Dialectics of Liberation conference in London in July 1967. Dialectics, he argued,

---

5 Ibid., 89–90.

6 Frederick Engels, "Ludwig Feuerbach and the End of Classical German Philosophy," in Karl Marx and Frederick Engels, *Selected Works* (New York: International Publishers, 1968), 597. The reversal of Hegel's conservatism Engels claims for the Marxist dialectic is verified by Hegel himself. "Immediate actuality is in general as such never what it ought to be; it is a finite actuality with an inherent flaw, and its vocation is to be consumed." Georg Wilhelm Friedrich Hegel, *The Logic of Hegel*, trans. William Wallace (Oxford: Oxford University Press, 1968), 266.

is liberation from the repressive, from a bad, a false system . . . by forces developing within such a system . . . I am intentionally using here moral, philosophical terms, values: "bad," "false" . . . I believe that in Marx too socialism *ought* to be . . . It is, we may almost say, a biological, sociological and political necessity. It is a biological necessity in as much as a socialist society, according to Marx, would conform with the very *logos* of life, with the essential possibilities of a human existence, not only mentally, not only intellectually, but also organically.[7]

Like many of Marcuse's lectures in this period, the text can be read at two levels. Superficially, the argument is one that any listener can understand: we must liberate ourselves from the unfree society in which we live. But at a deeper level, there is a lot more going on indicated by the phrases "false system," "ought," "*logos* of life." In what sense can a system be not just bad but "false?" And what does it mean to associate an "ought" with a "logos"?

Critics point out that the bare statement of these values is insufficient, both practically and philosophically. If we do not know how to realize them nor how to justify them philosophically, we are not much advanced. But this unflattering evaluation of Marcuse's program is unfair.[8] In fact, he grounded his normative claims in Hegel's dialectic.

---

7 Herbert Marcuse, "Liberation from the Affluent Society," in *The Dialectics of Liberation*, ed. David Cooper (Harmondsworth: Penguin, 1968), 175–6.

8 This was the complaint of the Habermasians who criticized Marcuse. See Richard Bernstein, "Negativity: Theme and Variations," in *Marcuse: Critical Theory and the Promise of Utopia*, ed. Robert Pippin, Andrew Feenberg, and Charles P. Weber (South Hadley, MA: Bergin & Garvey, 1988). I commented on this paper at the memorial "Symposium on the Thought of Herbert Marcuse," University of California, San Diego, March 14–15, 1980. Bernstein argued that Marcuse avoided the "hard questions." I responded that such a dismissive criticism reflects a rather narrow notion of what to ask, namely, only the questions posed by Habermas.

Real Possibility

Marcuse remarks that

> the dialectical categories construct a topsy-turvy world . . . Hegel
> plays up the absurd and paradoxical character of this world, but he
> who follows the dialectical process to the end discovers that the
> paradox is the receptacle of the hidden truth and that the absurdity
> is rather a quality possessed by the correct schema of common
> sense.[9]

One might apply this reversal to Marcuse's own writings. In his discussion of Hegel's *Science of Logic*, Marcuse focuses on a particular concept, "real possibility," and extracts from it a foundation for social critique.

Kant's *Critique of Pure Reason* contrasted real possibility with formal or logical possibility. According to his argument, the human mind can construct imaginary objects that are incompatible with possible experience. Such objects are merely formal possibilities that cannot be realized. An example would be an event without a cause. Since causality is an essential property of experience, such an event, while logically possible, can never actually occur. Real possibility thus refers to possible objects that conform with the essential properties of experience.[10] This type of possibility is a subset of the infinite variety of imaginable entities.

This, then, is the category that enters Hegel's "topsy-turvy" world, where it becomes the basis for Marcuse's interpretation of the historical dialectic. Hegel appropriates the general concept of real possibility, but it is no longer defined by the properties of experience in general. Instead, real possibility now relates to the logic of the thing itself of which it is the possibility.

What Hegel calls the "actual" entity has real possibilities that follow it as it develops. Marcuse writes, "Actuality controls a certain horizon

---

9 Herbert Marcuse, *Reason and Revolution: Hegel and the Rise of Social Theory* (Boston: Beacon Press, 1960), 130–1.

10 Immanuel Kant, *Immanuel Kant's Critique of Pure Reason*, trans. Norman K. Smith (London: Macmillan, 1961), 239–42.

(*Umkreis*) of possible determinations, and in every case its mode of being-there realizes a certain possibility within this horizon."[11] One might reformulate this to say that what is really possible are the many different configurations of the actual thing that conform with its essence. These alternative configurations could take the place of the thing given certain contingent circumstances. The thing itself, just as it is, is only one of these many possible configurations, itself occasioned by contingent circumstances. Thus, actuality seems to lose its privilege with respect to (real) possibility, or conversely, one could conclude that the possible is already in some sense actual in principle if not in practice.

Hegel complicates this picture further by considering real possibilities as not merely intrinsically compatible with the essence of the thing but as latent in the thing itself. Marcuse explains, "Possible is only that which can be derived from the very content of the real."[12] Implied in this interpretation of possibility is necessity, the next category of the *Logic*. Real possibilities are necessary where they belong to the developmental sequence of the thing itself. This differs from mere random changes, as, for example, the shattering of a vase into fragments. The realization of the possibility—fragments—is not an advance toward the "truth" of vase, except in the sense that the truth of any finite being is its destruction. Its shattering is thus without significance for the vase itself. It is not "necessary," not implicit in the "life" of the vase.

Where organic growth is concerned, on the contrary, what is possible *must* become real. Marcuse explains,

> The reality that is actual is the one wherein the discrepancy between the possible and real has been overcome. Its fruition occurs through a process of change, with the given reality advancing in accordance with the possibilities manifest in it.[13]

Necessity attaches to development insofar as it is intrinsic to the thing itself. The development is occasioned and not imposed by external

---

11 Herbert Marcuse, *Hegel's Ontology and the Theory of Historicity*, trans. Seyla Benhabib (Cambridge, MA: MIT Press, 1987), 93.

12 Marcuse, *Reason and Revolution*, 150.

13 Ibid., 153.

contingencies. In Hegel's words, "Being posited by another and its own becoming are one and the same."[14] The dependence of the thing on circumstances thus appears as a limit overcome at a higher stage where the living subject governs its own process of development. Marcuse writes, "Its process is *of necessity*, because it follows the inherent law of its own nature and remains in all conditions the same."[15]

Marcuse interprets Hegel's theory of real possibility as an alternative to utopian and formalist normative theories. In so doing, he distinguishes real possibility from the merely logically thinkable by its essential relation to what is actual. This narrows the gap between the possible and the real and so escapes Hegel's rejection of critique, but, by the same token, it seems conservative. Indeed, as we have seen, Hegel argues that what is "actual" is necessary.[16] This, of course, begs the question of what Hegel means by "actual." Some commentators take it to be equivalent to what exists, which would explain his reconciliation with the Prussian state. Adorno, for one, writes:

> According to Hegel's distinction between abstract and real possibility, only something that has become real is actually possible. This kind of philosophy sides with the big guns. It adopts the judgment of a reality that always destroys what could be different.[17]

Ernst Bloch is equally critical: what Hegel "calls real possibility is wholly surrounded by the circle of what reality has already become."[18]

However, there is another way of reading Hegel's theory of real possibility—an alternative Adorno hints at on the very next page of his discussion. He takes back his harsh critique, saying that for Hegel,

---

14 Georg Wilhelm Friedrich Hegel, *The Science of Logic*, vol. 2, trans. W. H. Johnson and L. G. Struthers (London: George Allen & Unwin, 1961), 202, translation modified.

15 Marcuse, *Reason and Revolution*, 154.

16 Hegel, *The Science of Logic*, vol. 2, 178–86.

17 Theodor Adorno, *Hegel: Three Studies* (Cambridge, MA: MIT Press, 1993), 83. For a discussion of Adorno's views on real possibility, see Iain Macdonald, "Possibilité et Actualité chez Hegel et Adorno," in *Les Normes et le Possible: Héritage et Perspectives de L'École de Francfort*, ed. Pierre-François Noppen, Gérard Raulet, and Iain Macdonald (Paris: Editions de la Maison des Sciences de l'Homme, 2012), 325–43.

18 Ernst Bloch, *The Principle of Hope*, vol. 1, trans. Neville Plaice, Stephen Plaice, and Paul Knight (Cambridge, MA: MIT Press, 1996), 245.

"'possibility' in the emphatic sense . . . is something that reality itself, however weakly, is putting out feelers to."[19] On this account, there would be room in Hegelian necessity for otherness, for "what could be different."

Those "feelers" can be traced in the contradictions of the society, its fractures and crises. Marx's critique of political economy is the objective standpoint from which the society reveals its own imperfection, the inner principle of its own destruction. That destruction awaits the class consciousness of the proletariat.

In consciousness real possibility implies a relation to time. Potential is not yet but can become. It depends on the "motility" of being, the perpetual dissatisfaction that propels the experienced time of the lifeworld. The time consciousness of a first-person subject is implied in these relations. As Lukács writes, "Only he who is willing and whose mission it is to create the future can see the concrete truth of the present."[20] That truth is the "feelers" pointing toward the future, what Marcuse calls the "bits and fragments" that are assembled in aesthetic experience. These possibilities are not only theoretical but belong to the lifeworld of the practical subject, where they are experienced as tensions and contradictions. A "second dimension" transcends the given and opens the world to dialectical comprehension and revolutionary transformation.

The Two Dimensions

When real possibility is considered in this double sense, as both developmentally and normatively "necessary," Marcuse calls it "potentiality." This term becomes the key to his approach. Indeed, it is the basis of his "two-dimensional" ontology, developed in his thesis on *Hegel's Ontology* and later in his essay on "The Concept of Essence," in *Reason and Revolution*, and in *One-Dimensional Man*. In this section, I will focus on his first attempt to explain that ontology in Hegelian terms.

---

19 Adorno, *Hegel: Three Studies*, 83. For a contemporary argument to this effect, see Rocío Zambrana, "Actuality in Hegel and Marx," *Hegel Bulletin* 40, special issue 1 (*Science of Logic*) (April 2019): 74–91.

20 Lukács, *History and Class Consciousness*, 204.

It was Aristotle who first proposed a notion of potentiality. Substances, he argued, have an essence that persists through change. This essence inhabits the substance and organizes it in a coherent whole. In the case of living things, the essence also governs capacities and development, which bring the potentialities of the organism into actuality in activity and growth.

The two dimensions of the thing are thus its empirically given form *and* its potentialities. Both are real, not just the given facts. It was on this basis that Aristotle confronted an ancient version of the positivist fetishism of the facts in the Megarian philosophical school. The Megarians denied the reality of latent capacities, the potential to act. Aristotle replied, "Something may be capable of being without actually being, and capable of not being, yet be."[21] Potentiality is real even in its unrealized condition. In this sense, Aristotle might be considered an early critic of one-dimensional thought.

In *Hegel's Ontology*, Marcuse introduced the two dimensions as aspects of beings in general with different manifestations depending on the type of being. The essence of being is *Bewegtheit*, usually translated as "motility." Being is movement, change, but not any random change. Rather, the motility of being must be conceived as a process of development driven forward toward potentialities. Marcuse writes that the two dimensions, actuality and potentiality,

> are not isolated and self-subsistent worlds that need to be brought subsequently in relation; they are dimensions of being which are from the beginning ontologically dependent on one another, and which only continue to exist through each other and which only move themselves within their conflictual unity.[22]

Aristotle's model of potentiality was life: living things realize a potential contained within themselves as they act and develop. Hegel's concept of life both returns to Aristotle and contains the seeds of the dissolution of the independent Aristotelian substance. As I argued in the previous chapter, Marcuse interprets Hegel's account of life against

---

21 Aristotle, *Metaphysics*, trans. Richard Hope (Ann Arbor: University of Michigan, 1960), 185.

22 Marcuse, *Hegel's Ontology*, 75.

a background of vitalist biology and Heidegger's concept of "world" as a system of references among things bound up with a subject. Accordingly, Marcuse emphasizes the role of subjectivity, systematically blurring the boundaries between organism and environment Aristotle took for granted.[23]

Marcuse argues that this conception is implied in Hegel's transformation of the inherited Aristotelian conception of essence. In Aristotle, the essence is "in" the thing without being an ordinary property. It preserves the thing in contact with an environment to which the thing relates only externally, accidentally. In the case of living things, the essence contains the potentials and the capacities the thing must strive to realize.

Hegel rejects Aristotle's metaphysical postulate of an internal essence behind the appearances of the thing. Instead, he seeks an explanation for potential in "the determinations, circumstances, and conditions" of a thing. "The Real Possibility of a case is the existing multiplicity of circumstances which are related to it."[24] Aristotle's essence is thus dissolved into the structure of the appearances and relations of the thing. They play the role of essence through bonds and tensions among themselves that both enable the thing to reproduce itself while undergoing accidental changes, and also give rise to internal sources of development.[25]

"Essence" describes this self-reproducing unity that preserves itself by realizing its potentialities through its relation to its circumstances. In so doing, it "appears"—that is, constitutes itself as an objective, meaningful entity within a world.[26] But this is not quite a Heideggerian "world." In Heidegger, "world" is merely a system of meanings without

---

23 As with "worldhood" so with vitalism, there is a temptation to reduce complex technical concepts to the specific political destination they reached in the 1930s in Germany. Marcuse did not resist this temptation in later comments, despite the imprint the concepts left on his thinking. The appropriation of similar concepts in French existentialism shows that they are not inherently reactionary.

24 Hegel, *The Science of Logic*, vol. 2, 179. Quoted in Herbert Marcuse, "The Concept of Essence," in *Negations: Essays in Critical Theory*, trans. Jeremy J. Shapiro (Boston: Beacon Press, 1968), 82.

25 These ideas are presented in both Marcuse's books on Hegel. See Andrew Feenberg, *Heidegger and Marcuse: The Catastrophe and Redemption of History* (New York: Routledge, 2005), chapter 3.

26 Ibid., 53–4.

the dynamic character of essence. Hegel emphasizes the *conflict* of organism and environment that Marcuse considers under the logical category of negation. Negation introduces a tension in the concept of world that allows for the unfolding of essence, the development of potentiality into the actuality. As Slavoj Žižek puts it, "For Hegel, external circumstances are not an impediment to realizing inner potentials, but on the contrary *the very arena in which the true nature of these inner potentials is to be tested*: are such potentials true potentials or just vain illusions about what might have happened?"[27]

This revision of the concept of essence has revolutionary implications. On this view, the environment is not a harmonious resting place for life but a scene of conflict and struggle. However, the fact of struggle is not ultimate. In overcoming the challenge of development, life absorbs the environment and the associated antagonism into itself. This is the process of realizing potentialities. "Through violence [*Gewalt*], passive substance is only posited as what it is *in truth*."[28]

Hegel thus saves Aristotle's central idea: potentiality is not an extrinsic goal imposed on the thing but belongs to the nature of the thing itself. But he overthrows the Aristotelian concept of the thing as a self-contained "substance" with an inner essence that is only accidentally related to its appearances and other things.[29] Aristotle's version of essence maintains the thing as what it is. But for Hegel, things are not; they *become*, and they do so through the interaction of their appearances and their environment, their inner and outer relations.

Here, we have another important influence on Marcuse's review of the *Economic and Philosophical Manuscripts*. Underlying the contingent causal relations and conflicts between life and environment, a more fundamental unity prevails. That unity is "world," the scene of a mutual correlation, a mutual necessity. The correlation of human being and nature is produced by labor in a struggle with natural constraints of all sorts, but through that struggle the potentialities of both are realized: human being comes to itself, and nature, too, achieves full reality—that is, actuality.

---

27 Slavoj Žižek, *Tarrying with the Negative: Kant, Hegel, and the Critique of Ideology* (Durham: Duke University Press, 1993), 142.

28 Hegel, *The Science of Logic*, vol. 2, 201. As quoted in Marcuse, *Hegel's Ontology*, 101.

29 Marcuse, *Hegel's Ontology*, 98–9.

From Philosophy to Social Theory

After Marcuse joined the Frankfurt School, he largely dropped phenomenological references, but the main lines of the early interpretation of the dialectic were retained. *Reason and Revolution* professes a Marxism that has transcended philosophy in social theory—one whose emphasis is now on objective knowledge of society. Many Marxists would prefer that this be Marcuse's position—among them, Adorno, whose early review of *Hegel's Ontology* first suggested a contradiction in Marcuse's approach between abstract ontology and actual history. This has become a theme of later criticism, even referenced by Marcuse himself.[30]

However, Marcuse's early ontology consists primarily in a formal account of the structure of motility. Its abstract character is not a fatal defect but, on the contrary, enables it to describe a dynamic of development. This is precisely what the Marxist account of actual history entails. His later presentations fill out the abstract forms of the dialectic with social content derived from Marx.

In any case, the argument is undeniably still philosophical, as Robert Pippin points out: "Although completely unacknowledged now, there are several passages that continue to make use of an unmistakably Heideggerian orientation."[31] However, during the 1930s and '40s, when Marcuse developed his mature interpretation of Hegel, he explicitly confined the dialectic to the domain of history, thus avoiding the suspicion of metaphysics that appeared in his early work and again after the war.

In the late work, once the dialectic is no longer confined to history but implicates nature, an ambiguity arises: Which nature? Is nature again divided into a "wider" and narrower form, the one accessible in the lifeworld and the other belonging to natural science? It is difficult to tell. Marcuse's late Hegelianism no longer marks a clean break with

---

30 Theodor Adorno, "Hegels Ontologie und die Grundlegung einer Theorie der Geschichtlichkeit," *Zeitschrift für Sozialforschung* 1, no. 3 (1932): 409–10. Alfred Schmidt, "Existential Ontology and Historical Materialism in the Work of Herbert Marcuse," in Pippin et al., *Marcuse*, 35.

31 Robert Pippin, "Marcuse on Hegel and Historicity," in Pippin et al., *Marcuse*, 82.

phenomenology, but he seems not to have known how to navigate the ambiguity that results from his increasing preoccupation with nature (an aspect of his work discussed in later chapters of this book).

The strictly historical approach to dialectics is evident in Marcuse's 1936 essay on "The Concept of Essence," in which he takes up the concept of real possibility but finds Hegel's definition too abstract. "Reality," he writes, "is no mere 'existing manifold of circumstances,' but rather a structure whose organization can be analyzed, and within which it is possible to distinguish between form and content."[32] Now, the socialist potentiality is identified with the suppressed content of the social system and its inadequate reality with its capitalist form.

Nine years after the publication of his first book on Hegel, Marcuse returned to its themes again with an explicitly political intent. In *Reason and Revolution*, he emphasizes the role of negation. The environing world is both necessary to life and a limit, an obstacle to be overcome. Marcuse comments, "Being is continuous becoming. Every state of existence has to be surpassed; it is something negative, which things, driven by their inner potentialities, desert for another state, which again reveals itself as negative, as limit."[33]

Going beyond the abstract exposition of *Hegel's Ontology*, this book offers a "given social system" as an example of the workings of becoming. That system, he writes, is unjust, but within it lie the elements of another social system capable of righting the injustice—for example, material forces of production, cultural achievements, and so on. These elements present in the given system are its "determinate negation," its undoing, the real possibility of an alternative:

> In such a case, the possibilities are not only real ones, but represent the true content of the social system as against its immediate form of existence. They are thus an even more real reality than the given . . . Hegel's famous proposition that "the fact [*die Sache*] *is* before it *exists*" can now be given its strict meaning. Before it exists, the fact "is" in the form of a condition within the constellation of existing data. The existing state of affairs is a mere condition for another

---

32 Marcuse, "Concept of Essence," 82.
33 Marcuse, *Reason and Revolution*, 136.

constellation of facts, which bring to fruition the inherent potentialities of the given.[34]

What are these potentialities? In "The Concept of Essence," Marcuse lists material achievements that make possible a higher stage of civilization. But his account also includes cultural aspirations that must be projected by the collective imagination: "the 'free' needs for gratification and happiness, for the 'good and the beautiful,' the availability, as material to be appropriated, of a wealth of cultural values in all areas of life."[35] Socialism thus includes more than material satisfactions; it aspires to a new state of humanity the outlines of which have emerged from generations of struggle. The memory of those struggles lives on in the projection of a redemptive future.[36] The validity of their claims, as more than fantasy, as true potentiality, is grounded in the objective factors.

Essence is now an object of political struggle rather than a purely conceptual category. As Marcuse argues in *Reason and Revolution*, the medium of philosophy has shifted from theory to practice. Or rather, the philosophical logos "is *theoretical and practical Reason* in one."[37]

In the 1960s, Marcuse draws political conclusions from his Hegelian version of Marxism. *One-Dimensional Man* explains the politics of essence in terms of the Hegelian critique of immediacy. According to Hegel, the concrete is not immediate appearance but rather the conceptual constellation of relations that make the object what it is. As Marx explains a similar point, "The concrete is concrete, because it is the sum of many determinations, [and] therefore a unity of diversity."[38] It is this multiplicity that gives a direction to development. As such, the context and relations of the object grant it its future possibilities—its

---

34 Ibid., 151–2.

35 Marcuse, "Concept of Essence," 72.

36 For a discussion of Marcuse's concept of historical memory, see Martin Jay, *Marxism and Totality: The Adventures of a Concept from Lukács to Habermas* (Berkeley: University of California Press, 1984), chapter 7.

37 Herbert Marcuse, "The Rationality of Philosophy," in *Transvaluation of Values and Radical Social Change*, ed. Peter-Erwin Jansen, Sarah Surak, and Charles Reitz (International Herbert Marcuse Society, 2017), 11.

38 Karl Marx, "Introduction" to the "Grundrisse," in *Texts on Method*, ed. Terrell Carver (London: Basil Blackwell, 1975), 72.

potential—and consciousness of that potential is the driving force of radical social change.

However, Marcuse argues, advanced capitalism blocks that change. The prevalent scientism with its

> radical acceptance of the empirical violates the empirical, for in it speaks the mutilated "abstract" individual who experiences (and expresses) only that which is *given* to him (given in the literal sense), who has only the facts and not the factors, whose behavior is one-dimensional and manipulated.[39]

The lost context that would restore the full content of the empirical data is known to the social critique, but it fails to find a place in social consciousness.

By the end of the decade, the emergence of a "new sensibility" in the New Left brought the dialectical concrete within the scope of experience. This was a sensibility informed by the aesthetic imagination. It resisted reified one-dimensionality and, insofar as it was a sensuous relationship to the world, it engaged with concrete reality, the "empirical." However, it went beyond the manipulated reality to the "factors" that explain it, not through theoretical insight but through resistance to the given way of life. Despite its limitations, the New Left strove to materialize potentialities hitherto confined to fantasy and art, which now entered the consciousness of significant groups within the society.

The Demands of Reason

Noteworthy in Marcuse's description of the socialist potential of capitalism is the mention of the "free" needs for the "good and the beautiful." The qualification "free" indicates that they differ from the basic needs for sustenance and protection from the environment. Freedom, in this sense, refers to cultural potentialities related to the role of rationality in human life.

---

39 Herbert Marcuse, *One-Dimensional Man: Studies in the Ideology of Advanced Industrial Society* (Boston: Beacon Press, 1964), 182.

The concept of reason is a constant theme in Marcuse's writings. In his inaugural lecture at the University of California, he writes that

> the philosophical quest is for the conditions under which man can *best fulfill his specifically human faculties* and aspirations. These conditions are *objective* ones because there is such a thing as "man" being a (potentially) rational animal finding himself under circumstances ... which allow the development of general concepts with *general validity*.[40]

This passage is a reminder of his early interpretation of Marx's concept of species-being as the capacity to understand the universal as well as the particular, the possible as well as the given.

According to Marcuse, the philosophical concept of reason signifies an authentic form of being. "Reason represents the highest potential of man and of existence; the two belong together."[41] In bourgeois philosophy, it is accommodated to a bad reality, but reason is inherently critical insofar as it posits potentialities. Reason conserves hopes for a better life that can only be fulfilled by the realization of its demands in reality—an outcome made possible by the material achievements of capitalism. On this view, the ideal promise of philosophy gives way to the creation of a rational society.

This theme harks back to the early Marx, who wrote,

> Reason has always existed, but not always in a rational form ... As far as actual life is concerned, the political state especially contains in all its modern forms the demands of reason, even where the political state is not yet conscious of socialistic demands.[42]

At the time he wrote these lines, Marx held that the principal "demand of reason" was the realization of the universal claims of morality in social life as a whole, not just in the duties of citizenship. In the

---

40 Marcuse, "Rationality of Philosophy," 4.

41 Herbert Marcuse, "Philosophy and Critical Theory," in *Negations*, 136.

42 Karl Marx, "Letter to Ruge," in *Writings of the Young Marx on Philosophy and Society*, trans. and ed. Loyd D. Easton and Kurt H. Guddat (New York: Doubleday & Co., 1967), 213.

Manuscripts, as we have seen, the demands of reason extend to reconciliation of all the antinomies of philosophy: individual and society, freedom and necessity, essence and appearance, subject and object.

In *One-Dimensional Man* Marcuse defined that project in terms of the concept of potentiality, conceived as the determinate negation of the existing society, but no agent existed capable of realizing that potentiality in reality. The intellectual protest was justified by the suffering of "those without hope," but prospects of radical change were poor or even nonexistent.[43] After 1968, Marcuse still could not identify an agent of revolution, but rationality was no longer purely theoretical.

In *An Essay on Liberation* and *Counterrevolution and Revolt*, Marcuse returned to his early interpretation of Marx's *Manuscripts*. There, he found a concept of sensuousness that, when joined to the concept of potentiality, gave a practical form to rationality. An "aesthetic *Lebenswelt*" shapes a "new sensibility." Under this horizon, the senses anticipate liberating possibilities:

> The senses do not only "receive" what is given to them, in the form in which it appears, they do not "delegate" the transformation of the given to another faculty (the understanding); rather, they discover or *can* discover by themselves, in their "practice," new (more gratifying) possibilities and capabilities, forms and qualities of things, and can urge and guide their realization. The emancipation of the senses would make freedom what it is not yet: a sensuous need, an objective of the Life Instincts (*Eros*).[44]

Here, then, was the form in which rationality could pass into practice and become a force in the world.

The introduction of sensuousness and need alongside thought transformed the subject of rationality, which was no longer a detached spectator on reality but an interested actor engaged with the life process. As Douglas Kellner writes, "The new sensibility would combine the senses and reason, producing a 'new rationality' in which reason would

---

43 Marcuse, *One-Dimensional Man*, 257.

44 Herbert Marcuse, "Nature and Revolution," in *Counterrevolution and Revolt* (Boston: Beacon Press, 1972), 71.

be bodily, erotic, and political."[45] This new rationality is still rational, that is, a relation to the universal. What is new, what grants this rationality its "bodily, erotic, and political" form, is the aesthetic nature of the universal to which it relates (a transformation in the concept of reason that will be explained in chapter 6).

Marcuse claims that reason has from the beginning been oriented by a specific value: the service and affirmation of life. This orientation is manifest in the technical relation to the natural world:

> Technics, considered as a historical process, is endowed with an internal meaning, a meaning of its own: it projects instrumentality as a means of freeing man from toil and anxiety, of turning his struggle for life into a more peaceful process. Therein lies the final cause of the methodical transformation of the world involved in technics. But technique, in the process of being developed as "pure" instrumentality, has disregarded this final cause, which no longer stands as the aim of technological development. Hence, pure instrumentality, without finality, has become a universal means of domination.[46]

The fact that Marcuse calls the final cause an "internal meaning" indicates that it is not merely an external goal but, rather, an intrinsic aspect of reason itself.

This is the classical understanding of the concept of final cause, the "logos of life." Indeed, Plato and Aristotle identified the final cause with the purpose of biological growth and technical activity. Plato explains in the *Gorgias* that technical fields have a "logos" that guides their operations.[47] The logos shapes the means internally; every tool

---

45 Douglas Kellner, "Marcuse and Radical Subjectivity," in *Herbert Marcuse: A Critical Reader*, ed. John Abromeit and W. Mark Cobb (New York and London: Routledge, 2003), 91.

46 Herbert Marcuse, "Reflections on Science and Technology," in *Philosophy, Psychoanalysis, and Emancipation*, ed. Douglas Kellner and Clayton Pierce (New York: Routledge, 2011), 143. See also the short article entitled "World without Logos," first published in the *Bulletin of the Atomic Scientists* in January 1964, and reprinted in Marcuse, *Philosophy, Psychoanalysis, and Emancipation*, 141-3.

47 Plato, *Gorgias*, trans. W. C. Helmbold (Indianapolis: Bobbs-Merrill, 1952), 23-6; E. R. Dodds, *Plato's Gorgias* (Oxford: Oxford University Press, 1959), 225.

and gesture of the craftsman is inhabited by a purpose that belongs to the nature of the craft and its materials. "Ought" and "is" are not separate but are joined in technē where the "ought" is the potentiality of the "is."

Marcuse argues that technē is superseded in modern times by the scientific mode of experiencing and understanding the world. The logos is purged from the empirical world of modern science. Science understands the world in terms of the "primary qualities," restricted to the measurable aspects of its objects. Scientific-technical rationality strips experience of much of its contents, the "secondary qualities," including values. Naturalism argues that this stripped-down version of the world is ontologically fundamental, but experience has a rich content lost in the scientific reduction to purified facts. This reduction is reification, reason's "irrational form" in capitalist society.

It is not so much the natural sciences that are "irrational" in Marx's sense but, rather, the reification of society and everyday consciousness. Much of *One-Dimensional Man* is devoted to explaining the workings of this new form of irrational reason.[48] According to Marcuse's argument, facts become ideological when they exclude all reference to the powers that institute them and the possibilities they could support. He agrees with Horkheimer and Adorno that "the new ideology has the world as such as its subject once the accurate depiction of the facts becomes a surrogate of meaning and justice."[49] The mass media are the scene on which this consecration of the facts plays out most effectively. Idealized images of cars and soft drinks return the individuals to their everyday life secure in the knowledge that they have it good. As sociologist Stanley Aronowitz writes, "The explosive thesis of *One-Dimensional Man* was to have freed ideology-critique from the mental realm and to have endowed it with onto-historical status."[50]

Marcuse develops this argument through a study of one-dimensional language. Critique, he argues, depends on the tension between words

---

48 For a detailed treatment of this theme, see Asger Sørensen, *Capitalism, Alienation and Critique: Studies in Economy and Dialectics* (Leiden: Brill, 2019), chapter 7.

49 Max Horkheimer and Theodor Adorno, *Dialectic of Enlightenment*, ed. Gunzelin S. Noerr, trans. Edmund Jephcott (Stanford: Stanford University Press, 2002), 119.

50 Stanley Aronowitz, "The Unknown Herbert Marcuse," *Social Text*, no. 58 (Spring 1999): 145.

and things, which advanced capitalism strives to relieve. The functions things perform in the existing system are routinely identified with their essential nature, although they may well contain other potentialities that could be actualized in a different social system. The reduction of concepts to their immediate instances has the effect of canceling any transcending content they might project. For example, if the concept of democracy is strictly defined on the terms of the existing political system, it can no longer serve in a critique of that system. Dialectics is thus not simply a philosophical method but is inherent in language that has not been artificially truncated to block its tensionful relation to the realities it signifies.[51]

Marcuse points to a second irrational form of reason: efforts to address social discontents with reforms that preserve the existing system. The translation of normatively charged demands for radical change into minor adjustments prolongs the fundamental injustice at the basis of capitalism: the alienation and exploitation of labor.

This is the work of management science, whose goal is to identify the operational components of workers' complaints and protests in order to defuse them short of disruptive action. As Marcuse argues, the sentiment expressed in the phrase "wages are too low" has a "transitive meaning" that goes beyond any particular situation to reflect a "sweeping indictment which takes the particular case as a manifestation of a universal state of affairs."[52] The researcher seeks to understand the personal situation of the worker who speaks this phrase in order to find a purely local "solution" to his "problem." The normative implications of the phrase are canceled along with its oppositional content.

As Wendy Brown points out, this aspect of Marcuse's argument resembles Foucault's approach to the role of technical disciplines in social life. Like the Frankfurt School, Foucault sought to address the betrayal of the Enlightenment promise of freedom in a totally

---

51 Marcuse, *One-Dimensional Man*, chapter 4.

52 Ibid., 109–10. For a discussion of Marcuse's philosophy of language and an application to British political discourse, see Mark O'Brien, "Marcuse and the Language of Power: The Unfair Discourse of 'Fairness' in the Coalition Government's Policy Presentation," *Radical Philosophy Review* 16, no. 1 (2013).

rationalized society. He called this the "fundamental problem we're all struggling with."[53] However, Foucault's approach was informed by detailed historical research. He did not trace the oppressive forms of rationality back to a capitalist origin, nor did he propose any measure of oppression other than the resistances it provokes.[54] Foucault has inspired much further research that goes well beyond Marcuse's remarks on management science. For example, Brown has developed a Foucauldian critique of neoliberal "political governance" that reprises themes from Marcuse's critique of operationalism, while showing concretely how "rational" economic criteria infiltrate the state and society.[55]

Foucault recognized late that he had much in common with the Frankfurt School, but one difference is clear: he had no theory of what a *rational* form of reason would be like. He was inhibited in this regard by his rejection of any general concept of reason and any anthropology, any idea of a human nature that would be satisfied by a different rationalization of the social world. This seems to have made it impossible for him to describe the form of fulfillment or happiness to be achieved by the emancipatory struggles he supported. These omissions correspond to the skeptical temper of our time, reflected in his preference, now commonplace, for "resistance" over "revolution."

Marcuse was not so inhibited. His Hegelian concept of potentiality, interpreted in terms of a psychoanalytic anthropology, grounds a positive concept of rationality distinct from its instantiation in particular technical disciplines. The forms of rationality depend on psychic structures that evolve historically but consistently display constructive and destructive tendencies of the human being. This has political implications; as Axel Honneth observes,

> It is precisely by locating his idea of a rational, emancipatory interest within his depth-dimensional theory of drives that allows Marcuse

---

53 Michel Foucault, "Interview with Michel Foucault," in *Power*, ed. James D. Faubion (New York: New Press, 2000), 273.

54 Michel Foucault, "The Subject and Power," in *Power*, 328–9.

55 Wendy Brown, *Undoing the Demos: Neoliberalism's Stealth Revolution* (Cambridge, MA: MIT Press, 2015), chapter 4.

to perceive an intimation of revolutionary transformation in the cultural renewals of the student movement that occurred during the 1960s.[56]

The Double Structure of Potentiality

Why is rationality so important? Marcuse does not place reason at the center of his theory from the simple love of pure thought, but because reason is the name given by the philosophical tradition to the encounter with the essence of things. That encounter transcends the subject's instinctive reactions as well as the limits of the object grasped as a simple matter of fact. The rational essence of humanity includes the capacity to formulate universals and thereby to relate to potentialities, both human and material.

In Marcuse's view, access to universal concepts is bound up with freedom. The ability to grant explicit meaning to objects and to reflect on their possibilities enlarges the subject's margin of decision and action. As he observes, "'Free' is firstly the being which can form concepts of things and consequently project and define their possibilities—project and define their transformation."[57] Hence, "Reason and Freedom are identical."[58]

It is through imagination that the potentialities of the present convey an image of the future. That anticipation transcends the given facts, but not arbitrarily. Rather, it is latent in the universals identified by reason. Marcuse focuses on a specific class of "substantive universals," those "that designate potentialities in a concrete historical sense."[59] Such is "democracy," a universal that achieves only partial realization at best in any given institutional setting, and that, therefore, "contradicts" its own realizations. Substantive universals are the basis of critical political discourse through which the dissonant

---

56 Axel Honneth, "Herbert Marcuse and the Frankfurt School," in *Radical Philosophy Review* 16, no. 1 (2013): 57.

57 Marcuse, "Rationality of Philosophy," 7.

58 Ibid., 8.

59 Marcuse, *One-Dimensional Man*, 214–15. Adorno calls something similar the "emphatic sense" of the universal.

"contents" of the society find a voice. (I will have more to say about this in chapter 5.)

On this view, potentiality is an aspect of both the world and the human subject. However, only a rational subject has the potentiality to know those worldly potentialities. Potentiality is thus not just an attribute of being in general but is consciously appropriated by a particular being: the human being. A rational society would be one that supports the potentiality of the subject to know potentialities, that is, to be itself rational.

To be capable of knowing is to be a certain kind of being with specific exigencies as such. Participation in critical discourse is not simply a cognitive concern but engages the subject of knowledge existentially, in terms of its own potentiality to be. The double structure of potentiality creates an obligation to struggle for freedom. For Marcuse, this is the ultimate "demand of reason," the demand that reason exist in a "reasonable form." He therefore argues that the defense of reason belongs to "the existential meaning of truth":

> The world is an estranged and untrue world so long as man does not destroy its dead objectivity and recognize himself and his own life "behind" the fixed form of things and laws. When he finally wins this self-consciousness, he is on his way not only to the truth of himself, but also of his world. And with the recognition *goes the doing*. He will try to put this truth into action and make the world what it essentially is, namely, the fulfillment of man's self-consciousness.[60]

With this double sense of potentiality, as worldly and subjective, Marcuse avoids reducing the political to a fixed human nature. The human essence is reason, the potentiality to know potentiality, rather than a moral quality such as greed or sociability. Knowledge of potentiality is animated by Freud's "eros": the life-affirming logos is both erotic and cognitive according to this Freud-inspired anthropology. The content of the erotic logos transcends the opposition of nature and

---

60 Marcuse, *Reason and Revolution*, 113, my italics. "It is manifest that behind the so-called curtain which is supposed to conceal the inner world, there is nothing to be seen unless we go behind it ourselves, as much in order that we may see, as that there may be something behind there which can be seen." G. W. F. Hegel, *Hegel's Phenomenology of Spirit*, trans. Arnold V. Miller (Oxford: Oxford University Press, 1979), 103.

culture. What appears as nature is always already inflected by society: "Cultural needs can 'sink down' into the biology of man."[61] Culture thus mediates the expression of nature in the social world.

Marcuse posits neither a substantive "human nature" nor an "end to history," but discovers a basis for critique in reason. His politics follows directly from the double structure of potentiality. Norms are not only concepts in the minds of human beings but appear negatively in the very structure of experience, in the objective injustices that obstruct human development and drive the social dynamic. This is the basis of Marcuse's rejection of a "false system" in the interests of an "objectively justifiable" "ought." Because reason itself is at issue, truth and objective value enter into the evaluation of societies.

On his view, the social system in which human beings encounter nature and each other either favors or obstructs the spread of rationality as the highest human potentiality. Advanced capitalist society has the resources to realize that potentiality in reality, but it continues to restrict human development long after the elimination of the scarcities that at one time made the full flowering of rationality the exclusive property of a small elite. The society can thus be judged bad, "false" at an existential level, to the extent that it blocks progress in rationality that could be realized on the basis of its own achievements. In sum, a radical change in the configuration of the whole is imperative.

Democracy: The Pursuit of Happiness

I shall conclude this chapter with a discussion of the controversy provoked by Marcuse's claim that values are objective. This claim contradicts the commonsense notion that values are a matter of personal preference rather than rational agreement. The subjectivity of values is a two-edged sword: on the one hand, it means that no experts or authorities can impose their own standards; on the other hand, it leaves society's victims with no rational basis for complaint. Marcuse insists on the objectivity of values in order to ground the appeal against injustice. But, who has the right to make judgments about values?

---

61 Herbert Marcuse, *An Essay on Liberation* (Boston: Beacon Press, 1969), 10; Feenberg, *Heidegger and Marcuse*, 119–22.

A similar ambiguity attaches to the related notion that needs are objective. If needs are without rational basis, individuals are free to conceive their bliss any way they choose. On the other hand, in a world of constant propaganda and advertising, choice may well be an illusion. To be truly free, Marcuse argues, we must make rational judgments about needs based on an objective scale of values.

This is a sticking point for many readers of Marcuse's writings. An objective definition of needs seems to disqualify the intuitions of ordinary individuals, shaped by personal feelings and social norms rather than philosophy. And manifestly, those feelings and norms contradict Marcuse's preferences and resist his call to revolution. But this raises a question that has preoccupied many of his critics: Is his a democratic project, or does it inevitably lead to a tyranny of reason? Did he intend for philosophers to rule as kings?[62]

In Marx's *Manuscripts*, needs are qualified as "ontological," which suggests a necessary connection with the means of satisfaction, but Marx also registers the corruption of that connection by money, both by poverty and riches. The consumer society exaggerates that corruption far beyond Marx's expectations. This is the background of Marcuse's distinction between true and false needs which first appears in the essay "On Hedonism" and later plays an important role in *One-Dimensional Man* and all his later work. Here, he argues that needs are not freely chosen but are relative to the structure of the society and the opportunities for gratification it affords. Whether specific types of gratification correspond to the objective potentialities of the human being must be decided by rational considerations, not unmediated feeling. This is especially so given the damage an unjust society visits on its members and on their understanding of their own chance for happiness. Marcuse concludes:

> In critical theory, the concept of happiness has been freed from any ties with bourgeois conformism and relativism. Instead, it has become a part of general, objective truth, valid for all individuals insofar as all their interests are preserved in it.

---

62 For a defense of the distinction between true and false needs, see Charles Rachlis, "Marcuse and the Problem of Happiness," *Canadian Journal of Political and Social Theory* 2, no. 1 (Winter 1978).

Hence, "In their completed form both, happiness and reason, coincide."[63] Here, we are at the very center of Marcuse's thought. As Stefano Petrucciani writes, his aim is "to establish a sort of circle, where the concepts of reason, freedom and happiness are strictly related to each other and, so to speak, define themselves reciprocally."[64]

Marcuse's objective concept of happiness derives from Freud's metapsychology, which provides the rational basis for the evaluation of needs. However, like Freud he remains at a very high level of generality with which it is difficult to imagine disagreement. Happiness is the fulfillment of erotic needs in a very broad sense: "The instinct seeks satisfaction in more than sexual relationships and objects: in cooperation, love, friendship; in the pursuit of knowledge, in the creation of a pleasurable environment."[65]

The question remains of how the manipulated individuals might come to experience the concrete needs corresponding to these generalities and so free themselves for the creation of a better society. In *One-Dimensional Man* Marcuse writes,

> No tribunal can justly arrogate to itself the right to decide which needs should be developed and satisfied. Any such tribunal is reprehensible, although our revulsion does not do away with the question: how can the people who have been the object of effective and productive domination by themselves create the conditions of freedom?[66]

---

63 Herbert Marcuse, "On Hedonism," in *Negations*, 191, 199. In *Reason and Revolution* Marcuse seems to devalue reason, writing that for Marxism, "the idea of reason has been superseded by the idea of happiness." Marcuse, *Reason and Revolution*, 293. But his objective analysis of happiness in his essay "On Hedonism" and throughout his later work gives the lie to this claim.

64 Stefano Petrucciani, "Marcuse, Politics, and Critical Theory," paper presented at the International Conference on Critical Theory, John Cabot University, Rome, May 22, 2008. See also Stefano Petrucciani, "Felicità e ragione: Il contributo di Marcuse all'idea di teoria critica," in *Eros, utopia e rivolta: Il pensiero e l'opera di Herbert Marcuse*, ed. Leonardo Casini (Milan: FrancoAngeli, 2004), 150–1.

65 Herbert Marcuse, "Cultural Revolution," in *Towards a Critical Theory of Society: Collected Papers of Herbert Marcuse*, ed. Douglas Kellner (London: Routledge, 2001), 133.

66 Marcuse, *One-Dimensional Man*, 6.

I call this "the dilemma of the first generation." It already preoccupied the philosophers of the Enlightenment, especially Rousseau, who wondered how a population corrupted by aristocratic governance could learn to display the virtues of citizenship required by a free society.[67] Marcuse's formulation of the dilemma revolves around the equally problematic role of need in the transition between forms of society. In the affluent society, the revolution must be motivated by new needs that cannot be satisfied by the existing repressive system, but only a non-repressive society seems capable of instituting such needs.[68]

Rousseau's solution was educational dictatorship. In *Eros and Civilization*, Marcuse argues that this was a reasonable response to the dilemma in earlier times, but no longer:

> The answer has become obsolete: knowledge of the available means for creating a humane existence for all is no longer confined to a privileged elite ... The distinction between rational and irrational authority, between repression and surplus repression, can be made and verified by the individuals themselves.[69]

Eros and Civilization leaves the definition of life-affirming policies to democratic debate.

Marcuse's commitment to democracy is confirmed by his few remarks on the political organization of socialist society that, for the most part, reference the heritage of council communism. This is a bottom-up, democratic socialism very different from the Soviet regime and its imitators. "Direct democracy," he writes, "the subjection of all delegation of authority to effective control 'from below,' is an essential demand of Leftist strategy."[70] Marcuse's comments on political action

---

67 This is a central problem of classical political theory. Rousseau solves it with religion and "la grande âme du législateur," citing Machiavelli's *Discourses* for his authority. Jean-Jacques Rousseau, *Du Contrat Social* (Paris: Éditions Garnier Frères, 1962), 263.

68 Marcuse, *An Essay on Liberation*, 18–19.

69 Herbert Marcuse, *Eros and Civilization: A Philosophical Inquiry into Freud* (Boston: Beacon Press, 1966), 225.

70 Herbert Marcuse, "The Left under the Counterrevolution," in Marcuse, *Counterrevolution and Revolt*, 45; see also 35, 42, 44. Marcuse relates the revival of council communism to *autogestion*, which played a major role in the political debates during the May events of 1968. For a selection of documents from those

in his late work also emphasize the role of dispersed grassroots resistance rather than vanguard party organization.[71]

But, as Christopher Holman points out, Marcuse seems to measure the legitimacy of democratic debate by its conformity with the erotic promise. Indeed, Marcuse writes, "The councils will be organs of revolution only to the degree to which they represent the people *in revolt*. They are not just there, ready to be elected in the factories, offices, neighborhoods—their emergence presupposes a new consciousness."[72]

The emphasis on the qualification of the participants raises the question of educational dictatorship in a way that becomes acute in Marcuse's famous essay on "Repressive Tolerance." This essay has been caricatured by Marcuse's critics more than once and recently blamed for the ravages of the so-called "cancel culture." In fact, its actual content is democratic. Here, Marcuse observes that the liberal ideal of the "free market in ideas" does not exist where independent thought is overwhelmed by ubiquitous propaganda. Even if dissenters can be heard, they are drowned out by a background consensus supported by powerful forces in society against which it is increasingly difficult to contend. Under these circumstances, tolerance of dissent is an alibi for domination rather than an invitation to challenge the status quo.

Marcuse proposes to reverse the situation by suppressing reactionary speech while privileging the progressive alternative, but this proposal turns out to be a mere provocation aimed at demystifying the myth of liberal tolerance:

> These same conditions render the critique of such tolerance abstract and academic, and the proposition that the balance between tolerance toward the Right and toward the Left would have to be radically

---

debates, see Andrew Feenberg and Jim Freedman, *When Poetry Ruled the Streets: The French May Events of 1968* (Albany: State University of New York Press, 2001), 147–84.

71 On New Left strategy, see Herbert Marcuse, "On the New Left," in *The New Left and the 1960s*, ed. Douglas Kellner (London: Routledge, 2005), 125–6.

72 Marcuse, "The Left under the Counterrevolution," 45. Christopher Holman, *Politics as Radical Creation: Herbert Marcuse and Hannah Arendt on Political Performativity* (Toronto: University of Toronto Press, 2013), 174.

redressed in order to restore the liberating function of tolerance becomes only an unrealistic speculation.[73]

After discussing the idea of educational dictatorship once again, he concludes, "The alternative to the established semi-democratic process is not a dictatorship or elite, no matter how intellectual and intelligent, but the struggle for a real democracy."[74]

The issue comes up again in Marcuse's late response to Rudolf Bahro's 1978 book *The Alternative in Eastern Europe*. Bahro grants the intellectuals a leading role in the transition to socialism. Marcuse interprets this in terms of the classical idea of educational dictatorship and seems to suggest that it is a necessary revision of Marxist theory in the light of the failure of the proletariat to make the revolution. Yet, despite this hint of antidemocratic elitism, he also agrees with Bahro on the democratic significance of workers' councils.[75]

The hodgepodge of positions is confusing. Although Holman sees a serious ambiguity here, I think that Marcuse merely intended yet another provocation. After all, he calls educational dictatorship a "scandal," and he rejects it in conversation with Habermas at about the same time as he was writing his review of Bahro's book.[76]

---

73 Herbert Marcuse, "Repressive Tolerance," in *The Essential Marcuse*, 54–5. See "Herbert Marcuse in 1978: An Interview by Myriam Miedzian Malinovich," in Herbert Marcuse, *Marxism, Revolution and Utopia* (London: Routledge, 2014), esp. 382.

74 Marcuse, "Repressive Tolerance," 58. Marcuse regarded dialogue and debate as an important part of that struggle. He engaged in public debate on the campus of UCSD with another professor who defended the War in Vietnam. What he thought should be resisted in practice was not honest disagreements over policy, much less clumsy jokes or verbal missteps, but such travesties of "freedom of speech" and "academic freedom" as government war propaganda, CIA recruiting on campus, and war research aimed at improving the targeting of American bombing raids on Hanoi.

75 Herbert Marcuse, "Protosocialism and Late Capitalism: Toward a Theoretical Synthesis Based on Bahro's Analysis," trans. Michael Vale and Anne-Marie Feenberg, in *Marxism, Revolution and Utopia*, 401–2. There is another confusing hint of dictatorship in *An Essay on Liberation*, again contradicted by the endorsement of bottom-up activism and administration. Contrast page 70 with chapter 4; and also in Gracchus Babeuf, *The Defense of Gracchus Babeuf before the High Court of Vendome*, ed. and trans. John A. Scott (New York: Schocken, 1972), which includes an essay by Marcuse.

76 Herbert Marcuse, "Theory and Politics: A Discussion with Herbert Marcuse, Jürgen Habermas, Heinz Lubasz and Tilman Spengler," *Telos* 38 (Winter 1978–79): 136.

That conversation is revealing. Habermas insists that rationality is located in free communication and has nothing to do with the structure of needs, the erotic level that Marcuse takes for essential. Marcuse replies that communication cannot even get off the ground without human beings whose needs permit and encourage a certain degree of solidarity. Solidarity founds communication, not the reverse. Where Habermas emphasizes the legitimacy of the widespread differences of opinion about the good life, Marcuse reminds him that not everyone is interested in the Good. Nazis and the Pentagon are unimpressed by Habermas's free and all-inclusive communication process.[77] In their case, Marcuse argues, "repressive tolerance" would be justified, were it possible.

Marcuse anticipates Chantal Mouffe's distinction between adversaries, with whom disagreement is appropriate, and antagonists, who fall outside the boundaries of discussion.[78] He grounds the distinction in a strong moral intuition he articulates in terms of one of Freud's most controversial theories, the instinct theory. The public exercise of rationality required by democracy, Marcuse argues, cannot be taken for granted, but presupposes the predominance of the erotic dimension of human nature. It is this dimension, not the communication process it makes possible, that is the source of rationality.[79]

The relevance of Marcuse's argument today is obvious. From the Enlightenment we inherit a natural bias toward thinking of politics in terms of opinion and deliberation. A rational politics based on self-interest and human rights was to replace a passionate politics of aristocratic honor and religious prejudice. Throughout the nineteenth century, the irregular but gradual progress of this rational politics supported faith in the eventual triumph of democracy. But it is impossible to understand the twentieth century on these terms. On the contrary,

---

77 Ibid., 139.

78 Chantal Mouffe, *The Democratic Paradox* (London: Verso, 2000).

79 Martin Matuštík translates this claim into the language of existentialism: "Existence is that concrete category in virtue of which claims to good and evil and those to procedural right can be raised and communicated in the first place." Martin Matuštík, "The Existential Dimension of the Great Refusal," in *The Great Refusal: Herbert Marcuse and Contemporary Social Movements*, ed. Andrew T. Lamas, Todd Wolfson, and Peter N. Funke (Philadelphia: Temple University Press, 2017), 326.

this was a period of rising political passions often diametrically opposed to rational interest and rights. Politics appears more and more clearly as a matter of identity, an existential stance, a way of being in the world, rather than as a matter of informed opinion.

The rising tide of authoritarian and racist politics raises fundamental questions about democracy. Those questions cannot be answered without recourse to psychological categories. However melodramatic Marcuse's quasi-Freudian vision may seem, politics is ultimately a life-and-death struggle. Indeed, the illusion that it is a matter of rational disagreement is periodically shattered by a brutal return to the reality of human destructiveness. The West lived such a shock on 9/11, and Donald Trump has reiterated the message, but no doubt observers in less fortunate regions mock those who require a reminder.

Marcuse's memory went back further, to still more horrific events. His disillusionment started early, with his participation in the German Revolution of 1918–19 as a student drafted into the army at the end of World War I. It was there that he learned not to count on rationality when the Soldiers' Council to which he was elected voted to reinstate the reactionary Prussian officers. As a witness to war, revolution, and reaction he was confronted with what he called a "depth dimension" of politics that defies explanation in rationalistic terms. He attempted to theorize it at first through Heidegger's philosophy and later through psychoanalysis.

Marcuse would not have been surprised by the racist appeal of right-wing populism today. As he said in a personal remark during his discussion with Habermas,

> I cannot understand what is happening today if I did not have Freud's concept of the destructive instinct as a basis, as an explanation, as a hypothesis. Today the intensification of this instinct is a political necessity for those in power. Without this hypothesis I must believe that the world has become crazy and that we are being ruled by madmen.[80]

Politicians like Richard Nixon and Ronald Reagan played on the irrationality of the mass of voters, but they themselves remained rational in

---

80 Marcuse, "Theory and Politics," 147.

a narrow instrumental sense. Reactionary politics today seems to confirm Marcuse's worst fears.

Nevertheless, his failure to confront the problem of democracy is, according to some commentators, "the most serious deficit in Marcuse's theory."[81] His ambivalent attitude toward democracy was surely influenced by its disastrous fate in Weimar Germany and the Cold War in the United States. Skepticism is also a heritage of both the traditional Marxist critique of the universalist claims of bourgeois right and the critique of mass society that begins with Kierkegaard and Nietzsche.

Douglas Kellner attributes Marcuse's ambivalence to the disappointed search for a revolutionary subject, arguing that he should have resisted the temptation to position the intellectuals in that role, even as a provocation. Kellner continues:

> Although I question whether there is a "revolutionary subject" defined as a universal revolutionary class, I do think it is important to specify the nature and conditions of revolutionary *subjectivity*, defined as a *universalizing consciousness* which formulates and translates society's needs into political action and prefigures alternative institutions, values and practices.[82]

Indeed, that is Marcuse's strength as a revolutionary theorist. The next chapter explains the Freudian basis of his theory of subjectivity.

---

81 John Abromeit and W. Mark Cobb, "Introduction," in *Herbert Marcuse: A Critical Reader*, 24. For a critique of Marcuse's views on democracy, see Helmut Dubiel, "Demokratie und Kapitalismus bei Herbert Marcuse," in *Kritik und Utopie im Werk von Herbert Marcuse*, ed. Institut für Sozialforschung (Frankfurt am Main: Suhrkamp, 1992), 61–100.

82 Douglas Kellner, *Herbert Marcuse and the Crisis of Marxism* (Berkeley: University of California Press, 1984), 317–18.

4

The Politics of Eros

Freudo-Marxism

Marcuse believed he was living in a sick society; he would certainly have subscribed to Freud's observation: "May we not be justified in reaching the diagnosis that, under the influence of cultural urges, some civilizations, or some epochs of civilization—possibly the whole of mankind—have become neurotic?"[1] Marcuse communicated the diagnosis in two ways: the dystopian exaggeration of the symptoms—*One-Dimensional Man*—and the depiction of a utopian state of health by which to judge the present condition—*Eros and Civilization*.

Marcuse's synthesis of Marx and Freud in the latter book is the most famous and influential version of Freudo-Marxism. While earlier versions in the work of Wilhelm Reich and Erich Fromm suggested the potential of the synthesis, Marcuse carries it further by incorporating it into a more theoretically sophisticated Marxism.

Just as Marx enlarged the concept of the political to include the economy, so Marcuse enlarges it to include the psychic dimension explored by Freud. This second enlargement is a response to the failure of the revolution, the absence of those "subjective factors" for which Marxists waited so patiently in the period leading up to World War I. Marcuse explains the psychological conditions of that failure and,

---

1 Sigmund Freud, *Civilization and Its Discontents*, trans. James Strachey (New York: Norton, 1961), 91.

correspondingly, of a radical transformation of civilization. The point is not to predict utopia but, as Fredric Jameson writes, to examine "*the conditions of possibility* of a society from which aggression will have been eliminated and in which libidinally satisfying work will be conceivable."[2] The abstract ontology discussed in the previous chapters now acquires concrete psychosocial content.

In Marcuse's interpretation, Freudian instinct theory becomes social theory and ontology. This involves some elaborate reconstructions. He introduces Marxist historical considerations into the relation between what Freud calls "eternal eros" and "his equally immortal adversary," thanatos,[3] and he devises an innovative ontology, a theory of being, starting out from Freudian psychology. This last operation is both complicated and obscure, positing the fundamental drives as aspects of reality, not just the psyche. It is not altogether clear whether Marcuse avoids old-fashioned metaphysics, but a charitable interpretation can draw on his background in phenomenology. As we saw in chapter 2, phenomenology allows him to treat what he calls "unpurged, unmutilated experience" as a fundamental ontological realm.[4]

This has strange consequences. All sorts of notions incompatible with the naturalistic worldview are thinkable within the realm of experience—for example, the constitutive power of labor, the liberation of nature, and a metapsychological theory of being.[5] This move contradicts Freud's naturalism, but because he rejected phenomenology after 1932, Marcuse cannot make explicit the assumptions behind his own experiential ontology. As a result, most commentators on his Freudo-Marxism focus on the political implications of his social psychology and ignore or reject his unusual ontology.

In the next section I will explain the background to Marcuse's synthesis in the philosophies of history of Marx and Freud, followed by an account of the consequences for his political theory and ontology.

---

2 Fredric Jameson, *Marxism and Form: Twentieth-Century Dialectical Theories of Literature* (Princeton: Princeton University Press, 1971), 115, my italics.

3 Freud, *Civilization and Its Discontents*, 92.

4 Herbert Marcuse, "The Rationality of Philosophy," in *Transvaluation of Values and Radical Social Change*, ed. Peter-Erwin Jansen, Sarah Surak, and Charles Reitz (International Herbert Marcuse Society, 2017), 15.

5 I will argue in chapter 6 that there are limits on this proliferation of entities.

The Synthesis of Marx and Freud

Both Freud and Marx dissented from the Enlightenment grand narrative of progress, but their alternative stories could not be more different. According to Freud, the human race was originally organized in small familial groups dominated by a father who monopolized the women for his own pleasure. Eventually, the deprived brothers rebelled, killed the father, and gained access to the pleasures formally denied them. However, they experienced guilt and internalized the repression that had been imposed on them by the father. Guilt thus became the basis on which civilized life was built, culminating in the ever more repressed and neurotic human beings of Freud's own day.

A structural foundation underlies Freud's story. He argues that there are two basic drives, a life instinct and a death instinct. Eros, the life instinct, aspires to create larger unities out of the fragments of the social world. Thanatos, the death instinct, wants to return to inorganic matter. Sexuality is an aspect of eros but eros includes much else besides—essentially all the life-affirming impulses of the human being. The ever-intensifying repression associated with the progress of civilization sublimates erotic energy and gives it expression in domains such as work, art, religion, friendship, and nonsexual love.

Eros and thanatos interact in the Freudian psyche. Eros strives to master thanatos in order to use its destructive energies for life, directing those energies toward the superego and nature. This is the basis of morality and technology. But, as technology develops, the competition between eros and thanatos for control of the psyche becomes ever more dangerous. World War I was a reminder that eros is not always in control.

Freud's story is apocalyptic in contrast with the liberal optimism inherited from the Enlightenment, but according to Marcuse his naturalism caused him to overlook the most radical implications of his own theory, hence the turn to Marx.

Marx's story begins with human beings living in tribal societies characterized by cooperation among their members. Such societies knew neither private property nor competition for scarce resources, but the level of individuality was necessarily low in these impoverished and tight-knit communities. With the coming of agriculture and large-scale social organization, cooperation declined and individuality developed, culminating in the modern individual free from superstition and conscious of real interests. However, at first, only a small minority enjoyed this advance. A ruling class monopolized the fruits of the labor of the great majority, causing untold suffering while also enabling social and technical progress.

The industrial revolution produced the first working class that not only resists but understands its exploitation. Capitalism is thus the last class society, soon to be superseded by a new form of social organization based again on cooperation but at a high level of individual development. The condition for this outcome is the enrichment of society by capitalism itself. The pattern of progress in Marx is dialectical: cooperation without individuality is succeeded by individuality without cooperation, and finally—the *Aufhebung*—communism combines the virtues of both earlier forms of life in a society based on cooperative individuality.

While Freud's story culminates in the present, in a world moving rapidly toward World War II, Marx's story concludes in a distant communist future that will have resolved social and national conflict. Freud's story is based on psychology, Marx's on economics. Both contest the liberal idea of continuous progress under a democratic capitalist regime, but they diverge in fundamental ways. How can they be reconciled, and why would anyone even try to reconcile such different perspectives?

The answer to the latter question is to be found in the peculiar situation of Marxist theory in the wake of World War I. The great socialist parties of the Second International betrayed their pacifist principles and supported mobilization for war except in Russia. The revolution Marx had predicted failed to occur in the rich capitalist West and instead took place in the most backward country in Europe.[6] Marxists searched for an explanation. They could no longer deny the yawning gap between the existing proletariat and the ideal agent of revolution postulated by the theory. What could explain this state of affairs?

---

6 Gramsci expressed the shock of his generation of revolutionaries in an article published in 1917 entitled "Una rivoluzione contro il 'Capitale'?" in *Scritti Politici,* ed. Paolo Spriano (Rome: Editore Riuniti. 1967), 80.

Marxists had assumed that despite its poverty and lack of education, the working class would be able to understand its situation and respond accordingly.[7] This assumption was derived from the old liberal story of progress, modified by the introduction of a revolutionary break. In reality, however, the rising rationality Marx foresaw was overcome by an irrational enthusiasm for violence against imaginary enemies. Nation trumped class. Clearly, as Freud argued, a psychological explanation would be required, but his explanation foreclosed the future and left little reason to hope. Grafting Freud's ideas onto Marxism would require major surgery.

Marx's rationalistic vision of the proletariat depended on the notion that people are ultimately moved by material needs. The needs of the proletariat cannot be satisfied in capitalist society, and the realization of this fact was supposed to motivate the revolution. But Marcuse was aware that human beings are moved not only by need but also by desire, by eros and thanatos. He knew that the structure of desire is more complex and less susceptible to a rationalistic explanation. Freud's account serves Marcuse as a starting point, but to it he adds a historical perspective derived from Marx.

Recall that in Freud, the infant's pursuit of pleasure is modified by the encounter with an unyielding reality. Libidinal energy is inhibited and an ego constructed capable of adapting to that reality. In the adult, the pleasure principle is subordinated to the reality principle. Genital sexuality prevails as the body is desexualized and suited to productive and social tasks. Moral limitations on the pursuit of pleasure sublimate libidinal energy and build larger social units and cultural achievements. This is what it means for the human psyche to adapt to reality as the condition of the possibility of civilization.

But, Marcuse asks, what is reality? Is it essentially the same for all time? Not according to Marxist theory. The reality to which the ego must adapt is radically different for class society as compared with the primitive communism of the tribe and a future communist society— discontinuities in the substance of the real that Freud ignored. Of course, Freud was aware of material progress, but he failed to see that a

---

7 See these remarkable texts of Engels: "The Peasant Question in France and Germany," in *Karl Marx and Frederick Engels: Selected Works* (New York: International Publishers, 1969); *The Housing Question* (Moscow: Progress Publishers, 1970).

qualitative change in the power of technology has transformed the relation of the pleasure principle to the reality principle. Differences in the level of economic development correlate with different psychic structures, not just different degrees of repression. Historicizing Freud's reality principle is therefore the key to Marcuse's synthesis.

Marcuse agrees with Freud that civilization requires repression. The question is, how much? The answer depends on the degree of scarcity. In poor class societies, most individuals must restrain their desires because the means of satisfaction are lacking. The degree of internal and external repression required to maintain civil order is accordingly high. Advanced capitalism has produced such a plethora of goods that absolute scarcity is no longer the primary reason for repression. Instead, a relative scarcity produced by the social organization imposes repressive structures long after the increased productivity of labor has made them technologically obsolete. Marcuse therefore distinguishes what he calls the "performance principle" from Freud's reality principle. The latter identifies natural constraints on pleasure that only technological advance can overcome, while the former describes socially constructed constraints that might be removed by social change. In other words, the performance principle adjusts the individuals to the artificial scarcities created by advanced capitalism.

Marcuse distinguishes between necessary repression and surplus repression, corresponding to the difference between the minimum renunciation of desire required by the reality principle and the excess imposed by the performance principle. Surplus repression could be reduced in a different organization of society without threatening the survival of civilization. Now the revolution can be reconceptualized in Freudian terms as the end of surplus repression and the associated performance principle. This new concept of the revolution requires a deeper probe of the psyche under capitalism and its possible future under socialism.

The Transformations

It is important to avoid a simplistic reduction of Marcuse's notion of eros to some sort of orgasmic mush. This is the error of many conservative critics who see only regression in his Freudo-Marxism. In fact, he is repeating in the domain of personality structures the dialectical pattern of development of Marx's philosophy of history. There is no return to infancy but rather a recapitulation of certain positive aspects of the early stage of development at the level of civilized adult personality. Nor does Marcuse reduce freedom to sexual freedom. Indeed, he recognizes that civilized life involves much besides. The triumph of eros, he argues, would not only liberate sexuality but would transform work, technology, creative activity, and human relations. This would be a total revolution.

Eros and Civilization formulates four different aspects of this revolution. First, the body will be released from its desexualized dedication to labor; the whole surface of the body will be eroticized and the sexual perversions condemned in class society de-stigmatized. Second, art and the imagination will no longer be excluded from the technical relation to nature in a socialist society. Third, a new concept of reason incorporating the imagination will accompany the social and economic changes brought about by the revolution; this reason will recognize as "real" the beauty of nature and human and social potentialities. Fourth, being itself will be transformed, such that the world, "reality," will appear as an aesthetic object of eroticized perception. In what follows, I will review these four utopian consequences of Marcuse's concept of revolution.

Sexuality

According to Freud, sexuality in the infant is not specialized but involves the whole body. This polymorphous sexuality conflicts with the reality principle. In the adult, genital sexuality emerges as a socially acceptable channel for desire while releasing the body for work. Marcuse concurs, arguing that capitalism is based on the working body, the privilege of genital sexuality, and the monogamous family under paternal authority. These structures are historically contingent, dependent on the adjustment of the psyche to scarcity and class rule. Once those conditions are overcome, their consequences can also be eliminated. Thus, the revolution will affect not only social and economic life but also the way the individuals understand and live their bodily existence.

Marcuse interprets this change in what can only be described as a double provocation for the times in which he was writing. *Eros and Civilization* offers a positive reevaluation of sexual perversion, and a related discussion in *One-Dimensional Man* criticizes the role of sexual liberation in consumer society.

The argument of *Eros and Civilization* is iconoclastic. For Freud, the perversions must for the most part be confined to phantasy. Perverse manifestations of sexuality bearing no connection to reproduction, work and the family conflict with civilized life. However, Marcuse argues that with the transformation of the reality principle, the original polymorphous sexuality can return and the phantasies be realized.

Remarkably for 1955, he offers a reasoned defense of sadomasochistic sexual play. Here is the passage in question:

> The function of sadism is not the same in a free libidinal relation and in the activities of SS troops. The inhuman, compulsive, coercive, and destructive forms of these perversions seem to be linked with the general perversion of human existence in a repressive culture, but the perversions have an instinctual substance distinct from these forms; and this substance may well express itself in other forms compatible with normality in high civilization.[8]

Today, we easily make the distinction for which Marcuse argues in this passage. Indeed, the stigma attached to unconventional sexual behavior has receded to the point where advertisements exhibit subtle or not-so-subtle references to activities that were unmentionable in polite company in 1955. In recent years, we have seen the legalization of nearly all forms of sexuality (at least in the West). But Marcuse's argument is not about civil rights or tolerance, which must have seemed out of the question at the time. Rather, he addresses a fundamental philosophical issue: namely, the mode of existence implied in various forms of sexual expression, in other words, what it is to be human and to have a body.

Marcuse's 1948 review of Sartre's *Being and Nothingness* anticipates his argument in *Eros and Civilization*. He notes that in sexual desire, the person is neither an instrumentalizing consciousness nor an instrumentalized object. The gap between subject and object is overcome in the caress that strips the body of its engagements in the social world

---

8 Herbert Marcuse, *Eros and Civilization: A Philosophical Inquiry into Freud* (Boston: Beacon Press, 1966), 203. See also Herbert Marcuse, "On Hedonism," in *Negations: Essays in Critical Theory*, trans. Jeremy J. Shapiro (Boston: Beacon Press, 1968), 189.

and discloses it as pure "flesh." Marcuse writes, "The '*attitude désir-ante*' thus reveals (the possibility of) a world in which the individual is in complete harmony with the whole."[9] Sexuality is emblematic of a freedom excluded in principle by Sartre's ontology, but, Marcuse argues, realizable through the revolution.

Sexuality, as an aspect of eros, is specifically related to the erotic significance of the body. For Marcuse, the revolution makes the erotic potential of the body available, reversing the desexualization of the body that suits it for alienated labor. The revolution will release sexuality from repression, but Marcuse argues that it goes far beyond mere physical enjoyment. The distinction depends on the subordination of sexuality to eros, the instinctive basis of sexuality. According to Freud, eros impels the human being toward creativity, love, and friendship as well as sex. The liberation of eros will give rise not only to new forms of sexual activity but "the eroticization of the whole personality."[10] The new sexual dispensation will affect all activities, especially labor, which will be invested with erotic significance and take on the features of play. This will be a "civilization evolving from and sustained by free libidinal relations."[11]

However, *One-Dimensional Man* cautions against overestimating the significance of sexual liberation under capitalism. After World War II, a shift occurs from a society that valued work and renunciation to a consumer society that revels in expenditure while releasing sexuality to some extent from the bonds of the old morality. The release from repression is blocked far short of general social emancipation by the focus on individual consumption and genital sexuality. These limitations enable capitalism to instrumentalize the change, binding the individuals ever more tightly to the system through their libidinal investments. Marcuse calls this "repressive desublimation," the partial return of libidinal energy to its normal channels of satisfaction under conditions that stabilize the existing society.[12]

---

9 Herbert Marcuse, "Sartre's Existentialism," in *The Essential Marcuse: Selected Writings of Philosopher and Social Critic Herbert Marcuse*, ed. Andrew Feenberg and William Leiss (Boston: Beacon Press, 2007), 150.

10 Marcuse, *Eros and Civilization*, 201.

11 Ibid., 207.

12 Herbert Marcuse, *One-Dimensional Man: Studies in the Ideology of Advanced Industrial Society* (Boston: Beacon Press, 1964), chapter 3.

Aesthetics

Marcuse notes that the concept of the aesthetic is ambiguous, associated with both sensuousness and artistic expression. Aesthetics offers "a synthesis, reassembling the bits and fragments which can be found in distorted humanity and nature. This recollected material has become the domain of the imagination, it has been sanctioned by the repressive societies in art."[13] Art is rooted in eros, presenting sensuous objects in their ideal form, stripped of contingent features that contradict their essence. In a non-repressive society, Marcuse argues, rationality would no longer be confined to adjustment and survival but can realize aesthetic form in reality. He emphasizes the contrast between an aesthetic logic of gratification and the existing repressive performance principle. As I will explain in chapter 6, this becomes a central theme in his projection of a reconstructed science and technology under socialism.

In *Eros and Civilization*, the "aesthetic dimension" is symbolized by two mythic figures, Orpheus and Narcissus:

> The Orphic and Narcissistic Eros awakens and liberates potentialities that are real . . . but in the un-erotic reality suppressed . . . The opposition between man and nature, subject and object, is overcome. Being is experienced as gratification, which unites man and nature so that the fulfillment of man is at the same time the fulfillment, without violence, of nature.[14]

Marcuse returned to this idea in 1969 in *An Essay on Liberation*, where he argues that the New Left did not simply advocate alternative policies but rather prefigured a different existential relationship to the world. An aesthetic *Lebenswelt* that privileged eros appeared as a critical alternative to a repressive reality. Marcuse notes that in the *Manuscripts*, Marx similarly introduced aesthetic considerations into the technological base, writing that unlike the animals whose relation to nature is determined entirely by need, "man constructs also in accordance with the laws of beauty."[15] Marcuse did not expect the New Left to make the

---

13 Herbert Marcuse, "Nature and Revolution," in *Counterrevolution and Revolt* (Boston: Beacon Press, 1972), 70.

14 Marcuse, *Eros and Civilization*, 165–6.

15 Karl Marx, "Economic and Philosophical Manuscripts," in *Early Writings*, ed.

revolution but rather viewed it as the living proof of the possibility of a world that obeyed "the laws of beauty" rather than those of profit.

Rationality

For Marcuse, the transformation of the concept of rationality has to do with the cognitive role of phantasy or imagination. In class society, phantasy is associated with perverse sexuality and art. From a Freudian standpoint, both are expressions of eros that lie outside "reality" as the object of adjustment. The ego must discipline phantasy in order to remain in touch with the conditions of survival. Under these conditions, phantasy has been stripped from the concept of reason, exiled to the realm of pure possibility.

Marcuse claims that the abolition of scarcity opens reason to the full content of experience. With the reduction of repression, it is possible to reunite the faculties and to institute a new concept of reason that incorporates phantasy and, with it, the possibilities formerly excluded by a reason oriented to survival:

> Owing to its unique capacity to "intuit" an object though the latter be not present and to create something new out of the given material of cognition, imagination denotes a considerable independence from the given, of freedom amid a world of unfreedom. In surpassing what is present, it can anticipate the future.[16]

Marcuse's defense of imagination is thus not a rejection of rationality but rather the projection of a new form of "libidinal rationality" no longer bound to the performance principle. "Eros redefines reason in his own terms."[17] So redefined, reason goes beyond the empirical facts to disclose an erotic reality, a reality that presents itself in the forms of beauty as containing potentialities awaiting realization. This would be a less aggressive and destructive form of rationality, but a form of rationality nevertheless. Imaculada Kangussu explains:

---

and trans. T. B. Bottomore (London: C. A. Watts, 1963), 128.

16 Herbert Marcuse, "Philosophy and Critical Theory," in *Negations*, 154.

17 Marcuse, *Eros and Civilization*, 224. See Gvozden Flego, "Erotisieren statt sublimieren," in *Kritik und Utopie im Werk von Herbert Marcuse*, ed. Institut für Sozialforschung (Frankfurt am Main: Suhrkamp, 1992), 187–200.

> Marcuse's original contribution lies in his attempt to link the mind process that Freud calls phantasy with that which Kant identifies as imagination (*Einbildungskraft*) . . . In *Critique of Pure Reason*, imagination realizes the connections between phenomena and concepts, a process known as "schematism" and responsible for knowledge, for finding the adequate concept of a phenomenon . . . Phantasy provides a schema (linking concepts and objects) according to which we judge and categorize objects and, more broadly, evaluate, estimate, consider, analyze, and categorize the world.[18]

The merger of Freudian phantasy with Kantian imagination opens reason to the categories under which things can be rationally evaluated in terms of their potentialities.

As discussed in chapter 3, the imaginative grasp of potentialities is not arbitrary but responds to the nature of life. Life has a direction of development and flourishes where it can fulfill its potentialities. Reason constructs social potentialities from indications it finds amid the given facts that signal such a direction of development.

This is not problematic in the case of biology, where criteria such as health or maturation enable an objective selection of facts supporting a concept of potentiality. The social case is more complicated. What qualifies as a potentiality of democracy, education, communication, family life? The answer again depends on a concept of development; but what are the criteria? The notion of life affirmation is too vague to decide difficult controversies. Marcuse proposes that philosophy and art can provide guidance, but in the end, they do not yield a consensus as does biology. This is why, he argues, the final word on social potentiality must be left up to political struggle and democratic debate.[19] The results of such struggles and debates are not arbitrary on this account but yield the existential truth insofar as it can be known. Fallibility, not relativity, is the limitation of the truths of the lifeworld.

---

18 Imaculada Kangussu, "Marcuse on Phantasy," in *Radical Philosophy Review* 16, no. 1 (2013): 388–9.

19 Marcuse, *Eros and Civilization*, 228.

Being

Our common sense tells us that reality is a sum of facts, the things we perceive in the world in their independent reality. We do not count our attitude toward these things as an aspect of their being but attribute it to the state of our psyche: being is independent of subjectivity. Once again, Marcuse rejects common sense. Just as he ontologizes Marx's social theory, so he argues that "it seems permissible to give [Freud's] conception a general ontological meaning."[20] Indeed, the common-sense view leaves out a great deal of the content of experience, including the objective correlates of the Freudian categories of eros and thanatos. For Marcuse, these are not merely subjective drives but reflect aspects of being itself.

The emphasis on the ontological role of experience appears to dissolve reality into consciousness. Freud would have objected that consciousness has no such privilege in defining the nature of reality. On the contrary! Reality, as defined by natural science, is indifferent to humanity. Marcuse follows Husserl's demonstration that the structure and concepts of natural science are based on the *Lebenswelt*. Science itself is grounded on something more fundamental and so cannot define being. It is not reality that is dissolved into consciousness, but consciousness that was always already there in what we use for reality, in the basic categories and types that define the world as science understands it.[21] It is thus wrong to treat all those aspects of experience excluded by natural science as mere illusions.

If physical reality is intertwined with subjectivity, it cannot transcend the historical world. Being is at stake in history.[22] Marcuse concludes:

The two layers or aspects of objectivity (physical and historical) are interrelated in such a way that they cannot be insulated from each other; the historical aspect can never be eliminated so radically that only the "absolute" physical layer remains.[23]

---

20 Ibid., 125.

21 Herbert Marcuse, "On Science and Phenomenology," in *Philosophy, Psychoanalysis, and Emancipation*, ed. Douglas Kellner (London: Routledge, 2011), 149, 151.

22 For an account of the role of this "absolute historicism" in Western Marxism, see Andrew Feenberg, *The Philosophy of Praxis* (London: Verso, 2017), chapter 1.

23 Marcuse, *One-Dimensional Man*, 218.

On this basis, he introduces a historicized notion of biological drives into the lifeworld: "Eros transforms being."[24]

Marcuse develops this idea in terms of Freud's theory of primary narcissism. The experience of the infant at first "engulfs the 'environment,' integrating the narcissistic ego with the objective world."[25] This notion, which in Freud describes a primitive psychological state, becomes the clue for Marcuse that the metapsychology hides a latent ontology implicating being itself in the workings of the instinctual drives. Accordingly, Marcuse projects the Freudian drives onto the human relation to nature.

> Eros reveals the world in its beauty as essentially correlated with human desire. Narcissism may contain the germ of a different reality principle: the libidinal cathexis of the ego . . . may become the source and reservoir for a new libidinal cathexis of the objective world— transforming this world into a new mode of being . . . which unites man and nature so that the fulfillment of man is at the same time the fulfillment, without violence, of nature.[26]

Eros now enters the world as a structuring principle of reality, not just of the psyche, and the same is true of thanatos. Beauty, as manifested in the objects of experience, is the objective correlate of the erotic drive, which plays the role of philosophical subject. A life-affirming social world unites subject and object.[27]

Habermas claims that this unusual interpretation of the instinct theory is based on Heideggerian ontology.[28] Presumably Habermas refers

---

24 Herbert Marcuse, *An Essay on Liberation* (Boston: Beacon Press, 1969), 10n1; Marcuse, *Eros and Civilization*, 171.

25 Marcuse, *Eros and Civilization*, 168.

26 Ibid., 169, 165–6.

27 Marcuse goes so far as to suggest that Kant should have considered a form of intuition of beauty alongside the intuitions of space and time. Marcuse, *An Essay on Liberation*, 32. See also Marcuse, "Nature and Revolution," 63.

28 "Whoever fails to detect the persistence of categories from *Being and Time* in Freud's categories of the drive theory, as Marcuse developed them in a Marxist historical construct, and in his recently reconstructed anthropology, will run the risk of serious misunderstandings." Jürgen Habermas, *Antworten auf Herbert Marcuse* (Frankfurt am Main: Suhrkamp, 1968), 10–11, my translation.

to the concept of worldhood; Marcuse is not stating facts of the sort that science could confirm but rather describing existential conditions common to the lifeworld. There is also a possible connection to the category of *Befindlichkeit*, which signifies inner states, moods, as modes of disclosure. This category is neither subjective nor objective but ties both together in being-in-the-world. Phenomenologically considered, moods are not only in the mind but manifest themselves also in perceived reality. The lifeworld is not disclosed as a collection of bare facts but in a mood, a general form that colors the substance of perception with a quality such as beauty or usefulness.

Film testifies to this ambiguity of inner and outer: each scene is revealed as frightening or heartwarming, exciting or expectant, meditative or triumphant, through a variety of objective means such as lighting, camera angles, and music. By analogy, eros is thus not only an inner state but reveals reality under its aspect. With this, Marcuse's version of worldhood acquires affective content.

This notion is thoroughly counterintuitive, and *Eros and Civilization* offers remarkably little argument for this transmutation of psychology into ontology. At one point Marcuse simply states that because the primary instincts pertain to both organic and inorganic matter, they imply an ontology.[29] The non sequitur seems too obvious to be accidental. He may have decided, at some point in the composition of his book, to simply leap over the objection that psychology has no necessary ontological implications. In this, he followed Marx, who made a similar claim in 1844, writing that feelings and passions "are true *ontological* affirmations of being (nature)."[30]

The leap has its sources and its justification in the metacritical reconstruction of the abstract categories of philosophy in social reality. Indeed, this is the hallmark of philosophy of praxis, an approach that begins with Marx's *Manuscripts*, is revived by Lukács in *History and Class Consciousness*, and continues in the Frankfurt School.[31] Marcuse proposes an erotic resolution of the antinomy of subject and object,

---

29 Marcuse, *Eros and Civilization*, 107.

30 Marx, "Economic and Philosophical Manuscripts," 189. I have discussed Marcuse's "leap" to ontology at greater length in Feenberg, *The Philosophy of Praxis*, 187–94.

31 These concepts are explained in chapter 2 above, in the section entitled "Marx's Philosophy of Praxis."

which classical German philosophy attempted to overcome at the purely cognitive level. He brings the concepts of subject and object down to earth with resources he finds in Freud, while treating their philosophical antinomy as politically contingent.

Apart from the strangeness of its claim that moods pertain to reality, this ontologized version of Freud's instinct theory raises a new difficulty: namely, it challenges Marcuse to reconcile the extended concept of narcissism with "human existence in its entirety," that is, with civilized life.[32] If "being is experienced as gratification," what further role can sublimation play, and what are the implications for culture that depends on sublimation?

Marcuse answers this question with the claim that eros aims at higher cultural ends under non-repressive conditions. Marcuse calls this the "self-sublimation of Eros." He believes he can find support for this notion in a brief remark in which Freud suggests that sublimation involves an initial redirection of libidinal energy toward the ego before it is attached to the new object. Whether or not this is a correct interpretation of Freud, he needs such a concept in order to argue for a "non-repressive mode of sublimation which results from an extension rather than from a constraining deflection of libido."[33] This hypothesis allows him to reconstruct the conditions of civilized life without surplus repression. "Sublimation would not cease but instead, as erotic energy, would surge up in new forces of cultural creation."[34]

---

32 Ibid., 158.

33 Ibid., 169–70. For critical discussions of this hypothesis, see Flego, "Erotisieren statt sublimieren," 187–200; Bernard Görlich, "Sublimierung als kulturelles Triebschicksal: Drei Brennpunkte der Sublimierungsfrage im Marcuse-Freud-Vergleich," in Institut für Sozialforschung, Kritik und Utopie, 171–86; Bernard Stiegler, Mécréance et Discrédit: 3. L'esprit perdu du capitalisme (Paris: Galilée, 2006), 99–102; Mitchell Aboulafia, Transcendence: On Self-Determination and Cosmopolitanism (Stanford: Stanford University Press, 2010), chapter 7.

34 Herbert Marcuse, "Progress and Freud's Theory of Instincts," in Five Lectures (Boston: Beacon Press, 1970), 40.

Technology

Although Marcuse does not describe an object of the death drive corresponding to the role beauty plays as the object of the life instinct, devastation would surely qualify. However, there is a more surprising correlate: technology responds to the destructive instinct which gains in strength in a society based on competition and struggle. He calls on Freud for help in explaining the mode of existence of the subjects of technological aggression and violence. After all, a simple obsession with instrumental control is insufficient to explain a world in which peace is maintained by the threat of "mutually assured destruction." Instrumentalism is inseparable from thanatos and must be mastered by a powerful erotic commitment to life to serve human flourishing.

Marcuse develops this argument from *Eros and Civilization* with greater specificity in *An Essay on Liberation*, where he claims that a "new sensibility" has emerged that considers nature as a subject with intrinsic potentialities. This sensibility requires a new aesthetically informed instrumental relation to nature. The concept of "subject" intended in this claim derives from Aristotle, Hegel, and the early Marx. The idea is not to engage in a conversation with nature, as Habermas once implied, but to seek a more harmonious technical relation to the potentialities of nature that favor human life.[35] This is not a simple matter of opinion; rather, it concerns a structure of sentiments and practices, an existential politics. The generalization of this politics would lead to a transformation of the mode of production under the influence of eros.

Marcuse recognizes the essential role of science and technology in any modern society, holding out hope for a different scientific-technical encounter with nature. The synthesis of Marx and Freud ties technological design to the instincts:

---

35 Habermas claimed that Marcuse's reference to nature as a "subject" intended a communicative relation. This is an obvious straw man, yet frequently repeated. Since Aristotle, "subject" can also refer to a being with potentialities, and this is what interests Marcuse. Jürgen Habermas, "Technology and Science as Ideology," in *Toward a Rational Society: Student Protest, Science, and Politics*, trans. Jeremy J. Shapiro (Boston: Beacon Press, 1970), 87–8.

Science and technology would have to change their present direction and goals; they would have to be reconstructed in accord with a new sensibility—the demands of the life instincts. Then one could speak of a technology of liberation, product of a scientific imagination free to project and design the forms of a human universe without exploitation and toil.[36]

Toward the end of his life, Marcuse recognized the power of eros in the environmental movement, which he interpreted as a resurgence of the life instinct countering the destructive energies embodied in the existing technology.[37] He also argued that feminism was implicated in this new object of radical protest. On his view, patriarchy has endowed women with specifically "feminine characteristics" that militate against the aggressive tendencies of capitalism and its technology. The generalization of these characteristics would make possible a "feminist socialism" which "would use the productive forces ... for making life an end in itself ... for the emancipation of the senses and of the intellect from the rationality of domination: creative receptivity versus repressive productivity."[38]

For Marcuse, the unity of humanity and nature is not only experientially validated, but validated scientifically by ecology as well. The aggressive struggle to dominate nature destroys "forces in nature which have been distorted and suppressed—forces which could support and enhance the liberation of man."[39] As such, theoretical and practical reason are truly united in the struggle to save the environment as a human lifeworld—considerations to which I shall return in more detail in chapter 6.

---

36 Marcuse, *An Essay on Liberation*, 19.

37 Herbert Marcuse, "Ecology and Revolution," in *The New Left and the 1960s*, ed. Douglas Kellner (London: Routledge 2005); Herbert Marcuse, "Ecology and the Critique of Modern Society," in *Collected Papers of Herbert Marcuse*, vol. 5, *Philosophy, Psychoanalysis, and Emancipation*, ed. Douglas Kellner and Clayton Pierce (New York: Routledge, 2017).

38 Herbert Marcuse, "Marxism and Feminism," in *The New Left and the 1960s*, 170. For a defense of Marcuse's feminism against the charge of essentialism, see Nina Power, "Marcuse and Feminism Revisited," *Radical Philosophy Review* 16, no. 1 (2013): 79. She writes, "So while Marcuse seems on the surface to uphold somewhat essentialist and constricting stereotypes of gender normativity, he does so not to remain with them but to help imagine a world where the true liberation of men and women will culminate in the overturning of the attachment of these characteristics to specific genders as such."

39 Marcuse, "Nature and Revolution," 66.

Conclusion: The Limits of Utopia

Marcuse's remarkable synthesis of Marx and Freud has been criticized as unfaithful to the true Marxist or Freudian doctrine.[40] However, there is a more fundamental issue, which I will address in conclusion. That issue concerns the implausibility of a non-repressive society. Does not such a conception presuppose, at best, an overly optimistic view of human nature, and at worst a coercive homogenization of society around a false promise of harmony? Joel Whitebook echoes a common critique: "The pursuit of 'integral satisfaction' that disavows the incomplete and conflictual nature of human existence brings us into the register of omnipotence and therewith raises the specter of totalitarianism."[41]

Marcuse's imagined utopia appears as a provocation and calls forth precisely such objections. Indeed, he willfully defies sober assessment of human nature. Of course, he is aware of the elementary objection to his position: given human nature as we know it, the peace and order of utopia could only be achieved by erasing individual differences. To counter this objection, he needs to affirm the possibility of individuality and conflict in a non-repressive society—a theme on which the last chapter of *Eros and Civilization* contains persuasive reflections.

To some extent, the issue is one of degree. It is obvious that a return to the infantile pleasure principle is incompatible with civilized life, indeed with life itself. However, Marcuse explicitly excludes regression. In that sense, his non-repressive society belongs on a continuum with the existing repressive society and should perhaps have been called the "less repressive society."

This more modest version of his thesis is obscured by his frequent invocation of a total revolutionary break, but he concedes that the

---

40 See, for example, Robert Steigerwald, *Herbert Marcuses dritter Weg* (Cologne: Pahl-Rugenstein, 1969); Sidney Lipshires, *Herbert Marcuse: From Marx to Freud and Beyond* (Cambridge, MA: Shenkman Publishing, 1974).

41 Joel Whitebook, "The Marriage of Marx and Freud: Critical Theory and Psychoanalysis," in *The Cambridge Companion to Critical Theory*, ed. Fred Rush (Cambridge, UK: Cambridge University Press, 2004), 89.

break would lead only to a drastic reduction in the level of repression, not its abolition. Thus, aggression would not disappear but would be better controlled by eros, with which it is essentially entangled in both Freud's and Marcuse's theories. Although this interpretation brings Marcuse closer to Freud, there is an important difference: Marcuse's revolutionary break changes personality structure in such a way as to diminish aggression while also diminishing repression. Freud thinks this is impossible, arguing that the progress of civilization requires increased repression, hence also with the spread of the neurotic plague.[42]

Marcuse recognizes that the very fact of human individuality leads to conflict. In *Civilization and Its Discontents*, Freud notes that the abolition of private property might be desirable—Marcuse would certainly agree—but would not eliminate conflicting sexual choices.[43] Marcuse takes up this point, which he relates to the ineradicable differences between the individuals. In a free society, he writes,

> men would really exist as individuals, each shaping his own life; they would face each other with truly different needs and truly different modes of satisfaction . . . The ascendency of the pleasure principle would thus engender antagonisms, pains, and frustrations—individual conflicts in the striving for gratification.[44]

Is this concession compatible with Marcuse's utopian vision? In *Dialectic of Enlightenment*, Horkheimer and Adorno distinguish human pleasure from animal satisfaction by the presence of social prohibitions and their overcoming.[45] The underlying Hegelian point is that human pleasure results from the satisfaction of desires that have been conceived as such, that are "reflected" rather than reflexive. Desire is thus individualized and does not obey sheer instinct. Marcuse agrees, adding

---

42 Freud, *Civilization and Its Discontents*, 90.

43 Ibid., 90, 60–1.

44 Marcuse, *Eros and Civilization*, 227–8. René Girard once told me in conversation, "Knowledge unites, but desire divides."

45 Max Horkheimer and Theodor Adorno, *Dialectic of Enlightenment*, ed. Gunzelin S. Noerr, trans. Edmund Jephcott (Stanford: Stanford University Press, 2002), 82.

that struggle is an aspect of "the rationality of gratification."[46] He suggests the possibility of a "libidinal morality" based not on repression, the superego, but on the very nature of human satisfaction.

This is a strange notion, and Marcuse's quasi-Freudian justification of it is hardly convincing, but there is a commonsense core to the idea that human desire has an intrinsic "moral" aspect. Desire is not a mere impulse to rush to the trough like a hungry pig. The pursuit of pleasure demands specific conditions and requires no Freudian repression to motivate a certain restraint. "What distinguishes pleasure from the blind satisfaction of want is the instinct's refusal to exhaust itself in immediate satisfaction, its ability to build up and use barriers for intensifying fulfillment."[47] The satisfaction of desire is all the greater where obstacles are overcome and the worth of the object and the virtue of the subject thereby confirmed.

This is especially true of personal relations. Challenge is of the essence and is implied in respect for the other. But even in the least repressive society, this implies also a risk of failure in the face of the contingency of satisfaction. Contingency would not be alienating in this case but would be a condition for achieving a fulfillment experienced as necessary. Coming to terms with this fact would not provoke violence or struggle for domination. "A society without conflicts would be a utopian idea, but the idea of a society in which conflicts evidently exist but can be resolved without oppression and cruelty is in my opinion not a utopian idea."[48]

The emergence of the New Left gave political substance to Marcuse's Freudo-Marxism, and a further generation of political struggles demonstrates the widespread desire for a society oriented toward peace and fulfillment. Marcuse argued that eros inspires movements around issues such as environmentalism and the rights of women and gender and racial minorities. The reactionary trend that increasingly prevails today testifies to the destructive potential of human nature, amplified by the present organization of society. Freud's *Civilization and Its*

---

46 Marcuse, *Eros and Civilization*, 228.

47 Ibid., 227.

48 Herbert Marcuse, "The End of Utopia," in *Five Lectures*, 79. In this text, exceptionally, Marcuse distinguishes between impractical utopias and progressive social change. The point, however, is clear.

Discontents proposed a theoretical explanation of these contradictions of political life—one that Marcuse attempted to do justice while finding grounds for struggle for a better world. He is truly one of the most important theorists of that struggle.

5

The Critique of Technology

An Ambiguous Critique

Marcuse's critique of advanced capitalist society embraced the familiar issues of the left: racism, imperialism, patriarchy, and the alienation and exploitation of labor. As he became a popular figure, he intervened actively in social movements, participating in demonstrations and addressing political meetings. He evoked the issues against the background of a critique of advanced capitalism. For him, it is not enough to oppose bad policies; the whole way of life that supports them must be challenged. Alienated labor, privatized consumption, and competitive individualism, he argued, are fertile ground for conservative hegemony.[1] Marcuse's critique of technology addressed one fundamental aspect of this capitalist way of life. In this chapter, and the next, I will present that critique and consider how it might be applied to our present situation.

One-Dimensional Man appeared in 1964, at a time when both Marxism and liberalism were unanimous in their praise for technical progress. Marcuse's critique of science and technology went against the current. It is now easy to attach his ideas to a tradition of Marxist

---

1 For an example, see Marcuse's critique of the Vietnam War, entitled "The Individual in the Great Society," in Herbert Marcuse, *Towards a Critical Theory of Society: Collected Papers of Herbert Marcuse*, ed. Douglas Kellner (London: Routledge, 2001), 59–80. This article was originally published by his students in an "underground" antiwar journal in 1966. Available at sfu.ca/~andrewf/pub_alternatives_magazine.html.

technology criticism, but at the time, such views were invisible to all but a few aficionados of twentieth-century European intellectual history. Such soon-to-be classics as Lukács's *History and Class Consciousness* and Horkheimer and Adorno's *Dialectic of Enlightenment* were untranslated and out of print, scarcely mentioned in the few articles and books that noticed their existence at all.[2]

Marcuse contributed to a rapidly growing climate of resistance to the technocratic dystopia feared by the newly emerging opposition of the 1960s. As his name became a symbol for these oppositional currents, his ideas were attacked as technophobic and antiscientific. This was the real scandal of *One-Dimensional Man,* which outraged readers on the right and the left as much by its critique of science and technology as by its revolutionary politics.

In this chapter, I will show that Marcuse's critique, while radical, does not imply irrational hostility to science, as is often supposed.[3] The demonstration will require not only a break with a widely accepted image of Marcuse, but also with the peculiar rhetorical strategy of his later works. His style is itself a conscious provocation, a refusal of the accepted canons of academic discourse—a strategy whose effectiveness can be measured by his remarkable impact. Sales quickly reached 50,000 per year, and translations appeared everywhere. However, while the constant compression of ideas into dramatic formulations emphasizes the dialectical connections, it sometimes obscures the meaning of the concepts so connected.

Marcuse's basic claim is that modern science and technology are *essentially* implicated in social domination.[4] By science and technology,

---

2 *History and Class Consciousness* practically disappeared after 1923, to be republished in Germany, with Lukács's permission, in 1967. It was available earlier, in 1960, in French translation, which is how I first read it. *Dialectic of Enlightenment* was what the French call a "confidential" publication. Horkheimer and Adorno refused to reprint its obscure first edition until 1969. I found a pirated edition in my student days, which appears to be a bound photocopy of the original Querido Verlag edition, with the possibly mythic added notice, "Edition 'Emigrant' Lichtenstein 1955."

3 There is a whole critical literature attacking Marcuse's critique of science. See, for example, Peter Sedgwick, "Natural Science and Human Theory: A Critique of Herbert Marcuse," *The Socialist Register 1966: A Survey of Movements and Ideas* 3 (1966): 163–92.

4 Herbert Marcuse, *One-Dimensional Man: Studies in the Ideology of Advanced Industrial Society* (Boston: Beacon Press, 1964), xv–xvi.

he means just what we would expect: research, machines, industry, but also the technical practices and patterns of thought that make these concrete achievements possible. His concept of domination refers to the suppression of the individual by society, both in the external form of exploitation and coercive power, and in the internal or "introjected" form of conformism and authoritarianism. He holds that, today, the machine is not merely *used* for the purpose of suppressing individuality but that it is the basis for new types of suppression that it alone makes possible and is destined to carry out.

Marcuse's dialectical style works on the ambiguities of certain terms in a way that is both illuminating and confusing. When he writes, for example, that science is "political" or that technology is "ideological," he makes the strong point that science and technology can only be understood in the context of the social world in which they function. Yet, in making his point in this way, he blurs the essential difference between science and politics, technology and ideology. He might be taken to mean that, as politics and ideology, science and technology are nothing more than the rationalization of the interests of a particular class. But, then, opposition to that class would include opposition to "its" science and technology. This view is undoubtedly irrationalist and resembles romantic critiques of modernity that call for a return to religious values or a simpler, pretechnological way of life.[5]

Yet this is not at all his intent. Despite his sharp criticism of "technological rationality," he still maintains the old Marxist faith in the ultimate liberating potential of technology. It still represents the material basis for overcoming scarcity and conflict, but capitalism "represses" this technical potential by creating an ever-renewed struggle for existence.

To avoid an irrationalist misrepresentation of his position, Marcuse is obliged to offer correctives to his strongest critical claims, asserting the neutrality, validity, and instrumental effectiveness of science and technology despite their political character. At one point, he states that "technological rationality, freed from its exploitative features" can be employed under socialism, but this seems to contradict his own

---

5 There was also a short-lived communist version of this critique in the 1920s supported by an organization called Proletcult. See Carmen Claudin-Urondo, *Lénine et la révolution culturelle* (Paris: Mouton, 1975), 47–60.

argument that "technology *as such* cannot be isolated from the use to which it is put."[6] He also asserts with equal assurance that "technology has become the great vehicle of *reification*," and that "science and technology are the great vehicles of liberation."[7] He writes:

> If the completion of the technological project involves a break with the prevailing technological rationality, the break in turn depends on the continued existence of the technical base itself. For it is this base which has rendered possible the satisfaction of needs and the reduction of toil—it remains the very base of all forms of human freedom. The qualitative change lies in the reconstruction of this base—that is, in its development with a view of different ends.[8]

The mutually canceling formulas do actually add up to a theory buried in the interplay of the concepts used to present it. However, Marcuse's rhetorical strategy is clear: from a variant of the Marxist position, he draws conclusions typical of the irrationalist critique. He wants to have his conceptual cake and eat it too, making the strongest possible critique of technology without paying the "Luddite" price.

Habermas, among others, has taken this to mean that Marcuse really believed in the neutrality of technology all along.[9] And Joachim Bergmann argues that without a distinction between the purely neutral technical resources of advanced societies and their actual realization in particular ideologically biased technologies, there can be no notion of a "repressed potential" that would be liberated under socialism.[10] How indeed would one measure this potential if it were not with respect to purely technical powers, abstracted from particular technologies and therefore also from whatever political or ideological function these technologies serve?

---

6 Marcuse, *One-Dimensional Man*, 235, xvi, my italics.

7 Ibid., 168; Herbert Marcuse, *An Essay on Liberation* (Boston: Beacon Press, 1969), 12.

8 Marcuse, *One-Dimensional Man*, 231; cf. 221–2.

9 Jürgen Habermas, "Technology and Science as Ideology," in *Toward a Rational Society: Student Protest, Science, and Politics*, trans. Jeremy J. Shapiro (Boston: Beacon Press, 1970), 88–90.

10 Joachim Bergmann, "Technologische Rationalität und spätkapitalistische Ökonomie," in *Antworten auf Herbert Marcuse*, ed. Jürgen Habermas (Frankfurt am Main: Suhrkamp, 1968), 99–100.

It is regrettable that Marcuse did not arrive at a clearer formulation of his theory in response to his critics. I will argue that many of his difficulties stem from the fact that his critique draws on two independent but related sources. The first of these sources is Marx's analysis of the adaptation of science and technology to capitalist society, an approach that informs his understanding of legitimation in advanced capitalist society, and his critique of Weber's theory of rationalization. Like Marx, Marcuse argues that technical progress can only provide universal benefits once freed from the imperatives of capitalism.

However, there is another strand to Marcuse's argument that holds that technical reason is a priori adapted to the maintenance of social domination not just under capitalism, but essentially, *in itself*. This position seems closer in spirit to critics of technology such as Heidegger or Ellul, whose views are frequently described as romantic. This "romantic" or, better still, "ontological" strand of the theory holds that "technological rationality," the prevailing form of technical reason, cannot serve a free society without fundamental transformation.

I am not convinced that Marcuse reconciled these positions successfully, but his attempt invites us to further reflection on technology. Can we, through the elaboration of his own concepts, bring these various approaches to the critique of technology together? Can they contribute to our understanding of the politics of technology today, such issues as climate change and surveillance on the internet? I will address these questions in this chapter and the next.[11]

The Neutrality of Technology

Marcuse argues that "the traditional notion of the 'neutrality' of technology can no longer be maintained."[12] Here is a claim that runs through his whole critique of technology. Yet, in reality, his rejection of the neutrality thesis is by no means so categorical as it seems. What is

---

11 For a discussion of the background of these various strands of Marcuse's theory in the Frankfurt School, see Patrick Murray, "The Frankfurt School Critique of Technology," *Research in Philosophy and Technology* 5 (1982): 223–48.

12 Marcuse, *One-Dimensional Man*, xvi.

the traditional notion of the neutrality of technology, and with what new conception does he propose to replace it?

The neutrality of technology consists, first of all, in its "value-free" indifference to the variety of ends it can be made to serve. As means, technologies stand under the norm of efficiency and are only contingently related to the substantive values that determine their applications. This is the meaning of the infamous slogan of the NRA according to which "Guns don't kill people, people kill people." This conception of neutrality is familiar and self-evident.

There is a second sense in which technology is said to be neutral. Not only is technology claimed to be indifferent with respect to ends, but it also appears to be indifferent with respect to social organization, at least in modern times, and especially with respect to the political distinction between capitalist and socialist society.[13] A hammer is a hammer, a steam turbine is a steam turbine, and such tools are useful in any social context, assuming the existence of a suitable technical infrastructure to support their employment. In this respect, technology appears to be different from legal or religious institutions, which cannot be easily transferred to new social contexts, because they are so deeply embedded in the culture of their society of origin. The transfer of technology, on the contrary, seems to be inhibited only by cost.

Third, the cultural neutrality of technology is usually attributed to its "rational" character and to the universality of the truth it embodies. That truth, like scientific truth, can be formulated in verifiable causal propositions that maintain their validity in every conceivable cultural context.

Fourth, the rational universality of technology also makes it possible to apply the same standards of measurement to technologies employed in different settings. Thus, the progress of technology is routinely said to increase the productivity of labor and social wealth in comparisons not only between different countries but also between different eras and different types of societies.

In opposition to these widely accepted views, Marcuse asserts that technology is fundamentally biased toward domination. His alternative

---

13 The qualification "modern" is necessary since modern technology is by no means culturally indifferent in premodern contexts. See Lauriston Sharp, "Steel Axes for Stone Age Australians," in *Human Problems in Technological Change*, ed. Edward H. Spicer (New York: Russell Sage Foundation, 1952).

position can be formulated in three theses, each of which summarizes an aspect of his argument:

1) Technology in advanced capitalism has become a total system, a world. It takes the place traditionally occupied by ideology in legitimating capitalist society. It thereby forecloses opposition to the wrongs of the society and perpetuates the domination inherited from the past.

2) Technology and its associated technical rationality are not politically neutral, because, even as they serve generic ends such as increasing the productivity of labor, their specific design and application under capitalism imposes top-down control in production and social life generally. In this sense, the means (technology) are not truly "value free" but can be said to include within their structure the end of controlling the labor force.

3) Scientific-technical rationality is a priori adapted to the maintenance of social domination.

These three theses contradict the commonsense notion of the neutrality of technology. Marcuse insists on linking means and ends, denies that technology is indifferent with respect to the alternative of capitalism or socialism, and challenges the apparent value-freedom of scientific-technical rationality.

Yet, he also insists on the possibility of a transition to socialism based on the reconstruction of existing technology. This prospect implies the neutrality of technology, albeit a different notion from the usual one. But what kind of neutrality would be compatible with Marcuse's claim that capitalist technology serves domination? Is this not a contradiction in terms? Or can neutrality and bias coexist?

The Bias of Technology

Typically, critics of technology like Marcuse find themselves accused of irrationalism. In denying that technology is neutral, they seem to be saying that it belongs to the shared myths of its society, like religious beliefs or social customs. The scientific-technical principles underlying technologies would thus resemble magical rituals or political doctrines, and the logical order of the scientific-technical disciplines would be as empty of intrinsic meaning as the rules of chess or bridge. This is clearly incompatible with Marcuse's Marxism, according to which the science and technology developed under capitalism, although biased by its demands, are nevertheless valid and form the basis for an advance to socialism.

Although nowhere does Marcuse explicitly formulate his alternative understanding of the relation between neutrality and bias, his theory rests on their coexistence. Bias, for him, is not the opposite of neutrality but cuts across the distinction between ideological and scientific-technical elements of social systems. In this section, I will propose an account of that relationship compatible with Marcuse's views.

This account derives from Marcuse's Hegelian-Marxist distinction between the "abstract" and the "concrete." For Hegel, the abstract is not the conceptually general but the part isolated from the whole to which it properly belongs. "Concrete" is the network of relations binding the parts to the whole.[14] The peculiar structure of capitalism results in the abstract parts appearing as independent, self-subsistent things. Each individual human being, each business enterprise, each government agency exists in reality only through its essential connections, but they appear separate, contingently related to their context. Because it has systemic consequences, this appearance is no mere illusion.

Lukács introduced the term "reification" to describe this aspect of capitalist society. In his terminology, a methodology is reified if it insists on working with such abstract elements, refusing to enlarge its horizon of explanation to the concrete whole (the totality) through which the parts take on their meaning. A society is likewise reified if its structure systematically obscures the inner connections between its various sectors and institutions, protecting them from critical scrutiny.[15]

On these terms, the technologies of advanced industrial societies exhibit a typical reification. Considered in isolation, technical devices

---

14 Georg Wilhelm Friedrich Hegel, *Texts and Commentary: Hegel's Preface to His System in a New Translation with Commentary on Facing Pages, and "Who Thinks Abstractly?"* trans. Walter Kaufmann (New York: Anchor Books, 1966).

15 Georg Lukács, *History and Class Consciousness*, trans. Rodney Livingstone (Cambridge, MA: MIT Press, 1971).

appear neutral, but in context their biased social role under capitalism becomes visible. Marcuse cites the assembly line, which appears as a neutral instrument for increasing productivity but which, in its social context, plays an essential role in the control of the labor force. A technology that appears neutral in purely technical terms exhibits its bias toward domination once the horizon is enlarged to include its social and political consequences.

To distinguish such biased technical arrangements from ideology and social customs, I call this a "formal bias." A formally biased device or system serves a substantive value of some sort, but it does so indirectly through its "form," its technical design, rather than directly through taste, prejudice, or discrimination. One-dimensional thought supports formal bias insofar as it fails to enlarge the contexts of explanation to encompass the concrete whole in which biased designs play a role.[16]

The traditional notion of the neutrality of technology is one dimensional, in the sense that it abstracts from contextual considerations. In isolation, and viewed from a purely technical standpoint, technologies appear neutral, but this is an illusion induced by a narrow perspective. Marcuse's method consists in recovering the lost contexts through which it is finally possible to develop a historically concrete understanding of technology. He argues that technologies and technical rationality are inseparable from social values, despite the fact that they embody objective knowledge of nature with a different epistemological status from phenomena such as customs, laws, or religious beliefs.

For him, values operate in the "fit" of technical designs to society at large. Capitalist innovation yields technologies that serve the pursuit of profit whatever the cost and consequences for humanity and nature. For example, the engineering design of a coal-fired power plant may be impeccable, but its place in the society is tied to the profits of the power company that owns it, regardless of the public interest in mitigating climate change. Similarly, surveillance on the internet has yielded a host of technologies designed specifically to service targeted advertising. Absent that financial incentive, internet technologies would be designed very differently for different purposes.

---

16 For the distinction between types of bias, see Andrew Feenberg, *Technosystem: The Social Life of Reason* (Cambridge, MA: Harvard University Press, 2017), 21–6.

This explains why reconstruction of technology is a necessary feature of the transition to socialism. The social environment of the transitional society is in flux, and the old fit, which favored the market at the expense of everything else, no longer works. The new society thus requires new technological designs and new materials.

The first two theses on technology that I attribute to Marcuse flow directly from these considerations, reflecting the consequences of class rule for social consciousness and technological design. These theses, treated in the next two sections of this chapter, summarize what I will call "the sociological moments" in his critique of technology.

The third thesis has a different status. It attributes intrinsic bias to scientific-technical rationality itself. This is the most radical strand in the Marcusean critique, the "ontological" moment, which aims to uncover the quasi-transcendental preconditions for the possibility of formal bias. Why, in fact, are formally biased systems so central to modern societies? Can it be an accident that formally neutral concepts and procedures lend themselves so readily to applications we consider misuse or abuse? Marcuse's response will be treated in later sections of this chapter.

The Sociological Moment: First Thesis

Marcuse first attempted to explain the impact of technology under capitalism in an essay published in 1941.[17] The essay was influenced by Marx, and also by Mumford and Veblen, with whose thought he became familiar during his American exile. Marcuse explains that the social conditions that supported autonomous individuality in the nineteenth century have been replaced by a bureaucratic order that imposes adaptation to society. The machine plays a role in this order by enforcing compliance with the given, obedience to the facts. Insofar as machinery spreads over the whole surface of social life, its lesson shapes thought and character and produces a conformist personality type. In this context, reason is identified exclusively with technical knowledge and the pursuit of efficiency. *One-Dimensional Man* develops this

---

17 Herbert Marcuse, "Some Implications of Modern Technology," in Herbert Marcuse, *Technology, War and Fascism*, ed. Douglas Kellner (London: Routledge, 1998).

argument further, explaining the ideological function of capitalist technical rationality in advanced industrial society.

This is quite different from Marx's approach. Marx criticized the harms suffered by workers chained to the narrow division of labor instituted in the manufacturing phase of development and perpetuated by industrial capitalism. He argued that industry required skilled workers to achieve maximum productivity, but that capitalism depends on the unskilled to control labor and costs. In turn, its machine designs are biased by this requirement. Since alienation had become an obstacle to the growth and development of the productive forces, the normative goal of creating a more humane society was seen as congruent with the technical goal of increasing economic productivity. The critique of capitalism could thus proceed on technical grounds without an explicit normative critique.

Marcuse argues that contemporary capitalism has invalidated this original Marxian position: the capitalist organization of production has proved its technical competence. Technological rationality can no longer serve, as it still did for Marx, as the basis of a critique of the prevailing relations of production. Capitalism now institutes a culture in which every injustice is addressed by technical problem solving within the framework of the existing system. Technical rationality replaces normative rationality and kills the hope for a radically different future.

Under these new conditions, technological rationality becomes the legitimating discourse of the society. Habermas summarizes this aspect of Marcuse's theory:

> At the stage of their scientific-technical development, then, the forces of production appear to enter a new constellation with the relations of production. Now they no longer function as the basis of a critique of prevailing legitimations in the interest of political . . . enlightenment, but become instead the basis of legitimation. *This* is what Marcuse conceives of as world-historically new.[18]

The problem is no longer the inability of capitalism to make effective use of the technologies it has developed, but rather the catastrophic human consequences of the effective use of these very technologies.

---

18 Habermas, "Technology and Science as Ideology," 84.

Not only is technical progress distorted by the requirements of capitalism, but the "universe of discourse"—public and eventually even private speech and thought—limits itself to the posing and resolving of technical problems within the constraints of the interest in domination that characterizes capitalist rationality. The universalization of technical modes of thought eliminates the subjective conditions presupposed by the Marxian theory of emancipatory struggle. This world has no place for critical consciousness: it is "one dimensional."

This explains why Marcuse, unlike Marx, not only attacks the dominant social interests that preside over technological choices, but also criticizes technical modes of thought and criteria of progress. The normative critique is thus forced to appear explicitly and independently; it can no longer hide behind the Marxian demand for a liberation of the productive forces to full development. Marcuse's critique targets "technological rationality," a self-propelling system of domination through technology, increasingly out of control of its human masters. He writes that "today, domination perpetuates and extends itself not only through technology, but *as* technology, and the latter provides the great legitimation of the expanding political power, which absorbs all spheres of culture."[19]

The Sociological Moment: Second Thesis

The twentieth century saw the extension of technology into every sphere of social life. Max Weber explained the consequences with his theory of rationalization. Marcuse's Marxist analysis of Weber's theory is based on Marx's distinction between the technical and the social aspects of technology under capitalism. According to Marx, capitalism has fused the drive to increase economic productivity with the maintenance of capitalist power on the workplace. Marcuse finds a similar fusion of the technical and the social in Weber's theory of rationalization.

Marx's argument follows from the consequences of the divorce of workers from the means of production. The control of their labor falls to the capitalist owners of enterprise, who must devise technological and managerial solutions to problems of labor discipline. Marx writes:

---

19 Marcuse, *One-Dimensional Man*, 158.

> The control exercised by the capitalist is not only a special function, due to the nature of the social labour-process, and peculiar to that process, but it is, at the same time, a function of the exploitation of a social labour-process, and is consequently rooted in the unavoidable antagonism between the exploiter and the living and labouring raw material he exploits.[20]

Technological choices, *like all* other aspects of capitalist production, are determined by the pursuit of control, not only over nature, but also over human beings. Technical progress proceeds under the aegis of dual goals, a purely technical and a socially specific goal, one serving generic human interests and the other serving class interests. The outcome is a technical system adapted to capitalism. This is what Marx calls the "real subsumption" of the means of production.

These considerations explain how the very same Marx who foresaw the liberation of humanity in a technologically advanced socialist society could also be the author of sharply critical diatribes against the division of labor and the use of machinery under capitalism. He wrote of science, for example, that it "is the most powerful weapon for repressing strikes, those periodical revolts of the working class against the autocracy of capital."[21] And, in another passage, he claims that "it would be possible to write quite a history of inventions, made since 1830, for the sole purpose of supplying capital with weapons against the revolts of the working class."[22] By contrast, socialism will release technology from enforcing top-down labor discipline and allow modern industry to flourish.

Weber generalized from Marx's theory of capitalism to a wider theory of modernity, but he lost Marx's critical edge in the process. The results show up in the theory of rationalization, which plays a pivotal role in the evolution leading from Marx to Marcuse.

Weber introduced the terms "substantive" and "formal" rationality to describe two different types of social thought and action. Rationality is "substantive" where it is determined by norms embodying a purpose, such as feeding a population, winning a war, or maintaining the social hierarchy. The "formal" rationality of capitalism characterizes

---

20 Karl Marx, *Capital*, trans. Edward Aveling (New York: Modern Library, 1906), 363.

21 Ibid., 475.

22 Ibid., 47–8.

economic arrangements that optimize calculability and control rather than the fulfillment of substantive goals. Formally rational systems thus lie under technical norms that have to do with efficiency in the organization of means rather than the achievement of specific substantive ends. As such, they are neutral with respect to ends.

Weber's distinction between these types of rationality plays out in his account of the social consequences of progress. According to him, premodern societies based on substantive rationality exhibit an explicit bias consecrated by a hierarchy of God-given functions and purposes. There is perfect consistency between the substantive form of rationality and the discriminatory social outcomes. The old kings of France had not a job but a divine mission, the purpose of which was to save the souls and protect the bodies of their subjects. Their superiority was fully justified on the terms of the dominant ideology.

"Rationalization" refers to the generalization of formal rationality in capitalist society at the expense of the substantively rational modes of action that prevail in traditional societies. God no longer consecrates the social hierarchy; rather, the great chain of being is replaced by equal exchange on the market. Souls and bodies are saved and protected, but not intentionally. Instead, entrepreneurs seeking profits provide products that achieve these desirable ends. They have not a mission but a business; their good works are incidental to their economic goal, and their focus is on the means to achieving that goal, not the ends which concern the consumer.

This does not have the democratizing effect one would expect. On the contrary, formal rationality supports new forms of discrimination despite (or because of!) its neutrality. For instance, rationalization favors the ambitions of certain social groups—capitalists and the bureaucracy—which rise to the top of a rationalized society. Yet the formally rational systems of accounting, control, production, and exchange that produce this effect are in themselves value free, neutral. Like Marx's theory of the market, Weber's rationalization theory leads to the recognition of the discrimination resulting from the normal operation of formally rational systems such as administrations, law, and the professions. The inconsistency between the neutrality of the means and the biased outcomes is paradoxical.

Marcuse's critique of Weber dissolves this paradox by reference to the Marxian theory of the dual criteria of progress under capitalism.

Proceeding from Marx's critique of *technology* to a critique of *technical reason*, he shows that Weber's "analysis has fallen prey to the identification of technical reason with bourgeois capitalist reason."[23] He accuses Weber of confounding specifically capitalist criteria of design and administration with rationality as such. Technical reason has been distorted by the same forces that have distorted technological development.

Marcuse argues that Weber's explanation of the general concept of formal economic rationality implicitly presupposes

> the separation of the workers from the means of production . . . (as) a *technical* necessity requiring the individual and private direction and control of the means of production . . . The highly *material*, historical fact of the private-capitalist enterprise thus becomes . . . a *formal* structural element of capitalism and of *rational* economic activity itself.[24]

As such, Weber's social theory treats the existing relations of production as an a priori basis of conceptualization.

The presupposition is not confined to Weber's sociology but is a general feature of reified thought in capitalist society. What Marcuse calls the "technological rationality" of this society is indelibly marked by the presupposition that domination is the necessary condition for effective action. Formal social and economic concepts, the prevailing definitions of social objects, concepts of efficiency, progress, and so on all exhibit an a priori bias. Domination is already present in the very notion of means/ends rationality since the means are deployed *in principle* from above to control the labor force. This explains why capitalist economic and managerial theories appear "value free" and do not require constant reference to an explicit ideology to be serviceable under capitalism.

The fusion of the technical and the social shapes the design of technologies as well. Marcuse does not, as some critics charge, substitute a technology critique for a critique of the antagonistic character of capitalism.[25] Rather,

---

23 Herbert Marcuse, "Industrialization and Capitalism in Max Weber," in *Negations: Essays in Critical Theory*, trans. Jeremy J. Shapiro (Boston: Beacon Press, 1968), 223.

24 Ibid., 212. Cf. Marcuse, *One-Dimensional Man*, 144–5.

25 Alberto Toscano, "Liberation Technology: Marcuse's Communist Individualism," *Institute for the Radical Imagination* 3, no. 1 (2009): 18.

he argues that technology is a site of that antagonism. Although he does not use the term "real subsumption," the following passage could be a definition of it:

> Specific purposes and interests of domination are not foisted upon technology "subsequently" and from the outside; they enter the very construction of the technical apparatus. Technology is always a historical-social *project*: in it is projected what a society and its ruling interests intend to do with men and things . . . The machine is *not neutral*; technical reason is the social reason ruling a given society and can be changed in its very structure.[26]

Here, we are at the threshold of the ontological critique, but Marcuse offers only a hint of the more elaborate theory presented in *One-Dimensional Man*. As a result, the critique of Weber leaves a confusing impression.

On the one hand, Weber is accused of confounding the technical with the social, which seems to imply the possibility of separating them and recovering a pure technical reason. The historically institutionalized forms of technical reason, whether they be technologies, professional specializations, or social sciences, fall before a critique that reveals not only their inhumanity but also their irrationality. Once the class bias is eliminated, "the consummation of technical reason can well become the instrument for the *liberation* of man."[27] This is the limitation of the sociological moment: its critique of the bias of rationality under capitalism gestures toward an abstract ideal of truly neutral technical reason, undistorted by power and ideology.

Yet Marcuse concludes his discussion of Weber by suggesting that the very notion of technical reason is ideological. Despite this claim, he does not question the validity of science and technology. On the contrary, he thinks they can provide the basis for a socialist society once reconstructed to support different goals. Clearly, if they are ideological, it must be in some different sense from the usual one. But what is that sense? Are they only ideological in their capitalist deployment,

---

26 Marcuse, "Industrialization and Capitalism in the Work of Max Weber," 224–5.
27 Ibid., 223.

or are they ideological in themselves? And if the latter, how can they serve in a future socialist society?

This is truly the parting of the ways. A version of critical theory was elaborated by Habermas and his followers compatible with one answer to these questions. In it, they adopted the main lines of the first socio-logical moment in Marcuse's critique of rationality while affirming the inherent neutrality of science and technology. Social critique was confined to protecting the lifeworld from intrusive technification. This position has the advantage of requiring no speculative concepts, and it can be elaborated against a background of commonsense assumptions about science and technology.

Unfortunately for those who took this approach, the burgeoning environmental movement wrong-footed their attempt to eliminate the critique of instrumental reason from critical theory. Other controversies around issues such as women's health, HIV/AIDS, and internet privacy and surveillance have made it clear that Marcuse was right to abandon the neutrality thesis. The design of technology and its consequences, good and bad, reflects the values of the social actors who influence the design process. For failing to pursue the critique of technology, critical theory lost relevance to important issues and struggles.

One-Dimensional Man goes beyond the critique of Weber, attacking the ontological roots of the problem in a speculative theory of reason more surely protected against technocratic ideology. This ontological critique is based on the refusal to separate reason from the social and cultural framework within which it operates and to which it contributes in practice. Under socialism, Marcuse argues, capitalist technical reason will not be purified but replaced by another form of technical reason free of domination.

The Ontological Moment: Third Thesis

Let us begin by recognizing the untimeliness of Marcuse's ontological critique. He was writing at the high point of technocratic ideology. A diminishing band of humanist critics, inspired by philosophers such as Bergson, agreed with the early Marx that science is "abstract" and alien to life, but they had little influence in the 1950s and '60s. Instead, the focus was on the marvelous, and sometimes terrible, applications of science. Science was widely believed to be value free, universal, and ultimately beneficial. While it received credit for its good applications, its bad ones were blamed on bad policies and not on science itself. However, cultural conservatives like Heidegger and radicals like Marcuse and his associates in the Frankfurt School disagreed. They argued that science was complicit in concentration camps, atom bombs, and media propaganda—all the disasters of the twentieth century.

Marcuse's most controversial thesis holds that there is an a priori connection between scientific-technical rationality and domination. According to this thesis, "science, *by virtue of its own method* and concepts, has projected and promoted a universe in which the domination of nature has remained linked to the domination of man."[28] This is a shocking claim, roundly condemned by Marcuse's many critics. Even such generally sympathetic ones as Habermas and William Leiss dismiss it as a vestige of romanticism.[29]

Although there are indeed problems with Marcuse's critique of science and technology, I do not think it can be so easily dismissed. We can rephrase his notion of the bias of rationality by asking: What is the significance of the general availability of formal systems such as technical disciplines for applications that favor domination? Is there something about them that opens them to such applications? What happened "originally" in the initial construction of the formal mode of abstraction that renders it pliable in this particular way?

To follow Marcuse's argument to this point is unsettling because we do not normally think of science and technology as *essentially* implicated in their applications. The executioner counts the intended victims, but it would be silly to blame arithmetic for their suffering. The involvement of science and technology in strategies of domination appears to be the sole responsibility of the subject who employs them. Marcuse's argument contradicts the commonsense view that bad applications are an abuse of a neutral system. He is seeking precisely to connect neutrality and domination as moments in a dialectical totality.

The ontological moment of the critique has two aspects, discussed in this and the next sections. In the first place, Marcuse argues that the

---

28 Marcuse, *One-Dimensional Man*, 166.

29 Habermas, "Technology and Science as Ideology," 85–6; William Leiss, *The Domination of Nature* (Boston: Beacon Press, 1974), 211–12.

instrumentalist orientation of "technological rationality" reduces being, including human being, to raw materials and system components, eliminating other dimensions essential to full understanding and the flourishing of life. This aspect of the critique was anticipated by Horkheimer and Adorno's *Dialectic of Enlightenment*, which first introduced the critique of instrumental reason into Marxism. A second aspect counters this technological reduction in terms of a broadly Hegelian logic.

Given the obvious filiation of Marcuse's considerations on science and technology in the earlier writing of Horkheimer and Adorno, we have to ask why Husserl and the later Heidegger play such an important role in *One-Dimensional Man*. The *Dialectic of Enlightenment* could be interpreted as a critique of instrumental rationality as such. The *metis* of Odysseus figures as a model of rational domination. This suggests that reason as such is the problem, and no escape from it is envisaged.[30] This poses a problem for Marcuse, who is engaged not only in critique but also in the utopian projection of a socialist form of rationality. Husserl's and Heidegger's considerations on science and technology ground the critique of instrumental rationality historically, although not specifically in capitalism. Despite this limitation, Marcuse was able to incorporate certain of their insights into his Marxist approach.

Chapters 5 and 6 of *One-Dimensional Man* are a Marxist response to Heidegger's essay "The Question Concerning Technology."[31] Although Marcuse relies primarily on Husserl in his discussion of scientific method, there is a striking parallel between the structure of these chapters and that essay. Both Heidegger and Marcuse begin with a discussion of Aristotle's teleological concept of technical practice and end with a critique of the modern mechanistic view of nature. According to Heidegger, and Marcuse is essentially in agreement, the Greeks recognize the potentialities of the matter that enters into technical practice, whereas the moderns treat nature as fungible stuff as they incorporate it into the industrial system. Modern science lies in the background of this change.

---

30 Theodor Adorno and Max Horkheimer, *Dialectic of Enlightenment*, trans. J. Cumming (New York: Herder and Herder, 1972).

31 Martin Heidegger, "The Question Concerning Technology," in *The Question Concerning Technology and Other Essays*, trans. Harriet Brundage Lovitt (New York: Harper & Row, 1977), 3–35.

Husserl claims that modern "Galilean" science refines practices current in the *Lebenswelt* of its society. Science introduces precision into ordinary practices of measurement and, on this basis, achieves foresight and control over its objects. A quantified, ideal world is substituted for the concrete world of experience. That quantified world consists of basic shapes and relations that can be manipulated independent of the substance in which they are discovered. Qualitative aspects and the potentialities associated with that substance are simply eliminated from science.[32]

Heidegger amplifies the Husserlian thesis, arguing that modern science projects a quantifiable idea of nature that is intrinsically oriented toward technical control. He calls this a "ground plan" that anticipates in advance the sorts of things that can appear as objects of research. His principal example is physics, for which nature consists of a self-contained system of motion of units of mass related in time and space. Here, "motion" means only change of place in a uniform continuum. This definition of the object suits it to exact mathematical measurement. Because modern science defines its object as the sort of thing that can be measured and counted, it can rely on such mathematical procedures.

Heidegger argues further that modern science produces an image or representation he calls a "world picture," that is, a supposedly exhaustive representation of reality. This seems self-evident: science gives us an image of the cosmos we accept as more or less accurate. But according to Heidegger, this is a uniquely modern way of understanding the real—one that makes possible prediction and technical manipulation. The connection between science and technology lies in the original ground plan that exposes nature to both representation by science and control by technology.[33]

For Heidegger, modern and ancient science have radically different conceptions of nature. The ancient view, exemplified by Aristotle's *Metaphysics*, is derived from biological growth. It corresponds closely with the everyday ontology of the lifeworld. The Greeks did not

---

32 Edmund Husserl, *The Crisis of European Sciences and Transcendental Phenomenology*, trans. D. Carr (Evanston, IL: Northwestern University, 1970).

33 Martin Heidegger, "The Age of the World Picture," in *The Question Concerning Technology and Other Essays*, 115–54.

identify the essence of reality with a picture but with a process. They encountered a self-creating, self-moving nature consisting of relatively stable things that realize intrinsic potentialities through change. This nature has a life of its own independent of the human subject. Its developmental process cannot be measured in quantitative terms. It is on this conception of nature that the Greek understanding of technical activity is based. Ancient craft realizes potentialities of nature that nature cannot realize by itself. The technē of a craftsman must intervene to bring those potentialities into actuality, just as the farmer brings forth nature's bounty through cultivation of the soil.

In Heidegger's view, the modern scientific picture of nature eliminates self-movement and intrinsic potentiality. Nature is meaningless and utterly dependent on the subject for which it serves as raw material (*Bestand*) dominated through instrumental control. Heidegger calls the reduction of the world to manipulable resources the *Gestell*, usually translated in English as "enframing." Modern technology differs from technē in that it involves no mutual interaction of subject and object in the realization of potentialities. Our model of technical action is not cultivation but clear-cutting.

As noted earlier, *One-Dimensional Man* follows the same pattern as Heidegger's essay. Chapter 5 discusses Aristotle's concept of essence and its relation to the notion of potentiality, and chapter 6 then considers modern technology on terms very similar to Heidegger's. Marcuse does not use Heidegger's terminology—*Gestell*, *Bestand*, and so on—but his argument repeats Heidegger's concern with the universalization of instrumentality. "When technics becomes the universal form of material production," Marcuse writes, "it circumscribes an entire culture; it projects a historical totality—a 'world.'"[34]

Marcuse's discussion of science follows, more or less, along the lines laid out by Husserl and Heidegger. He, too, argues that science is based on a concept of nature which exposes it to quantification and control, quoting Heidegger as saying, "Modern man takes the entirety of being as raw material for production and subjects the entirety of the object world to the sweep and order of production."[35] Modern science

---

34 Marcuse, *One-Dimensional Man*, 154.

35 Quoted in Marcuse, *One-Dimensional Man*, 153–4; Martin Heidegger, *Holzwege* (Frankfurt: Vittorio Klostermann, 1950), 266.

eliminates intrinsic potentiality in favor of measurable facts. The Greeks conceived potentialities as real properties of objects—essences— but essences are now dismissed as mere cultural prejudices. Since reality no longer offers any guidance for action, all goals appear equally arbitrary, and science and technology are surrendered to the prevailing social and economic powers.

Both Heidegger and Marcuse agree that there is no fundamental difference between science and technology—in other words, that science cannot be separated from its applications. In contemporary terms, we would say that they propose a critique of technoscience. Marcuse writes, "The science of nature develops under the technological a priori which projects nature as potential instrumentality, stuff of control and organization."[36]

> Scientific-technical rationality and manipulation are welded together into new forms of social control. Can one rest content with the assumption that this unscientific outcome is the result of a specific societal *application* of science? I think that the general direction in which it came to be applied was inherent in pure science even where no practical purposes were intended, and that the point can be identified where theoretical Reason turns into social practice.[37]

Are these similarities between Marcuse's and Heidegger's critiques a coincidence? That is unlikely, given Heidegger's fame at the time. Everybody involved with continental philosophy, and certainly Marcuse (who, lest we forget, was once Heidegger's student), read "The Question Concerning Technology" and thought deeply about it. The references to Husserl and Heidegger in *One-Dimensional Man* and several earlier essays show that Marcuse was still seriously engaged with the phenomenological critique of science and technology.[38] Chapters 5 and 6 of *One-Dimensional Man* respond to Heidegger by incorporating aspects of phenomenological ontology into Marxism, creating an original theory.

---

36 Marcuse, *One-Dimensional Man*, 153.

37 Ibid., 146.

38 Herbert Marcuse, "From Ontology to Technology: Fundamental Tendencies of Industrial Society," Herbert Marcuse, *Philosophy, Psychoanalysis, and Emancipation*, ed. Douglas Kellner and Clayton Pierce (New York: Routledge, 2011).

That theory has a political aspect absent in these phenomenologists. What Marcuse calls "one-dimensionality" is the generalization of instrumentalism as common sense, replacing normatively charged ideas and attitudes that formerly shaped the everyday relation to the world. This change is politically significant. The potentialities of the social world are obscured where it is reduced to a vast collection of measurable facts subject to technical control. Such potentialities are now treated as mere values, subjective wishes of individuals rather than objective realities able to guide technical practice. On these terms, society can be modified in this or that respect but not fundamentally changed. Operationally effective reforms can eliminate the desire for change short of any challenge to the prevailing organization of social life. The problem is thus not only the destructive power of science and technology but the elimination of the potential for a just society.

Excursus: Heidegger or Marcuse

In 1949, Heidegger declared that

> agriculture is now a mechanized food industry, in essence the same as the production of corpses in the gas chambers and extermination camps, the same as the blockading and starving of countries, the same as the production of hydrogen bombs.[39]

Is this what he learned from his Nazi experience and the war? Technology, he laments, has obliterated the human subject and occluded man's "needed belonging to revealing."[40] There is no escape from this condition. The attempt to realize "human values" only confirms the disaster. The very fact that humanity has become a "value" served by technological means demonstrates the ontological point: technology now prevails over all being.

---

39 Martin Heidegger, "Positionality," in *Bremen and Freiburg Lectures: Insight into That Which Is and Basic Principles of Thinking*, trans. Andrew J. Mitchell (Bloomington: Indiana University Press, 2012), 27.

40 Heidegger, *The Question Concerning Technology and Other Essays*, 76.

It may be tempting to interpret Marcuse in this vein. After all, he dismisses minor reforms of the system, arguing that they only serve to perpetuate one-dimensionality. His "Great Refusal" could be taken for a complete rejection of technological society. The containment of the negative forces that formerly promised radical change seems to confirm the ontological permanence of the technified world. Yet the argument is really quite different.

Where for Heidegger the emergence of values as the correlate of technology is an episode in the history of being, Marcuse is concerned with the *social procedures* that reduce potentialities to values, to operational components in the bureaucratic and technical systems of capitalism. For Marcuse, certain values have a "transitive" content indicating the blocked potentialities of the society. The persistence of that content, despite efforts to eliminate it, contains a promise. Thus, *One-Dimensional Man* opens by acknowledging an ambiguity: the book, he says, will waver between despair and the hope "that forces and tendencies exist which may break this containment and explode the society."[41]

Heidegger's *Gestell*, the mathematical skeleton of a technified society, is not so contingent. It is nearly total, bearing no hidden transitive content. For him, action cannot alter the technological revealing; indeed, Heidegger seems to believe that an attempt to change it would simply reproduce its dominion. There is no reciprocal action of the ontic on the ontological. At best, we can preserve a sense of the possibility of an alternative through philosophical reflection while waiting for "a God" to save us.[42] But insofar as Marcuse's Marxist version of ontology depends on social practice, it cannot maintain such a sharp separation of the ontological and ontic levels. As in Lukács's theory of reification, which it resembles, the interaction between levels in Marcuse's theory takes place through struggles by which social actors intervene in the constitution of society.

---

41 Marcuse, *One-Dimensional Man*, xv.

42 Martin Heidegger, "'Only a God Can Save Us': *Der Spiegel*'s Interview with Martin Heidegger," in *The Heidegger Controversy: A Critical Reader*, trans. Maria P. Alter and John D. Caputo, ed. Richard Wolin (Cambridge, MA: MIT Press, 1993). See Dana Belu and Andrew Feenberg, "Heidegger's Paradoxical Ontology of Technology," *Inquiry* 53, no. 1 (2010): 1–19.

For Marcuse, those struggles are supposed to issue in a new concept of reason, that is, a new ontological dispensation oriented toward life and able to guide the transformation of science and technology. But unlike Lukács, with his confidence in class struggle, he has no strategy for breaking the grip of technological rationality. This is, after all, understandable: during his lifetime, the revolutionary class struggle was defeated, and only the first stirrings of new forms of resistance had emerged. While Marcuse supported those resistances, he failed to reconstruct his concept of reason around their lessons for science and technology.

How might that reconstruction have gone? Perhaps Marcuse would have revised his ontological critique of scientific-technical rationality in view of the social forces imposing environmental constraints on industry and humanizing technical disciplines such as medical practice. This unexpected public contestation of science and technology presupposes the achievements of the sciences but incorporates them into reformed disciplines and procedures oriented by a concern for life. The one-dimensional thought that blocked contestation of the technical framework of life recedes. It would have been interesting to see how Marcuse would have reacted to the paradoxical decline of one-dimensionality in an ever more technified world—a question taken up in the next chapter, which will propose a possible alternative to the pessimism of *One-Dimensional Man*. One thing is certain: he would not have confounded industrial production, essential for *any* modern society, with the holocaust.

Epochal Openings

Marcuse's decision to draw on phenomenology in a social critique of science is puzzling. Why not just say that science is capitalist ideology without the frills? In fact, he uses the term "ideology" to describe science and technology. This is a powerful rhetorical tactic, but it is nevertheless confusing since ideology is usually understood to be epistemologically "particular," class related, the cover for special interests. Ideology is essentially false, and science refutes it. But what about science? If it is ideological, would it then be false too? And if so, by what standard? In order to criticize science at a fundamental level, and not

just specific uses or abuses of science, Marcuse has to elaborate a different type of historical account. He wants to show that science is shaped
by its epoch, the capitalist epoch, but also that it is universal for its
epoch—in other words, that it is not just a cloak of false beliefs associated with the interests of a particular class. But, then, what is its status
if it is both historically situated and valid? Science and technology fall
into a gap between universal and particular, truth and falsehood.

What Marcuse needed was something like Thomas Kuhn's para-
digms or Foucault's epistemes. These are historically situated openings
within which a realm of truth and falsity appears, a space for the
proposal and testing of particular ideas. Openings are biased by the
epochal spirit, but they are not class ideologies.

There are different ways of constructing such a theory. Heidegger
proposed what he called a "history of being," according to which each
epoch falls under a specific horizon of intelligibility. An epochal
dispensation is a system of meanings and practices, an experienced
"world" in something like the phenomenological sense of the term.
Science belongs to a particular historical epoch—modernity, the epoch
of technology, characterized by the pursuit of prediction and control.
This theory is interesting, but it is based on a speculative concept of
being as the source of epochal dispensations.

Marxism, too, has an epochal conception based on the history of
modes of production, but the relation of that conception to natural
science has never been fully clarified. Marx quickly abandoned his
early critique of science in the *Manuscripts*. He and Engels believed
that while the natural sciences were historical products of the capitalist epoch, they were nevertheless valid, unlike the philosophical
and social scientific heritage of the bourgeoisie. They criticized the
confusion between the lawfulness of nature and the historical contingency of society, but they did not distinguish different types of
rationality.[43]

Lukács's *History and Class Consciousness* was the first attempt within
Marxism to achieve a penetrating theoretical explanation for the bias of
rationality under capitalism. The concept of "reification" develops

---

43 For a study of Marxist theories of science, see Pietro Daniel Omodeo, *Political
Epistemology: The Problem of Ideology in Science Studies* (Cham: Springer Nature
Switzerland, 2019).

Marx's concept of commodity fetishism, relating it to the processes Weber had summed up under the category of "rationalization." Lukács identifies a general "form of objectivity" that shapes perception and action in capitalist society, reducing the objects of everyday experience to isolated facts.

Reified thought obscures the dialectical character of social life and the role of the subject in the constitution of the social world. It exposes society to the same sort of scientific-technical rationality that prevails in the study of nature. Lukács writes:

> What is important is to recognize clearly that all human relations (viewed as the objects of social activity) assume increasingly the form of objectivity of the abstract elements of the conceptual systems of natural science and of the abstract substrata of the laws of nature. And also, the subject of this "action" likewise assumes increasingly the attitude of the pure observer of these—artificially abstract—processes, the attitude of the experimenter.[44]

Lukács condemns reification insofar as it distorts *social* knowledge and action. In so doing, he brings to light the congruence of a mode of thought that seeks the laws governing social facts and the fragmentation of capitalist society. This could have opened the way to a general critique of scientific-technical rationality, but Lukács confines his attack to the social sciences and the institutions of capitalism. He argues that the universalization of commodity exchange creates the cultural framework within which methods appropriate to the study of nature serve social domination when applied to society.[45]

Marcuse extends the critique of reification to science and technology, which now have a political function in advanced capitalism. The formal rationality of science ties it to class domination. In *One-Dimensional Man*, Marcuse claims that science corresponds to a specific world of experience essentially related to a corresponding

---

44 Lukács, *History and Class Consciousness*, 131.

45 Ibid., 6–7. For a review of Lukács's approach to this relation, see János Kelemen, *The Rationalism of Georg Lukács* (New York: Palgrave Macmillan, 2014), chapter 3.

subject.[46] The nature of such a world is determined by a civilizational project. This is the Husserlian thesis of the grounding of science in the lifeworld. And, just as he historicizes Freud's "reality principle," so Marcuse introduces history into the phenomenological lifeworld that, he argues, is shaped by capitalism.

Marcuse's analysis thus differs from Heidegger's in arguing that the instrumentalist conception of nature is due not to modernity as such but specifically to its capitalist form. He writes:

> Individual, non-quantifiable qualities stand in the way of an organi-
> zation of men and things in accordance with the measurable power
> to be extracted from them. But this is a specific, socio-historical
> project, and the consciousness which undertakes this project is the
> hidden subject of Galilean science.[47]

Marcuse refers here to Sartre's concept of "project," which he calls a *Vorhaben*—a "having in advance."[48] Husserl employed this term to refer to the opening of a horizon. It also appears as one of the three existentials of understanding in Heidegger's *Being and Time*, which influenced Sartre. The project is not a particular plan but the projection of a world within which plans become possible. Recall the discussion of the carpenter's workshop in chapter 2; Heidegger shows us how it "projects" an opening within which a myriad of specific projects become possible.

The capitalist project is prediction and control, the reduction of the real to fungible stuff available for exploitation and commodification. This is a "one-dimensional" world. Marcuse writes: "The projection of nature as quantifiable matter ... would be the horizon of a concrete societal practice which would be *preserved* in the development of the scientific project."[49] This would explain why modern science and technology have arisen at the same time as capitalism and serve it well.[50] The phenomeno-logical concept of world correlates with a constitutive subject, hence not just a "one-dimensional" world, but also a "one-dimensional man."

---

46 Marcuse, *One-Dimensional Man*, 162.
47 Ibid., 164.
48 Ibid.
49 Ibid., 160
50 Ibid., 162–5.

Experience is socially constructed under the a priori of a project, but this is not the Kantian transcendental a priori. Marcuse brings it down to earth; it is a "specific mode of seeing . . . within a purposive practical context."[51] The construction reflects the hegemonic economic system. Capitalist social practices thus underlie the one-dimensional concept of an objective world. The capitalist *Lebenswelt*, which in the following passage he identifies with "empirical reality," "is the framework, and the dimension in which the pure scientific concepts develop. In other words, the empirical reality constitutes, in a specific sense, the very concepts which science believes are pure theoretical concepts."[52]

What precisely can this mean? What concepts are in question? The answer is Galileo's stripped-down idea of nature's primary qualities, characterized by "calculable, predictable relationships among exactly identifiable units."[53] This is the source of what, following the French phenomenologist Suzanne Bachelard, Marcuse calls "the instrumentalist horizon of mathematical physics."[54] Under this horizon, nothing has inherent potentialities; everything is subject to technological manipulation. Science is thus essentially technological at its basis.

Note that instrumentalism, in this sense, is not the only possible technical relation. Other relations such as cultivation and artistic creation respond to the potentialities of their objects. They may employ methods similar to those of science and use modern techniques in a context organized around those potentialities—a point developed further in chapter 6.

Marcuse's critique of science is not the usual ideology critique. For him, the basic principles of science do not reflect any substantive idea or interest that would be tied to a specific class. It has a subtler bias; indeed, its neutrality with respect to values *is* its bias. That neutrality eliminates the notion of potential through which certain values were granted objective reality in the traditional teleological conception. This is what it means to view the world as raw materials: to deny potentialities is to leave a free space of exploitation. Insofar as it is value neutral,

---

51 Ibid., 164.

52 Herbert Marcuse, "On Science and Technology," in *Philosophy, Psychoanalysis, and Emancipation*, 149.

53 Marcuse, *One-Dimensional Man*, 164.

54 Ibid., 156n18.

science is adapted to the needs of capitalism in advance of any application. The science/ideology dilemma is resolved.

The attribution of the rise of science to a specific socioeconomic system suggests the possibility of change through political action. Marcuse believed that a revolution would modify not only economic arrangements but being itself. Socialism would integrate science and art in a new, more benign technology respectful of nature. This would be the revival of something like ancient technē, and with it the recovery of the teleological idea of potentiality, banned from the modern scientific idea of nature.[55] It is to this concept of potentiality that I turn in the next section.

Transcendental Logic as Critique

Marcuse's 1941 essay "Some Implications of Technology" describes the split between critical and technical reason in contemporary capitalism.[56] While *One-Dimensional Man* returns to this theme, here his treatment depends on his dialectical ontology, based on the distinction between "substantive" and "logico-mathematical" or "formal" universals. This approach resembles a transcendental logic that studies the relation of logic to experience.

Marcuse's theory of formal universals depends on his interpretation of formal logic. These universals refer to the abstract qualities and quantities that can appear in propositions such as "S is P." The formal logical structure of such propositions, Marcuse explains, determines a specific type of knowledge:

> In this formal logic, thought is indifferent toward its objects. Whether they are mental or physical, whether they pertain to society or to nature, they become subject to the same general laws of organization, calculation, and conclusion—but they do so as fungible signs or symbols, in abstraction from their particular "substance." This general quality (quantitative quality) is the precondition of law and order—in logic as well as in society—the price of universal control.[57]

---

55 Ibid., 238–40.

56 Herbert Marcuse, "Some Social Implications of Modern Technology," in *Technology, War and Fascism*, 39–66.

57 Marcuse, *One-Dimensional Man*, 140.

Formal universals decontextualize their objects and evacuate their "content"—that is, their essential nature—reducing them to an assemblage of accidental qualities and quantities. These can be classified and quantified in terms of the function they serve in a system of instrumental controls. Thus, rather than identifying the essential potentialities of its objects, which determine an intrinsic trajectory of development, formalism exposes them to extrinsic technical manipulation. Marcuse argues that this is no accident but belongs to the very essence of this mode of abstraction. This explains the phenomena I describe with the term "formal bias," understood as an intrinsic dimension of reason itself.

By contrast, dialectical logic works with substantive universals. These universals involve idealization, a reduction of contingency that makes possible the conceptualization of an essence. In the case of social universals such as peace, freedom, and justice, the essence does not refer directly to their given instantiations but rather expresses historical potentialities that go beyond the limited facts of life in any existing society. For Marcuse, these potentialities are not merely ideal but are immanent in things themselves, where they appear as internal contradictions. For example, peace is maintained by nuclear missiles; freedom coexists with a vast archipelago of prisons; justice systematically perpetuates racist discrimination. Thus, substantive universals transcend the split between "ought" and "is," and as such provide the basis of a critical consciousness that learns in the course of history to struggle for their realization.

The theory of substantive universals depends on a unique form of conceptual realism. Particular things are not isolated and independent, but their essential connections are perceptible only through concepts. These concepts

are identical with and yet different from the real objects of immediate experience. "Identical" in as much as the concept denotes the same thing; "different" in as much as the concept is the result of a reflection which has understood the thing in the context (and in the light) of other things which did not appear in the immediate experience and which "explain" the thing (mediation) . . . By the same token, all cognitive concepts have a transitive meaning; they go beyond descriptive reference to particular facts.[58]

---

58 Ibid., 105–6.

According to Marcuse, the dialectical concepts reflect a demand for freedom that is implicit in philosophy from the very beginning. However, philosophical thought has been blocked and distorted throughout history by the overwhelming realities of scarcity and domination. As a result, the potentialities it identifies appear as a metaphysical dimension beyond the given.

Philosophy thus suffers the same fate as the imagination and artistic creation. In all these domains, the demand for a better reality is blunted through marginalization of the dangerous visions in which the truth attempts to shine forth. Reality contradicts metaphysical and artistic truth, and is subject to purely formal understanding. In Hegelian terms, the given is delivered over to "immediate facticity." Formal thinking reflects the split between essence and existence that results from the conditions of life in class society.

From the standpoint of formal thinking, the substantive universals that reveal the potentialities of being appear as mere phantasy. The split between these logics is reflected in the corresponding split between reason and imagination, fact and value, reality and art. The "content" that dialectics identifies as pointing toward suppressed potentialities is redefined as mere "value," subjective and arbitrary, without normative validity.

Here is the core of Marcuse's argument. Formal universals are value free in the sense that they do not prescribe the ends of the objects they construct conceptually as means. However, they are value laden in another deeper sense: namely, that the very conception of value from which formal universals are "free" is itself a product of the abstractive process in which formalism suppresses potentialities. Thus, formalism is not in fact neutral with respect to the alternative of actual and potential in its objects. Rather, it is biased toward the actual, what is already fully realized and present at hand.

Methodologically, this bias appears in the refusal—or the inability—to integrate history and social contexts as the scene of development. Formal abstraction restricts its range to the artificially isolated, reified object as it immediately appears. In so doing, it comes under the horizon of the existing society and its technical mode of practice. Its objects can be used, but not transformed; they can be adapted to the dominant social purposes, but not transcended toward the realization of higher potentialities in a possible, better society.

This explains why formal bias is an intrinsic aspect of formal systems. In abstracting objects from their contexts, it ignores the dimension of reality that points toward "real possibilities" of progressive development. Instead, objects are conceptualized as isolated and unchanging in themselves but available for manipulation from without. Formal bias arises when the so-conceptualized objects are integrated into a real world of historical contingencies. Then, the abstraction of the concept of the object from the material content and contexts from which it was abstracted is revealed as a precondition of domination.

Marcuse concludes that "formalization and functionalization are, *prior* to all application, the 'pure form' of a concrete societal practice."[59] He applies this logic to science and technology in general:

> The hypothetical system of forms and functions becomes dependent on another system—a pre-established universe of ends, in which and *for* which it develops. What appeared extraneous, foreign to the theoretical project, shows forth as part of its very structure (method and concepts); pure objectivity reveals itself as *object for a subjectivity* which provides the Telos, the ends. In the construction of the technological reality, there is no such thing as a purely rational scientific order; the process of technological rationality is a political process.[60]

So long as formal universals coexist with the "second dimension" of substantive universals, culture reflects the contradictions of class society. Transcending potentialities of the society can be formulated in such a divided culture, if only in a religious, artistic, or metaphysical form. With the emergence of capitalism, those potentialities are increasingly interpreted in historical terms. Social criticism can finally become mass consciousness and lead to revolutionary change. Indeed, Marxism was elaborated under just such conditions.

However, in advanced industrial societies, Marcuse argues, the second dimension is increasingly replaced by concepts drawn from the apparatus of technological rationality. As every aspect of social life comes to be articulated exclusively through formal universals,

---

59 Ibid., 157.
60 Ibid., 168.

transcending thought and action are blocked. Social crises and injustices no longer call for fundamental change but instead are interpreted as technical problems. Standard modes of action and organization, which presuppose domination, function as a priori constraints on the "solutions" offered, and so technological rationality reinforces the status quo in responding to the very wrongs it inflicts.

The link between this form of instrumentalism and domination becomes apparent in the paradox of advanced societies, which are increasingly effective in controlling not only nature but also human beings. Every advance in the power of formalistic thought also advances the suppression of human beings and the potentialities for peace and freedom made possible by technical progress itself. At its most absurd, pure formalism may someday materialize in the destruction of the earth through the untrammeled exercise of technical power in nuclear war.

Conclusion: Neutrality as Bias

The market does not play favorites, and no one controls its movements; nevertheless, it is not a neutral mediator of human desires but has a dynamic of its own. It has effects independent of its role in joining buyers and sellers to their mutual advantage, and some of those effects are disastrous—for example, periodic crises, the alienation of labor, and the degradation of the natural environment. Marx's idea of socialism was based on a critique of these consequences of capitalism and the hope that a conscious agent, the proletariat, could construct a better world.

Marcuse supplements Marx's critique of political economy with a critique of the technical systems of capitalism—systems that now constitute the social world along with, and to some extent in place of, the market. Like Marx's critique, this new critique shatters the illusion of neutrality. The administrations, technologies, and technical disciplines that organize life in industrial societies exhibit biases similar to those Marx identified in the capitalism of his day, but now they penetrate every domain of social life. Contemporary critique must therefore address both market and technosystem, identify the problems in both, and discover the new sources of social change.

Weber's concept of rationalization was an important advance in understanding the new developments, but he presupposed control from above. He thus excluded a priori any more democratic organization of society. Marcuse argues that the source of the bias of Weberian rationalization is the separation of workers from the means of production under capitalism. This critique of Weber could be taken to imply the neutrality of a hypothetical technical reason purified of class bias; but according to the ontological critique, the bias of rationalization is a consequence of the very nature of technical reason. Technical reason is, indeed, neutral at some level, Marcuse will argue, but its very neutrality subserves it to domination and so ties it to class society.

This solution to the conundrum of neutrality and bias is paradoxical. Where the irrationalist critique of reason attempts to undermine the claim of science to neutrality by showing it to be an ideological veil for hidden interests, Marcuse argues that it is the very neutrality of science that supplies the link between instrumentalism and domination. He writes:

> This interpretation would tie the scientific project (method and theory), *prior* to all application and utilization, to a specific societal project, and would see the tie precisely in the inner form of scientific rationality . . . It is precisely its neutral character which relates objectivity to a specific historical Subject—namely, the consciousness that prevails in the society.[61]

With this, Marcuse squares the theoretical circle and demonstrates that neutrality is itself a form of bias. His critique of scientific-technical rationality is not irrationalist but open to an alternative dialectical form of rationality. What is that alternative? Could there be a modern form of reason that recognizes potentialities? How would it enter into human projects? I will address these questions in the next chapter.

---

61 Ibid., 159, 156.

6

A New Concept of Reason?

The Two Natures

In the background of Heidegger's and Marcuse's critiques of science, there lies a sense of loss of the immediate relation to living nature that characterized premodern times and that is recollected in art. The scientific representation of nature as measurable facts is radically simplified. The generalization in public understanding of that simplified nature impoverishes experience. Heidegger writes, "The botanist's plants are not the flowers in the hedgerow; the 'source' which the geographer establishes for a river is not the 'springhead in the dale.'"[1]

Heidegger feared that human beings had come to see themselves as mere resources in this new technological world. This complaint is familiar from a tradition of critique that deplored the reduction of a rich concrete lifeworld to abstract measurements and equations. As Goethe's Mephistopheles says, "Gray, my dear friend, is every theory, and green life's golden tree."[2] Heidegger's famous essay on "The Question Concerning Technology" was only the latest in a long line of such critiques.

When Marcuse wrote *One-Dimensional Man*, he too believed that everyday consciousness now corresponded to the one-dimensional

---

1 Martin Heidegger, *Being and Time*, trans. John Macquarrie and Edward Robinson (New York: Harper & Row, 1962), 100.

2 Johann Wolfgang von Goethe, *Faust*, ed. and trans. Walter Kaufmann (New York: Anchor Books, 1962), 206. "Grau, teurer Freund, ist alle Theorie und grün des Lebens goldner Baum."

worldview of natural science. The dystopian perspective of these philosophers was justified by the seemingly universal acceptance of the technified world. Apart from a few critics like themselves, there was practically no resistance to the developing technocracy. The socialist movement was dead in the United States, and its prospects as an emancipatory force appeared poor everywhere. The environmental movement was still minuscule. Only philosophy, literature, and art conserved human values, and they were weak vessels on which to pin one's hopes.

Walter Benjamin explained the fate of lived nature in the context of film production. His remarks can be taken as referring metaphorically to modern life:

> In the studio the mechanical equipment has penetrated so deeply into reality that its pure aspect freed from the foreign substance of equipment is the result of a special procedure, namely, the shooting by the specially adjusted camera and the mounting of the shot together with other similar ones. The equipment-free aspect of reality here has become the height of artifice; the sight of immediate reality has become an orchid in the land of technology.[3]

In sum, there is no immediate that is not already mediated by technology.

If this is so, there is no way back to nature, but perhaps it is possible to go *forward*. This would require a transformation of the form of rationality presiding over the technological mediations, hence Marcuse's call for a new concept of reason. The prevailing concept, modeled on modern science, structures a technified form of capitalism. A socialist rationality would have to preserve the achievements of science while reflecting socialist values.

According to *One-Dimensional Man*, this new concept of reason belongs to a "transcendent" historical project. Here is Marcuse's description of that project:

---

3 Walter Benjamin, *Illuminations*, trans. Harry Zohn (New York: Shocken, 1969), 233. The translator has done well to communicate Benjamin's intent, but in fact the "orchid" is a *blaue Blume*, symbol of romantic longing in Novalis's novel *Heinrich von Ofterdingen*. See Walter Benjamin, *Das Kunstwerk im Zeitalter seiner technischen Reproduzierbarkeit* (Frankfurt am Main: Suhrkamp, 2010), 52.

(1) The transcendent project must be in accordance with the real possibilities open at the attained level of the material and intellectual culture.

(2) The transcendent project, in order to falsify the established totality, must demonstrate its own *higher* rationality in the threefold sense that

    (a) it offers the prospect of preserving and improving the productive achievement of civilization;

    (b) it defines the established totality in its very structure, basic tendencies, and relations;

    (c) its realization offers a greater chance for the pacification of existence, with the framework of institutions which offer a greater chance for the free development of human needs and faculties.[4]

Socialism corresponds to these requirements, and the Marxist dialectic validates it rationally. However, *One-Dimensional Man* offers little hope for its realization. What would it take to fulfill that last requirement? Two conditions: a social revolution, and a new science and technology. The two conditions are inseparable in practice: in a technified society, fundamental social change is technical change.

At least for a time, the New Left refuted Marcuse's pessimism. Critical theory was relayed by widespread consciousness of a second dimension of purpose and growth in the context of a life-affirming ethos. The new sensibility broke through reification in artistic creation, struggle, and protest, demanding the "Union of liberating art and liberating technology" under socialism. Marcuse found an anticipation of this future in the proclamations of the students of the Beaux-Arts in Paris in 1968.[5] The aesthetic imagination, he argued, would enrich the data on which science relies. This would be a future scientific revolution, the reconstruction of science around a logos, an acknowledged telos of its objects.

Marx's *Manuscripts* inspired the notion of a new science. Marx writes, "Hitherto [industry] was not conceived in its connection with

---

4 Herbert Marcuse, *One-Dimensional Man: Studies in the Ideology of Advanced Industrial Society* (Boston: Beacon Press, 1964), 220.

5 Herbert Marcuse, *An Essay on Liberation* (Boston: Beacon Press, 1969), 48.

man's *essential being*, but only in an external relation of utility." He continues:

> *Industry* is the *actual*, historical relationship of nature, and therefore of natural science, to man. If, therefore, industry is conceived as the *exoteric* revelation of man's *essential powers*, we also gain an understanding of the human essence of nature or the natural essence of man. In consequence, natural science will lose its abstractly material— or rather, its idealistic—tendency, and will become the basis of *human* science, as it has already become—albeit in an estranged form—the basis of actual human life, and to assume *one* basis for life and a different basis for *science* is as a matter of course a lie.[6]

Marx's point is not that science depends on technical progress, but rather that technology *discloses* nature in two forms, to science and to "man"—that is, to the subject of the lifeworld. Marx argues that a *"true science"* will unite these dual natures that have been wrongly separated, and that it will be based on the liberated senses in the "twofold form of *sensuous* consciousness and *sensuous* need."[7]

On Marcuse's terms, this is a way of marking the role of potentialities in the new science. Sensuousness relates to potentialities of nature that correspond to human needs. That relation is immediate insofar as it is given to the senses, but, as we saw in chapter 2, the senses themselves are historically mediated and have a cognitive aspect. They have become "human" senses through the evolution of human being from its crude origins to its developed form in civilized society. The sensuous basis of science implicates humans in nature not simply as indifferent observers, but also as active beings informed by culture.

Marcuse's late essay on "Nature and Revolution" argues that every historical epoch objectifies nature in accordance with a specific social a priori. The prevailing capitalist a priori is uniquely destructive and so has become the object of political struggle. A socialist a priori, in contrast, recognizes nature as a subject in its own right. Nature's potentialities are its own, even as it serves human needs. Marcuse resolves

---

6 Karl Marx, "Economic and Philosophical Manuscripts," in *Early Writings*, ed. and trans. T. B. Bottomore (London: C. A. Watts, 1963), 163–4.

7 Ibid., 164.

this seeming contradiction as follows: "Is nature only a productive force—or does it also exist '*for its own sake*' and, in *this* mode of existence, for *man*?"[8] The ambiguity of the second "for" in this phrase means that nature qua subject belongs to the lifeworld even as it acts independently of human aims.

Marcuse acknowledges the "metaphysical" implications of the idea of "nature as a manifestation of subjectivity."[9] Like Kant, he intends to avoid metaphysics while nevertheless retaining something very much like a concept of teleology. Our experience of nature, he argues, recognizes aesthetic qualities excluded from natural science. Marcuse follows Kant in interpreting this aspect of nature under the category of freedom, which nature exhibits where it displays the "capacity to form itself."[10] We have an intuitive sense of exactly what this means: the plant grows without obstacle toward the light; the child learns new words each day; the lake is clear and populated by fish and wildlife. Each of these examples suggests the freedom of a natural "subject" to develop unobstructed—albeit, Marcuse notes, without any final end in view. Kant, in his discussion of artistic beauty, calls something similar "purposiveness without purpose."

Environmentalism valorizes the everyday sense of nature as fraught with potentialities, recalling human beings to their responsibilities toward that nature. This everyday idea of nature has always existed, but modern science was founded on its rejection. Ever since Bacon, science has resisted the "idols of the tribe"—a resistance Gaston Bachelard formulated in his theory of the "epistemological rupture." Science, he argued, "must be formed against nature, against all that comes from nature's impetus and instruction, within us and outside us, against natural allurements and colourful, diverse facts."[11] Everyday experience is presumed to be the domain of error, of prejudice and a flat earth.

---

8 Herbert Marcuse, "Nature and Revolution," in *Counterrevolution and Revolt* (Boston: Beacon Press, 1972), 62.

9 Ibid., 65.

10 Marcuse quotes from *The Critique of Judgment*, in ibid., 67.

11 Gaston Bachelard, *The Formation of the Scientific Mind: A Contribution to a Psychoanalysis of Objective Knowledge*, trans. Mary McAllester Jones (Manchester: Clinamen Press, 2002), 70, 33. For more on Bachelard and the relation of his thought to science and technology studies, see Bas de Boer, "Gaston Bachelard's Philosophy of Science: Between Project and Practice," in *Parrhesia* 31 (2019): 154–73.

Indeed, like everything human, experience is fallible. Marcuse would certainly have agreed that some errors—the belief in the flatness of the earth, for example—should simply be corrected by science, but a wide range of phenomena stem from a different disclosure of reality accessible in the lifeworld. This is most obvious with respect to social life, but it also applies to many socially embedded scientific-technical disciplines and the concept of nature they project. Marcuse's concept of life affirmation adjudicates between social and technical phenomena, those that stem from destructive impulses such as prejudice, and those that are normatively valid, such as protection of the environment.

With these qualifications, the lifeworld can play an indirect role in revising scientific conceptualization. It makes a return as a valid source of knowledge capable of orienting science toward essential concerns:

These potentialities [of nature] can be . . . bearers of *objective values.* These are envisaged in such phrases as "violation of nature," "suppression of nature." Violation and suppression then mean that human action against nature, man's interrelation with nature, offends against certain objective *qualities* of nature—qualities which are essential to the enhancement and fulfillment of life. And it is on such objective grounds that the liberation for man to his own humane faculties is linked to the liberation of nature—that "truth" is attributable to nature not only in a mathematical but also in an existential sense. The emancipation of man involves the recognition of such truth in things, in nature.[12]

What is the relation of "existential" to "mathematical" truth? This question lays out clearly Marcuse's problematic: *the coordination of experienced potentialities with objective nature.* One belongs to the life-world, which has standards of validity that apply in the first person, the other to the sciences with their ideal third-person standpoint. Potentialities are disclosed to sensuousness and are articulated in art and philosophy. For Marcuse, the gap between these disciplines and natural science must be overcome.

This chapter will explore Marcuse's reflections on art, science, and technology. I will begin with his concept of aesthetics and then show its

---

12 Marcuse, "Nature and Revolution," 69.

relation to the transformation of natural science. Later sections will take up the theme as it applies to technology and to the socially embedded scientific-technical disciplines that shape a technified society. As I will show, the contestation of these disciplines by social movements, notably the environmental movement, sheds a new light on Marcuse's argument for a new concept of reason.

The Laws of Beauty

Marx's *Manuscripts* propose an unusual distinction between human beings and animals. It is not language or reason, but aesthetics that marks the difference. Unlike animals, bound by need, "Man constructs also in accordance with the laws of beauty."[13] Marcuse comes back to this sentence several times in his various writings over the years, first in his interpretation of the *Manuscripts*, later in *Eros and Civilization*, where he signals its source in Schiller, and then again, in his essay on "Nature and Revolution."[14]

This latter text contains other echoes of Marcuse's interpretation of the early Marx. He writes:

> Aesthetics of liberation, beauty as a "form" of freedom. It looks as if Marx has shied away from this anthropomorphist, idealistic conception. Or is this apparently idealistic notion rather the *enlargement of the materialistic base*? For "man is directly a *natural being*; he is a corporeal, living, real, sensuous objective being" who has "real sensuous objects" as the objects of his life . . . This is . . . the extension of Historical Materialism to a dimension which is to play a vital role in the liberation of man.[15]

---

13 Marx, "Economic and Philosophical Manuscripts," 128.

14 Herbert Marcuse, "New Sources on the Foundations of Historical Materialism," in *Heideggerian Marxism*, ed. Richard Wolin and John Abromeit (Lincoln and London: University of Nebraska Press, 2005) 97; Herbert Marcuse, *Eros and Civilization: A Philosophical Inquiry into Freud* (Boston: Beacon Press, 1966), 189; Friedrich Schiller, *On the Aesthetic Education of Man: A Series of Letters*, trans. Reginald Snell (New York: F. Ungar Publishing, 1963), 112; Marcuse, "Nature and Revolution," 67.

15 Marcuse, "Nature and Revolution," 67–8.

The human senses perceive properties that go beyond the primary qualities recognized by natural science. Those properties include beauty as a real "dimension" of the objective world. As we saw in chapter 4, that dimension is an erotic mode of disclosure articulated not only in aesthetic judgment but also in the affirmation of life.

The notion that beauty has "laws" suggests an objectivist aesthetic. In fact, Marcuse refers to an article by Stefan Morawski in which the objectivist position is laid out in three principles: that objective properties of objects are defining for their aesthetic value, that these properties determine aesthetic experience, and that they provide a basis for aesthetic judgment.[16]

Marcuse proposes several different versions of an objectivist aesthetic. As explained in chapter 4, he identifies beauty with that which is "life enhancing." "For the aesthetic needs have their own social content: they are the claims of the human organism, mind and body, for a dimension of fulfillment" denied by the established society.[17] That content is manifested in art.

The late essay on "Art and Revolution" explains the cognitive significance of that manifestation:

"Truth" in art refers not only to the internal consistency and logic of the *oeuvre*, but also to the *validity* of what it says, of its images, sound, rhythm. They reveal and communicate facts and possibilities of the human existence; they "see" this existence in a light very different from that in which reality appears in ordinary (and scientific) language and communication. In this sense the authentic *oeuvre* has indeed a meaning which claims general validity, objectivity.[18]

In *An Essay on Liberation*, Marcuse suggests that Kant should have considered a form of intuition of beauty alongside the intuitions of space and time, thereby grounding the validity of aesthetic perception

---

16 Herbert Marcuse, "Art and Revolution," in *Counterrevolution and Revolt*, 87. See Stefan Morawski, "Artistic Value," in *Journal of Aesthetic Education* 5, no. 1 (January 1971): 23–59.

17 Marcuse, *An Essay on Liberation*, 27.

18 Marcuse, "Art and Revolution," 88–9. There is an echo here of the distinction between validity, *Geltung*, and factual existence explained in chapter 2.

in the correlation of consciousness and objectivity.[19] We are once again reminded of the *Manuscripts'* emphasis on the ontological status of beauty.

One-Dimensional Man offers a more expansive notion of this specifically aesthetic seeing, which Marcuse calls the "rationality of art." He refers to Hegel's notion of an "aesthetic reduction" that eliminates the contingent aspects of the objects of representation to allow them to express themselves freely:

> In the aesthetic Form, the content (matter) is assembled, defined, and arranged to obtain a condition in which the immediate unmastered forces of the matter, of the "material," are mastered, "ordered." Form is the negation, the mastery of disorder, violence, suffering, even when it presents disorder, violence, suffering.[20]

The reduction creates a distance between art and reality, a distance in which an idealized world is revealed. That world is a realm of potentialities in which the actual world would be fulfilled if only the means existed to reconcile human beings with each other and with nature, freedom with necessity, subject with object. As such, art gives substance to the idea of potentiality Marcuse finds in Hegel.

It is in this sense that aesthetics holds the answer to the questions posed at the end of the last chapter. Only through a merging of technological rationality with the rationality of art can science and technology transcend their instrumentalization in the interests of domination. This is Marcuse's response to the pessimism of Horkheimer and Adorno's *Dialectic of Enlightenment*, which offers no concrete escape from the logic of domination (although Adorno, like Marcuse, would later find a utopian promise in aesthetics).

Formulated in the terms of Horkheimer's *Eclipse of Reason*, Marcuse seeks to transcend the antinomy of "subjective" reason, concerned only with means, and "objective" reason, which posits ends that were once justified by a metaphysics that is no longer credible. Horkheimer's solution to the antinomy, the "self-critique of reason," is far too abstract to satisfy

---

19 Marcuse, *An Essay on Liberation*, 32. See also Marcuse, "Nature and Revolution," 63.
20 Marcuse, *An Essay on Liberation*, 43.

Marcuse who instead seeks a concrete social alternative.[21] Charles Reitz calls Marcuse's solution "an aesthetically oriented philosophy of praxis."[22]

Marcuse worked this out in three stages. First, in *One-Dimensional Man*, he argues for revising scientific-technical rationality to incorporate the aesthetic imagination. This new concept of rationality would support a technology reconciled with nature. Second, in *An Essay on Liberation* and several unpublished essays, he argues for the possibility of the total realization of the new rationality, transcending the gap between actuality and potentiality and canceling the independence of art. Third, in the essay on "Art and Revolution" and in *The Aesthetic Dimension*, he reaffirms the unbridgeable separation of art and life, without abandoning the idea of an aesthetic transformation of rationality and society. In the next section, I will discuss these three versions of Marcuse's aesthetic. Later sections will explain and criticize Marcuse's call for a new science based on the aesthetic dimension.

Art and the Concept of Reason

Marcuse imagines an ideal history of reason that begins with the free play of the imagination, uniting science, philosophy, and art in a unified faculty that addresses both the real and the possible. This original form of reason is later broken up, such that science rationalizes the world practically through technical advance within limits set by the established social organization, while philosophy and art transcend those limits in thought without the capacity to change reality. This is the differentiation of logos and eros that underlies civilization and culminates in capitalist modernity.

For Marcuse, philosophy and art postulate another state of being, an erotic world oriented toward the flourishing of life, unconstrained by the logic of domination. Until modern times, that world could exist only in imagination. The immense power of modern technology can support a way of life based on solidarity and the fulfillment of needs while respecting natural limits. Thus, only now can a reunion of

---

21 Max Horkheimer, *Eclipse of Reason* (New York: Oxford University Press, 1947), 177.

22 Charles Reitz, *Art, Alienation, and the Humanities: A Critical Engagement with Herbert Marcuse* (Albany: State University of New York Press, 2000), 181–2.

science, philosophy, and art be envisaged. Saint-Simon's famous sequence of stages, from metaphysics to science, can now be reversed and the metaphysical concepts realized in a radically new type of modern society Marcuse identifies with socialism:[23]

> This is the notion of the rupture with the continuum of domination, the qualitative difference of socialism as a new form and way of life, not only rational development of the productive forces, but also the redirection of progress toward the ending of the competitive struggle for existence, not only abolition of poverty and toil, but also reconstruction of the social and natural environment as a peaceful, beautiful universe: *total transvaluation of values*, transformation of needs and goals.[24]

What form would the new concept of reason take? Marcuse envisages a renewal of the ancient concept of technē that united technical and aesthetic considerations in craft labor. Technē had two presuppositions alien to modern science and technology: the matter of craft was seen as containing the potentiality for its own transformation, and craft was oriented by a logos in the sense of an intrinsic purpose. These presuppositions are reflected in Marcuse's "outrageous" demand for the "liberation of nature" in the context of a transformed technology, and in his equally shocking demand that science "become political."[25] A new science and technology, he argues, will respect the potentialities of nature rather than reducing it to raw materials, mere fungible stuff, and it will incorporate values into theory and design.

Artistic beauty now plays a new role. It is no longer confined to a separate realm of unrealizable ideals with no consequences in the real world. Instead, its idealizations are an imaginative grasp of potentialities that can guide technical practice. The split between a technical reason serving established power, on one hand, and an impotent aesthetic, on the other, is overcome. In Marcuse's words, "The rationality of art, its ability to 'project' existence, to define yet unrealized

---

23 Marcuse, *One-Dimensional Man*, 239.

24 Herbert Marcuse, "Re-examination of the Concept of Revolution," in *Marxism, Revolution and Utopia*, ed. Douglas Kellner (New York: Routledge, 2014), 204–5.

25 Ibid., 233; Marcuse, "Nature and Revolution," 69.

possibilities could then be envisaged as *validated by and functioning in the scientific-technological transformation of the world.*"[26]

This would put an end to the neutrality of scientific-technical reason. Science would no longer be subservient to capitalism but would be guided by consciousness of potentialities. The "liberation" of nature "would not be an external event which would leave the scientific enterprise in its structure intact: it may well affect the scientific method itself, the scientific experience and projection of nature."[27] This is the emancipatory response to the ontological critique discussed in the previous chapter. The technoscientific "projection" of nature as the stuff of domination would be replaced by another projection based on erotic, life-affirming values.

Marcuse pursued these reflections further in the wake of the French May Events of 1968 and the rise of the New Left. He argued that the "new sensibility" of the New Left restored an erotic relation to the environment. An "aesthetic *Lebenswelt*" had emerged on a mass scale, a new mode of experience prefiguring the revolutionary future. Drawing on these themes, Marcuse's most optimistic book, *An Essay on Liberation*, imagines a world in which the distinction between art and technique has been overcome. Under the cultural revolution,

> technique would then tend to become art and art would tend to form reality: the opposition between imagination and reason, higher and lower faculties, poetic and scientific thought, would be invalidated. Emergence of a new Reality Principle: under which a new sensibility and a desublimated scientific intelligence would combine in the creation of an *aesthetic ethos*.[28]

Socialist technology would pursue idealizing strategies similar to those of art. Misery, injustice, suffering, and disorder would be removed not just from the artistic illusion, but eliminated practically by appropriate technological solutions. The merger of art and technique would

---

26 Marcuse, *One-Dimensional Man*, 239.

27 Herbert Marcuse, "Remarks on a Redefinition of Culture," in *The Essential Marcuse: Selected Writings of Philosopher and Social Critic Herbert Marcuse*, ed. Andrew Feenberg and William Leiss (Boston: Beacon Press, 2007), 27.

28 Marcuse, *An Essay on Liberation*, 24.

mean the end of art and the realization of the essential potentialities of humans and nature in a new form of society.

> No return to precapitalist, pre-industrial artisanship, but on the contrary, perfection of the new mutilated and distorted science and technology in the formation of the object world in accordance with "the laws of beauty." And "beauty" here defines an ontological condition—not of an *oeuvre d'art* isolated from real existence . . . but that harmony between man and his world which would shape the form of society.[29]

With this, Marcuse renews the ambition of the early twentieth-century avant-gardes, who hoped to overcome the separation of art from life in an aestheticized existence. He invokes the surrealist notion of *hasard objectif*, according to which "human faculties and desires . . . appear as part of the objective determinism of nature—coincidence of causality through nature and causality through freedom."[30] Marx's conception of objectification echoes in this phrase.

As the New Left offensive receded, Marcuse became more cautious, conceding that the realization of art in reality would always be incomplete. Perhaps this is the "correction" to which he alludes in the acknowledgments that precede the text of his next book, *Counterrevolution and Revolt*. There, he insists on the inevitable estrangement of art, which reflects both the exigencies of aesthetic form and the limits of human nature. Art can communicate the idea of a better world but cannot be dissolved into that world without remainder. "At the optimum, we can envisage a universe common to art and reality, but art would retain its transcendence."[31]

This is also the position he takes in his last book, *The Aesthetic Dimension*. There, he still envisages the realization of aesthetic potentialities in the social world and its technology, but, even under these ideal

---

29 Herbert Marcuse, "Cultural Revolution," in *Towards a Critical Theory of Society: Collected Papers of Herbert Marcuse*, ed. Douglas Kellner (London: Routledge, 2001), 138–9. I wonder if there is not a typo here: "now mutilated" would make more sense than "new mutilated."

30 Marcuse, *An Essay on Liberation*, 31.

31 Marcuse, "Art and Revolution," 121.

conditions, "art bears witness to the inherent limits of freedom and fulfillment."[32] There will be no "end of art." Apparently, the "laws of beauty" cannot transform the real world in its totality after all.[33]

Marcuse's Dilemma

Marcuse's most radical speculations follow Marx's call for a new science. He envisages a merger of the two dimensions in a physical science informed by aesthetics. The high ideals of art and philosophy would be realized in a future natural science and its associated technology. Metaphysical claims that appear exaggerated are necessarily deflated in the social context they now enter. Such deflation is not intended to diminish a noble heritage but rather to raise the material world to a higher level. Unfortunately, Marcuse's rhetoric promises results it cannot deliver. There is a peculiar dissonance between the quasi-eschatological tone of his account of the relation of art to science, echoing Marx's "resurrection of nature," and the few (rather poor) examples with which he illustrates his thesis.[34] This discordance signals serious problems with his theory.

Marcuse's rhetorical strategy was effective in the midst of the social turmoil of the late 1960s and early '70s. He called for "a new idea of science, of Reason," at a time when modern societies suffered a crisis of legitimacy that extended to the project of material progress on which they were based.[35] It later became clear that his position suffered from two serious flaws.

On the one hand, a literal reading of many passages in Marcuse's work invites skepticism, so extraordinary are his claims for a new concept of reason. It is as though he has himself constructed a straw man for his critics.[36] On the other hand, the critique of quantitative

---

32 Herbert Marcuse, *The Aesthetic Dimension* (Boston: Beacon Press, 1977), 28–9.

33 For a discussion of Marcuse's late aesthetics, see Reitz, *Art, Alienation, and the Humanities*, chapter 9.

34 Marx, "Economic and Philosophical Manuscripts," 157.

35 Marcuse, *One-Dimensional Man*, 231.

36 The most influential such attack was that of Jürgen Habermas in "Technology and Science as Ideology," in *Toward a Rational Society: Student Protest, Science, and*

scientific-technical rationality seems to imply the validity of a qualitative science such as Aristotle's. This Marcuse explicitly rejects. While potentiality and secondary qualities are to play a role in a future science, we never learn how. If science is to remain a quantitative venture, how does Marcuse intend to avoid the implications of his quasi-Heideggerian critique? Not surprisingly, these problems have proven fatal to attempts to defend Marcuse's theory from attacks from all quarters.

Both of these problems are evident in several passage where Marcuse explains the transformation scientific method must undergo in a socialist society. In one unpublished text, he writes:

> In this context, the "sensuous basis of all science" means something more and other than empirical verification by sense certainty: it means that the scientist, without in any way abandoning the logic and rigidity of scientific method, is guided in his research by the (emancipated) sensuous needs for the protection and amelioration of life. If the satisfaction of these needs, instead of being a mere by-product of science (a by-product which seems to become increasingly rare and feeble), would become the rationale of science, it may well lead to a different conceptual foundation of the natural and human sciences.[37]

It is encouraging to learn that Marcuse approves of the "rigidity of scientific method," but is that not precisely what reduces the world to primary qualities? How can a "rationale"—a logos—be inserted into such a world?

Marcuse proposes two distinct answers to this question, seemingly without registering the difference between them. On the one hand, he argues that under socialism, "scientific rationality as a whole" will incorporate ideas it rejected in the past—presumably potentialities and affective qualities. This would be a successor science. "The scientific

---

Politics, trans. Jeremy J. Shapiro (Boston: Beacon Press, 1970). See also Peter Sedgwick, "Natural Science and Human Theory: A Critique of Herbert Marcuse," *Socialist Register 1966: A Survey of Movements and Ideas* 3 (1966): 163–92.

37 Marcuse, "Cultural Revolution," 138.

concepts could project and define the possible realities of a free and pacified existence,"[38] while "formerly metaphysical ideas of liberation may become the proper object of science."[39]

On the other hand, Marcuse draws on Gilbert Simondon's concept of translation to articulate a notion of the future of science and technology. Simondon called for overcoming the split between ethics and technical design.[40] Marcuse develops Simondon's idea:

> The historical achievement of science and technology has rendered possible the *translation of values into technical tasks—the materialization of values*. Consequently, what is at stake is the redefinition of values in *technical terms*, as elements in the technological process. The new ends, as technical ends, would then operate in the project and in the construction of the machinery, and not only in its utilization. Moreover, the new ends might assert themselves even in the construction of scientific hypotheses—in pure scientific theory.[41]

The final sentence of this passage appears to promise a successor science, but the application of the idea of translation to technology suggests a more plausible approach. As I will show in later sections, Marcuse gestures here toward a realizable transformation of the technology, but the next paragraph offers examples that deflate the expectations raised by these remarks. He suggests that the alternative to a discredited "qualitative physics" is "quantifying" values such as the resources required to free human beings from want and to care for the sick and disabled.[42] There is nothing new about this; it consists merely in calculating the means to the chosen ends without calling into

---

38 Marcuse, *One-Dimensional Man*, 231.

39 Ibid., 233.

40 Gilbert Simondon, *Du Mode d'Existence des Objets Techniques* (Paris: Aubier-Montaigne, 1958), 151.

41 Marcuse, *One-Dimensional Man*, 232. I was surprised recently when I noticed Marcuse's use of the term "translation." A related concept was developed in science and technology studies thirty years later, for example, by Bruno Latour. This way of thinking becomes obvious to everyone studying science and technology by the 1990s, but something similar, with a more restricted application, is there in Marcuse in 1964.

42 Marcuse, *One-Dimensional Man*, 166, 232.

question the means themselves. We are returned to the classic notion of economic planning, despite the introduction of the suggestive concepts of "translation" and "materialization" that figure in this passage.

A number of other hints are offered to explain the concrete significance of the merger of art and technology, but none of them are very convincing. Marcuse mentions parks and reservations as examples of respect for aesthetic values under the limits set by capitalism. He argues for relating to nature through "cultivation" of its potentialities, rather than through reducing it to raw materials. He refers to examples of crafted objects he finds meaningful for his project but also rejects a return to preindustrial techniques of production. He mentions the aestheticization of consumer goods, mere gadgets in those days before smartphones, and remarks on the limitations of such examples: confining aesthetics to parks and consumer goods leaves out the more important issues involving industrial destruction of the environment, alienation at work, and preparation for war.[43]

An uncharitable interpreter could rest the case at this point. Indeed, the rhetoric rises to improbable heights and, when it is time to pay off, descends to the depths of banality. Nevertheless, I do not think Marcuse can be so easily dismissed. His presentation is flawed, to be sure, but the intent behind it is valid, as I will show.

Successor Science and Translation

Marcuse anticipates what Thomas Kuhn calls a "scientific revolution" that would overthrow science as we know it, that is, Kuhn's "normal science." Normal science is based on a "paradigm" that functions as an a priori foundation for scientific work. Kuhn writes, "The commitments that govern normal science specify not only what sorts of entities the universe does contain, but also, by implication, those that it does not."[44]

In defining the acceptable entities in terms of "calculable, predictable relationships" and thereby excluding potentialities, science

---

43 Marcuse, *An Essay on Liberation*, 50.

44 Thomas Kuhn, *The Structure of Scientific Revolutions* (Chicago: University of Chicago Press, 1962), 7.

abandons its original logos, the service of life. Under socialism, the logos returns: beauty is the a priori of a new object construction that would restore the logos by granting potentialities epistemic validity. An aestheticized successor science would evolve from contemporary physics and, like it, apply to being as such. In Marcuse's words, "Scientific hypotheses, without losing their rational character, would develop in an essentially different experimental context (that of a pacified world); consequently, science would arrive at essentially different concepts of nature and establish essentially different facts."[45]

There is something incoherent about this idea of a new scientific revolution. Natural science leads a triple life: first as scientific methods (experimentation, quantification, and formalization); second as a worldview, a picture of the real as consisting exclusively of primary qualities; and third as one-dimensional consciousness for which reality is the exclusive object of technical control. In Marcuse's imagined scientific revolution, there is no intrinsic connection between the methods, which remain the same, and the corresponding worldview and form of consciousness, which are transformed.

He claims that the "logic and rigidity of scientific methods" can be employed in the context of an aesthetic worldview that would restore the connection between scientific rationality and the lifeworld. Scientific methods and the aesthetic content of perception meet in a new natural science. In this overly ambitious projection, an aestheticized natural science would continue to occupy the same foundational role in theory and consciousness while still employing formal quantitative methods.

Did Marcuse fail to heed the strict separation of philosophical and factual inquiry achieved by neo-Kantianism and phenomenology? In chapter 2, I explained that these traditions assigned science the exclusive role as concerns factual knowledge, consequently rejecting metaphysics as a source of truths about the natural world. Marcuse's argument for a scientific revolution certainly suggests a return to metaphysics, a philosophical claim to knowledge of facts, for that is what potentialities would be, conceived as scientific data. That these facts will be discovered in the future rather than dogmatically posited in contradiction to existing science does not erase this suspicion.

---

45 Marcuse, *One-Dimensional Man*, 166–7.

Marcuse's attempt to validate his imagined future science phenomenologically introduces other problems without resolving this one.

As Ian Angus points out, Marcuse relies on Husserl's claim that the return of the lost content of the *Lebenswelt* can heal the wound inflicted by scientific naturalism. Similarly, the aesthetic revolution is intended to revoke the strict reduction of being to primary qualities, but the nature of modern science prohibits any such return to the concrete.[46] The formalization of being that renders it mathematically calculable cannot be compensated with the concrete content from which it is abstracted. Formalization cuts the connection to content and substitutes abstract variables for concrete objects.

Here is an example to clarify Angus's point. The referent of d in the physics equation $d = v * t$ ("distance equals velocity times time") is any and every possible measure of spatial separation, all concrete qualities excluded. Angus argues that this distinguishes the formal abstractions of modern science from mere generalizations, which can be filled out with lost content by specifying details as desired. "Drilling down" to the concrete basis of a generalization can call it into question or modify it. Filling out a variable—d in the example—does not achieve concreteness: it is still just a measurable quantity with no concrete qualities. Angus therefore concludes that the attempt to infuse natural science with the content of aesthetic perception is doomed to fail.

Indeed, there is no way back from the geographer's "source" to the "springhead in the dale." But the "source" is a construction that can be defined in terms of the values associated with the vernacular concept of a "springhead." For example, the purity of the water can be identified as a significant aspect of the construction and appropriate means mobilized to measure and eventually protect that characteristic. Such measures thus carry with them an implicit normative content in the lifeworld: pure water is better than polluted water. There is a connection between the two objects—the experiential and the scientific—but this is a connection established by translation, not through a merger of

---

46 Ian Angus, "Galilean Science and the Technological Lifeworld: The Role of Husserl's Crisis in Herbert Marcuse's Thesis of One-Dimensionality," in *Symposium* 21, no. 2 (Fall 2017): 133–59. I would like to thank Ian Angus for giving me access to the manuscript of his new book on phenomenological Marxism: Ian Angus, *Groundwork of Phenomenological Marxism: Crisis, Body, World* (Lanham: Lexington Books, 2021).

incompatible attitudes toward nature. The translation relates the scientific calculation of contaminants in the water to vernacular expressions of the human suffering and the violation of nature. These two linguistic forms are not equivalent, nor can the first replace the second.

This is evident in the case of climate change. The science predicts civilizational disaster in numerical calculations and graphs. Those extrapolations are neutral, in the sense that they are equally useful to investors seeking profits from climate change and the public seeking climate mitigation.[47] And, as Marcuse explains, that neutrality favors what Adorno calls "the big guns," the investors rather than the public.

Yet something has changed that Marcuse did not anticipate. Science has not transcended its limits. Rather, its focus has evolved in response to social concern for a livable world. A new "project" intervenes that does not correspond to the imperatives of capitalism. It is articulated in public opinion, protests, and philosophical reflection and translated by the science on scientific terms. The translation modifies the object of the science to include aspects formerly ignored or downplayed. In doing so, it creates an implicit reference to public concerns. However, science can only track the issues; it cannot dictate a response. In itself, out of a social context, it has no normative implications.

Clearly, we need both interpretations of nature, the scientific and the nonscientific. Science alone is not enough, for its explanations abstract from the human meaning of its object. The statement "My C fibers are firing" is not equivalent to "I am in pain." One is a statement of fact based on a scientific abstraction; the other is also a call for help and implies a concrete social context absent from neurobiology. Where two such propositions meet, as in medicine or ecology, next "goes the doing," as Marcuse says in his discussion of the existential meaning of truth.[48] The "doing," the medical or environmental intervention,

---

47 As one mainstream commentator on *The Limits to Growth* wrote with respect to its predictions of civilizational collapse, "Conceivably, if you believe their predictions of extremely short time spans before the exhaustion of resources, there are many speculative killings to be made." Leonard Silk, "Questions Must Be Raised about the Immanence of Disaster," *New York Times*, March 13, 1972, 35.

48 "The world is an estranged and untrue world so long as man does not destroy its dead objectivity and recognize himself and his own life 'behind' the fixed form of things

follows from reflection on the situation revealed and explained by science, but only if the objects of science are appropriately constructed by a consciousness attuned to what Marcuse calls the "life instincts."

I need to make one final point, lest it seem that philosophy adds only "values" to a world adequately described by science. Science and experience both arise from the infinite complexity of the lifeworld, but they focus on different aspects. The fact that they share the same source should enable communication between them. Marcuse worries that this communication has broken down and only those aspects retained by science are considered real. In this situation, the surplus of experiential meaning reflected in the categories of philosophy and art is rejected, while values appear subjective and scientific abstractions are identified with being as such. Restoring the epistemic status of concrete experience, he argues, is therefore essential to full understanding.

An Experiment

As we have seen, Marcuse fails to find a plausible concretization of physics, and with that, his strategy in the philosophical revision of reason falls. His political argument concerning technology fares better, but, with the exception of management science, he omits an essential mediation: the many socially embedded scientific-technical disciplines that shape the technified world of advanced capitalism. Disciplines such as medicine, accounting, meteorology, nursing, architecture, interior and product design, dietetics, criminology, urban planning, automotive, traffic, and civil engineering, computer science, and many more are the foundation of what I call the "technosystem" that organizes modern life.[49] The critical theory of these disciplines, and

---

and laws. When he finally wins this self-consciousness, he is on his way not only to the truth of himself, but also of his world. And with the recognition *goes the doing*. He will try to put this truth into action and make the world what it essentially is, namely, the fulfillment of man's self-consciousness." Herbert Marcuse, *Reason and Revolution: Hegel and the Rise of Social Theory* (Boston: Beacon Press, 1960), 113, my italics.

49 Andrew Feenberg, *Technosystem: The Social Life of Reason* (Cambridge, MA: Harvard University Press, 2017), 32–5.

especially the medical and environmental sciences, reveals another more plausible way of achieving Marcuse's new concept of reason.

The difference has to do with the range of considerations these socially embedded disciplines translate. Where physics responds to a narrow range of practical relations to the world, corresponding to the poverty of the primary qualities, these disciplines contend with manifold relations in many different registers. They can achieve "concreteness" in something like a Hegelian-Marxist sense, as a synthesis of many determinations, if not through a return to the immediate or a final totality. Traversed by multiple considerations, they evolve by translating a wide range of objects.[50] These translations are objectifications in Marx's sense of the term. As we saw in chapter 2, Marcuse's interpretation of the *Manuscripts* emphasized the objectification of meaning in artifacts which thereby reflect human capacities and needs. Between 1844 and the present, work has been transformed by the intervention of these scientific-technical disciplines. The objects of these disciplines constitute the meanings that are objectified, which now reflect not just generic capacities and needs but a way of life embodied in the design of the built world. Public interventions into the objects of these disciplines, that is, into the meanings they intend, translate between the "narrower" and the "wider" nature, between scientific nature and the nature of the lifeworld. In turn, the choice among those objects determines their relation to "the recovery of the life-enhancing forces in nature."[51] Marcuse calls this the "materialization" of values in technological design. It is in the critique of these disciplines that Marcuse's philosophical and political concerns meet. Through political struggles, modern artifacts must acquire a logos.

In the remainder of this chapter, I will try an experiment with Marcuse's concepts. Let us apply his notions of translation and successor science, potentiality and the dialectical concrete, formal, and substantive universals, not to physics but to the scientific-technical disciplines that actually organize life today. This is a departure from the Husserlian background of Marcuse's critique of science. The focus will no longer be on physics, but on the structures of the disciplines that shape

---

50 Andrew Feenberg, *Critical Theory of Technology* (New York: Oxford University Press, 1991), 191–5.

51 Marcuse, "Nature and Revolution," 60.

society. This will allow me to show both the limits and the relevance of his approach.

The limits are obvious. For example, consider the tremendous development of research in science and technology studies since Marcuse's day, providing a wealth of sociological detail crossing the boundary between science and society.[52] I will allude to some of that detail in what follows. Marcuse's claim that modern science has been shaped by capitalism is a philosophical anticipation of the constructivist critique of "technoscience," according to which natural science cannot be separated from the social forces that influence its development and govern its applications.[53] "Technoscience" signifies that commercial and political considerations play a central role not only in technical fields but also in the sciences.

While constructivism has entered philosophy primarily around epistemological issues, its implications for social philosophy are equally significant. Feminist and postcolonial scholars have demonstrated the gender and racial bias of science and technology, arguing that the exclusion of these groups has epistemic consequences.[54] Marcuse's phenomenologically inspired approach makes a similar argument for the human being as such. Discrimination is not only an issue of gender and race but also takes the form of the systematic exclusion of ordinary people, the users and victims of technology, from a role in the design of the technified world in which they live. Marcuse thus enables us to enlarge the range of research to embrace the many

---

52 Feenberg, *Technosystem*, chapter 2.

53 Andrew Feenberg, "Technoscience and the Dereification of Nature," *Filosofia Unisinos* 21, no. 1 (January–April 2020): 5–13. The term "technoscience" is controversial. For alternative definitions, see the essays in Alfred Nordmann, Hans Radder, and Gregor Schiemann, eds., *Science Transformed? Debating Claims of an Epochal Break* (Pittsburgh: University of Pittsburgh Press, 2011.) The reluctance of the practitioners in these fields to call themselves "technoscientists" suggests that there is a useful distinction between science and technology despite the mutual dependence. Basic science is pursued in far more sheltered institutions than most technology, and while social forces do affect it, they usually do so indirectly. Technical fields are more deeply embedded in the social world.

54 Sandra Harding, *The Science Question in Feminism* (Ithaca: Cornell University Press, 1986). Sandra Harding, *The "Racial" Economy of Science: Toward a Democratic Future* (Bloomington: Indiana University Press, 1993).

emancipatory struggles over science and technology that challenge this exclusion.[55]

The connection between science and society Marcuse established on phenomenological grounds is now verified empirically in science and technology studies. For instance, Michel Callon and his collaborators have studied the role of social struggles over science and technology in orienting research in several fields.[56] Sheila Jasanoff has developed a similar theory of "co-production" of knowledge and society.[57] Perhaps the contribution most closely resembling Marcuse's views is the theory of "postnormal" science of Silvio Funtowicz and Jerome Ravetz, who argue that the sciences I refer to as "socially embedded" involve uncertainty and risk, in contradistinction to Kuhn's "normal science." They note the changed situation of science in a highly technified society and focus on public contestation of the disciplines. According to them, no paradigm establishes a consensus under these unprecedented circumstances—a development that has had a destabilizing effect, as now values intervene in scientific practice. In response, they advocate for an "extended peer community," including multiple disciplines and public stakeholders.[58]

Katharine Farrell argues that "postnormal science can be interpreted as a manifestation of the new modality of science predicted by Marcuse."[59] Translated into Marcuse's philosophical language, similarities do appear. For one, the reference to public stakeholders suggests the return of the lifeworld as a source of valid knowledge. Also, the difficulty of separating facts from values relates to the

---

55 For more on the relation of Marcuse's work to science and technology studies, see Andrew Feenberg, *Heidegger and Marcuse: The Catastrophe and Redemption of History* (New York: Routledge, 2005), 103–6.

56 Michel Callon, Pierre Lascoumes, and Yannick Barthe, *Acting in an Uncertain World: An Essay on Technical Democracy* (Cambridge, MA: MIT Press, 2009.)

57 Sheila Jasanoff, ed., *States of Knowledge: The Co-production of Science and Social Order* (New York: Routledge, 2004.)

58 Silvio Funtowicz and Jerome Ravetz, "A New Scientific Methodology for Global Environmental Issues," in *Ecological Economics: The Science and Management of Sustainability*, ed. Robert Costanza (New York: Columbia University Press, 1991), 137–52.

59 Katharine Farrell, "The Politics of Science and Sustainable Development: Marcuse's New Science in the 21st Century," *Capitalism Nature Socialism* 19, no. 4 (2008): 82.

uncertainty of the attributions of potentialities to the phenomena. Thus, as Marcuse wrote in *One-Dimensional Man*, science must become political. Farrell writes, "The production of good quality postnormal science needs to be supported by a structured combination of scientific knowledge production and political discourse."[60] She believes that Marcuse would have approved of the methodology of postnormal science, as applied to contentious issues such as cloning, climate change, and nanotechnology.

I would go further and argue that "postnormality" applies wherever disciplines have immediate effects on the social world and vice versa. The socially embedded disciplines serve valuative dimensions of experience inscribed in the objects they construct. This is quite different from the ghostly universe of matter in motion, bleached white like Melville's whale, that troubles Marcuse.

The term "technoscience" is appropriately applied to some of these disciplines. This is not simply a question of the technical applications of theoretical knowledge, itself generated by technical instruments. The deep connection between theory and technology has been known since Galileo, at least to scientists if not always to philosophers of science. What is new is the disappearance of the gap between theory and applications, or rather, the formation of a chiasmus that implicates each in the other. This is most obvious in fields such as pharmaceutical research, where the science and the commercial product emerge simultaneously from the lab—the research *is* the technological application. Compounds are run through tests, which add to knowledge of their properties while also identifying their commercial prospects as medicines. Other sciences are directly implicated in changed public attitudes and practices that are then translated into new scientific objects and technologies.

A growing number of disciplines similar to the technosciences participate in the technification of society without actually being sciences in the proper sense of the term. For instance, management science and other disciplines of social control emulate science without the requisite methodological basis. They construct a tissue of formal concepts and purported causal relations that apply to social institutions and individuals, while a questionable use of quantification and experiment offers a veneer of scientificity. Unlike the natural sciences, these

---

60 Ibid., 73.

disciplines have immediate and unintended causal impacts on their objects. For example, some versions of management science encourage behaviors and attitudes on the part of management that generate the need for management. Similarly, public awareness of the science of psychology has changed the psychology of modern individuals.

Despite the dissolution of the New Left in the 1970s, in recent years so much resistance has emerged to policies governing a wide range of these socially embedded disciplines that Marcuse's dystopian fears no longer seem justified. And, contrary to his expectations, the real, historically active challenge does not involve physical science but the many disciplines that are actually at issue in social struggles. Recognition of the threats generated by the externalities of industry defies the one-dimensional reduction of experience and activates the perception of potentialities relevant to human well-being. Experiential nature thus emerges amid the world of technology, as Benjamin supposed, but it does so negatively—not as pristine but as damaged and dangerous.

As we saw in chapter 4, Marcuse was aware of the emerging environmental movement of the 1970s and discussed it positively in two late speeches.[61] His argument is primarily political and references the Freudian war between eros and thanatos. Capitalism is a destructive force that is countered by "the politicization of erotic energy" in defense of nature and a peaceful and fulfilling life. The erotic world relation that environmentalism must restore is the capacity to recognize our participation in the natural world through revulsion at its destruction and recognition of its beauty.

These speeches show that Marcuse's focus on aesthetics belonged to a larger project that could have applied not just to physics but to all the sciences implicated in modern society. Aesthetics signified the life-affirming impulses denied by the existing society and determining for scientific-technical development under socialism.[62] Today, a normative concept of life challenges the technified world. The climate movement, discussed later in this chapter, is the contemporary nexus between this

---

61 Herbert Marcuse, "Ecology and Revolution," in *The New Left and the 1960s*, ed. Douglas Kellner (London: Routledge 2005), 173–6; Herbert Marcuse, "Ecology and the Critique of Modern Society," in *Philosophy, Psychoanalysis, and Emancipation*, ed. Douglas Kellner, 206–13.

62 Ibid., 212.

notion of aesthetics and the politics of technology. Despite Marcuse's difficulties articulating his insight in a form we can accept today, our situation reveals just how prescient he was.

His very prescience raises a question: Why did Marcuse not extend his critique to all the scientific-technical disciplines that engage the social world, as we would be inclined to do? After all, the various disciplines that address the social and natural environment reveal dimensions of reality hidden to physics. Marcuse's phenomenological approach could have validated the multiplicity of truths revealed by these disciplines, but instead, he persisted in his vision of a future transformation of physics that was supposed to be able to encompass that multiplicity.[63]

I think the answer has to do with the role of physics as the paradigmatic science, the transformation of which would have the most far-reaching significance. Ever since Kant's first *Critique*, physics has been the model of pure reason. During and after World War II, it played a dramatic role in the world, commensurate with its philosophical significance. Indeed, it seemed that the most basic natural science was also the ultimate source of the most basic social problems. Perhaps those problems could be addressed by infusing science with the imaginative resources of art.

Given the exorbitant prestige of physics and the weakness of social struggles over science and technology, such a notion was plausible in the period in which Marcuse developed his ideas. Back then, the principal protest movement that addressed issues of science and technology demanded nuclear disarmament. Although influential with academics, this movement was quite small in the United States.[64] Neither medicine nor the environment were prominent on the agenda of public discussion when Marcuse developed his critique of science and technology.

---

63 For a discussion of multiplicity in this sense, see Lorraine Daston, "Toward a History of Reason," in *Aurora Torealis: Studies in the History of Science and Ideas in Honor of Tore Frängsmyr*, ed. Marco Beretta et al. (Sagamore Beach: Science History Publications, 2008), 165–80.

64 The critical spirit of the times is exemplified by Federico Fellini's great film of 1960, *La Dolce Vita*. The film depicts the corrosive effects of consumer capitalism on art, while also staging the technology issue through a character who kills himself and his children over despair at the prospect of nuclear war. See Andrew Feenberg, *Alternative Modernity: The Technical Turn in Philosophy and Social Theory* (Los Angeles: University of California Press, 1995), chapter 3.

Later, small movements of radical professionals in science, engineering, medicine, and planning were inspired by the New Left, but Marcuse failed to theorize their significance as innovative attempts to create successor sciences in their fields.[65] In his estimation, the reconstruction of scientific reason was a task for a distant socialist future. In the meantime, he focused on more relevant contemporary movements against war and racial and gender discrimination. I see this as a significant missed opportunity.

The next sections will consider an alternative application of Marcuse's concepts of successor science and translation to disciplines such as medicine and climate science. I will argue that potentialities can enter these disciplines through the construction of their objects, if not as aesthetic data—in sum, as meanings rather than as facts. In this context, Marcuse's aesthetic concept of life affirmation suggests the possibility of revolutionary scientific change.

Object Construction

In chapter 3, I argued that Marcuse follows the precedent of ancient philosophy in relating ethical values to rationality, the logos. He cites the association of art and technique, both of which are signified by the term "technē" in ancient Greek. The point of this reference to the Greeks is not to prove the validity of values but to show that they are or should be conceived as potentialities guiding technical practice.

Plato claims that the authentic craftsman is guided by a logos, a meaning or purpose.[66] In the case of medicine, the logos consists in the idea of health and the means of providing it. Plato distinguishes a proper technē such as medicine from a mere collection of rules of thumb such as "cookery," which lacks a logos but pretends to provide the good of the body. Technē is based on knowledge of its object, and that knowledge is normative insofar as it includes the object's potentialities—that is, health. Neutral means that are indifferent to any proper end are employed by fakers, such as orators and makeup artists, who

---

65 Lily Hoffman, *The Politics of Knowledge: Activist Movements in Medicine and Planning* (Albany: State University of New York Press, 1989).

66 Plato, *Gorgias,* trans. W. C. Helmbold (Indianapolis: Bobbs-Merrill, 1952), 23–4.

profit from simulacra of the achievements of moral argument and healthy exercise.

In one respect, Plato's theory is quite modern, although he formulates it objectivistically, not in our neo-Kantian terms. Still, it is not difficult to see that he is actually explaining the construction of the object of a technical discipline by distinguishing the "true" object from a false simulacrum. The very fact that he must make this distinction suggests the role of subjectivity in the process. Today, we would not hesitate to reference the constructive activity of the subject of knowledge. The object of medicine is not simply there, out in the world, waiting to be discovered like the bones of the dinosaurs; rather, it is actively constructed through experiments, conjectures, and choices. Such rational procedures produce a meaningful object worthy of study, a true object in Plato's sense as opposed to seductive nonsense. The true object embodies the logos of the science through its definition and boundaries.

In chapter 5, I showed that Husserl, Heidegger, and Marcuse share the modern notion of object construction as it applies to science and technology. Like Plato, they hold that each field of research defines a specific kind of object through its methods and concepts. Physics studies matter in motion, while biology considers organisms, and so on. In one sense, this is obvious, but these philosophers regard such definitions as only the beginning of a far more detailed specification of the way in which a certain cross section of reality is carved out for investigation. And they contend that one such cross section has acquired ontological significance in modern society as the very definition of the real: the object of physics now prevails as being as such.

Kant argued that the connection between science and being depends on a "transcendental" subject. He invented the transcendental approach, which he explained as an operation the subject performs on the givens of experience. Transcendental forms, he famously demonstrated, were imposed by the mind on the raw content of sensations. Those forms correspond to the objects of mathematics, geometry, and Newtonian physics. The basic categories of science structure the very world science explains.

In Kant, the transcendental is universal and timeless, a constant feature of all possible experience. But Husserl, Heidegger, and Marcuse agree that the forms are changeable, their universality confined to a specific historical period. Husserl identified the Renaissance as the decisive turning point in epistemic history, and Heidegger calls the succession of forms "the history of being." Marcuse, for his part, attributes the changes to the evolution of modes of production. In all these cases, an anonymous historical process rather than an individual mind is responsible for the imposition of form on content. This approach should therefore be called "quasi-transcendental," since the source of the forms is time bound and, in Marcuse's case, inner-worldly.

In *One-Dimensional Man*, a phenomenologically inspired critique of the object of physics explains the prevailing concept of reason. Marcuse draws on Husserl's notion that the source of the scientific concepts lies in the refinement of ideas and practices circulating in the lifeworld. Since the capitalist lifeworld is oriented toward the domination and exploitation of human beings and nature, science has taken up this practical heritage in its conceptual structure. According to Marcuse, it does not translate any specific social practice but rather refines certain general practices of manipulating physical objects. In a capitalist context, the practices it privileges are those such as measurement and prediction that can be quantified and formalized. In turn, a science rooted in these elementary practices can serve in the unrestrained manipulation of human beings and nature.

As Marcuse points out, these are not the only technical practices. Throughout most of history, technique required careful cultivation, craft skills, and artistic ability—all forms of recognition of the potentialities of the materials. What Husserl calls "Galilean" science gives power over the things it explains while eliminating any such notion of potentiality that might guide recognitive interaction with them. This object construction flows from reification, that is, the general condition of instrumental action under capitalism: control through the laws of the phenomena. Under capitalism, this feature of science is deployed without measure. "In this project," Marcuse writes, "universal quantifiability is a prerequisite for the *domination* of nature."[67]

I argue that science cannot be redeemed by the introduction of potentialities as a new form of data, nor is it possible to revert generally to earlier forms of technical practices. Control belongs to the essence of

---

67 Marcuse, "On Science and Technology," in *Philosophy, Psychoanalysis and Emancipation*, 164.

modern science, but it can be contextualized by potentialities in the object constructions of the socially embedded discipline, for example, in medicine. As Plato argued, medicine is a science based on potentialities, although how they enter into the science depends on the cultural context.

Let us consider briefly the various ways in which medicine constructs its object. Medicine does not just apply technical principles to the body in its immediacy, but rather organizes those principles around a specific conception of the body as an object. That conception, based on "humors" in Plato's time, differed from the cosmic conception of the Chinese, the modern mechanical conception, and so on. The anthropologist Claude Levi-Strauss, describes an indigenous medical system that employs a spoken narrative of the patient's struggle with the disease. Curative objects, what we call "medicines," are simply props in the story recounted to the patient. What could be more alien to our notion of scientific medicine? Yet the "symbolic efficacy" of such story-telling is attested to by those it heals.[68]

Modern medicine, too, comes loaded with implicit valuative content that does not depend on the subjective desiderata of a user but flows from cultural beliefs and practices inscribed in a conception of the medical body. In contrast with these earlier healing arts, valuative content now takes a modern scientific form. For example, health and sickness are signified by a blood test through a list of quantities of various parameters: how much vitamin B12, how much creatinine, and so on. There is nothing "human" about those results which look no different from any other list of objective measurements, but within the science of medicine, the test measures only parameters that correspond to the well-being of the human body as a living whole. Literally millions of other parameters could be measured, but these are the ones that make a difference in terms of a value—health—and they define the medical body.

Unlike the object of physics, which relates to pure instrumentality in physical systems, the object of medicine contains an implicit life-affirming teleological reference. In this context health, the logos of medicine, appears as a potentiality of the human body *within* the science.

---

68 Claude Levi-Strauss, *Structural Anthropology*, trans. Claire Jacobson and Brooke G. Schoepf (New York: McGraw-Hill, 1968), 198.

The Structure of Technoscientific Revolutions

Today, to a far greater extent than in Marcuse's time, the "existential truth" now intervenes to introduce new objects of science reflecting potentialities that were formerly ignored. Fields such as medicine, computer science, engineering, and ecology are more and more constrained to construct their objects in terms of norms imposed by social movements, regulation, and public opinion without abandoning scientific methods. The interactions between experience and the socially embedded disciplines thus engage a mutual co-construction.

The process of critique and reconstruction reflects a particular historical situation. Technology and the socially embedded disciplines have evolved over several centuries in a capitalist environment—one in which the elaboration of specialized knowledges was influenced by the concerns of capitalist owners and their representatives.[69] As a result, the disciplines developed blind spots, clashing with the needs of workers and communities who were excluded from the process.

Only in the lifeworld do the undesirable effects of the bias of the disciplines become visible. Interestingly, Plato once again anticipates our current notions. In *The Republic*, he writes, "It follows, then, that the user must know most about the performance of the thing he uses and must report on its good or bad points to the maker."[70] Users—and, it must be added, victims—of technical arrangements bring to light phenomena hidden to "makers" and through their protests inspire progressive development.

This dynamic justifies intrusions into the world of science that violate its presumed autonomy. This was, in fact, the role of workers' protests in stimulating Marx's radical transformation of economic science. Indeed, one could argue that *Capital* is the original successor social science. Marcuse attempted to prolong the Marxian critique to sketch the outlines of a future successor natural science. I have argued that he was not successful in this project; nevertheless, his critique of Weber's theory of rationalization does extend the Marxian approach to the modern social sciences.

---

69 Jean-Baptiste Fressoz, *L'apocalypse Joyeuse* (Paris: Le Seuil, 2012).

70 Plato, *The Republic of Plato*, trans. F. M. Cornford (New York: Oxford University Press, 1960), 332.

There is a significant difference between Marcuse's critiques of natural science and the socially embedded science of management he discusses in his essay on Weber. While both critiques apply the notion of object construction, the latter is concerned not with being as such but with the specific region of being constituted by organized human activity. Within that region, a particular object—capitalist management—is taken up and formatted for rational investigation. The capitalist requirement of control from above is reified, treated as a natural constraint, although it is historically contingent on the separation of workers from the means of production. The critique uncovers the hidden presuppositions of management in capitalist society: namely, the translation of particular social practices into the object of a technical discipline. In turn, such translation opens a domain of objective research while biasing its results.

What is true of management science applies equally to many other socially embedded disciplines. They are based on particular patterns of behavior and particular attitudes observed in the everyday life of society. Refined and formalized, these vernacular materials are translated into technical concepts and an object construction. They apply scientific methods to discover "calculable, predictable relationships" in the context of various regional ontologies reflecting diverse aspects of social life. Although they claim the same neutral status as natural science, their bias is due to specific features of capitalist social relations taken up into their objects. By contrast, natural science depends on no specific feature of capitalism; its bias depends on a selection among the several types of generic instrumental relations.

Just as Marcuse criticizes Weber's theory of rationalization, so critical researchers in these fields expose the hidden socioeconomic constraints that reify the objects of their disciplines. The critique opens up new objects of research reflecting neglected potentialities. The researchers remain within the general framework of their discipline, but they subordinate the application of scientific methods to the social demands translated by these new objects. The new objects are formally indistinguishable from the neutral objects of physics, but their specific construction places them in the service of potentialities their disciplinary tradition has neglected in the past.

Writing a bit later than Marcuse, Foucault formulated the new situation of professionals in contested fields such as these. He introduced the concept of the "specific intellectual" to signify resistance *in* the sciences. Unlike traditional "universal" intellectuals, the public activities of specific intellectuals are based on normative concerns arising from a position in the technical division of labor.[71] Foucault mentions, for instance, J. Robert Oppenheimer, who led the creation of the atom bomb and then called for disarmament and world government to deal with the consequences. A similar case could be made today with respect to the many computer professionals who contributed to the creation of the internet and now struggle to redesign it in accordance with ethical and democratic principles.[72]

The success of these scientific dissenters in reshaping their discipline often depends on public pressure. Science and society meet through public protest and dialogue, policy and translation. Although institutionally differentiated, they form a single whole that cannot be disaggregated into mechanically separated parts. Co-construction, the interaction of the public with the sciences, transgresses the differentiation of theory and practice in the translation between scientific objects, technology, and vernacular understanding. In turn, the vernacular uptake of theoretical knowledge leads to a richer conception of the object and improved technological designs in function of public concerns.

In this way, science responds to properly epistemic questions posed by researchers while simultaneously addressing other questions posed by corporations, governments, and the public. And, as Isabelle Stengers argues, these are all legitimate questions responding to different concerns and different understandings of nature.[73] As the environmental movement has shown, they can often be reconciled around the reconstruction of the research object and the corresponding technologies.

This understanding of science gives new meaning to Husserl's claim that the essence of science is method, not a one-dimensional ontology.

---

71 Michel Foucault, *Power/Knowledge*, trans. Colin Gordon et al. (New York: Pantheon, 1980), 127–8.

72 I participated in a 2019 Dagstuhl seminar on "Values in Computing." The report gives an idea of the preoccupations of many computer professionals today. Christoph Becker et al., eds., "Values in Computing," *Dagstuhl Reports* 9, no. 7 (2019): 40–77, available at drops.dagstuhl.de.

73 Isabelle Stengers and Thierry Drumm, *Une autre science est possible!* (Paris: La Découverte, 2013), 129–34.

There is no one foundation to which everything can be reduced, no singular truth of the whole. Marcuse's ambition to derive a new concept of reason from a transformation of natural science was misguided. A multitude of objects have emerged in public consciousness, each with different properties and demands. Technoscience introduces a polyphony of reasons corresponding to these objects, making possible a fruitful interaction of value and fact, "existential" and "mathematical" truth.

Interaction between experience and science orients scientific work and answers Marcuse's requirement that science recover a notion of potentiality. But can we call such transformations of the technosciences "revolutions" in Kuhn's sense of the term? While they do not change scientific method as radically as Kuhn's examples, they do change the scientific notion of the "sorts of entities the universe . . . contain[s]."[74] This has provoked many small "revolutions" in the socially embedded disciplines.

Communicating Rationalities

In this section, I will argue that the concept of rationality must be revised to account for the role of translation in object construction. Technical and everyday language constitute two different instances of rationality. They are not incommensurable but, on the contrary, communicate frequently, despite having radically different presuppositions. Communication between them is essential for the well-being of both science and society, and has particular relevance to environmental issues.

The nature environmentalists hope to protect is the one in which we all participate: the experiential nature encountered in everyday life. It has a teleological aspect science does not recognize, yet it depends for its well-being on scientific and technical knowledge that is itself imbricated in language and history.

"Pollution," for example, was at first a sacred category. Purified of normative content by scientists studying the environment, the term came to represent the presence of certain chemical compounds in air and water. This scientific concept of "pollution" is no longer just a technical concept but has entered the vernacular. There, it once again

---

74 Kuhn, *Structure of Scientific Revolutions*, 7.

receives normative content. Nature is now conceived as sick or healthy, abused or protected, and not simply as nonsocial "stuff" available to study or use as a resource. In other words, its condition is evaluated in terms of potentialities that serve as normative criteria.

It is a paralogism to contrast these potentialities, reduced to values, directly with the scientific facts. The former are not "subjective" and the latter "objective." Correctly understood, there is complementarity between science and the lifeworld. They relate to the same reality and employ similar concepts to articulate its meaning. For example, the very term "potentiality," which plays such an important role for Marcuse, has a scientific equivalent: "potential energy." Potential energy is energy that is latent but can be released, for example, by a change of position. There is certainly some common intuition behind both the philosophical and the scientific concept of potential, but they have subtly different meanings, and the difference is important.

Potential energy can be quantified, but only because it trades precision and lawfulness for the freedom that gives potentiality (in the philosophical sense) a relation to the new, to the transcendence of the given. Furthermore, potential energy, like every other scientific concept, is void of intrinsic teleological intent.[75] If only the scientific concept is considered valid, then it becomes difficult to articulate the demand for social change, which appears now as a mere subjective "value." However, from Marcuse's standpoint, that so-called value is the trace in one-dimensional language of the potential for a new organization of the society.

In practice, respect for potentialities is translated into scientific-technical language in order to engage the technical systems of a modern society in preservation and repair. The interaction of lay and expert shows that the barrier between common sense and modern science is not absolute.

Consider the example of the water crisis that began in 2014 in Flint, Michigan.[76] The presence of lead in the municipal water supply became known through a combination of direct observation of color and smell and through testing by a scientist who aided the community. The scientist

---

75 Henri Atlan, *Tout, Non, Peut-Être: Éducation et Vérité* (Paris: Le Seuil, 1991), 121–3. See also Feenberg, *Technosystem*, chapter 7.

76 Carla Campbell, Rachael Greenberg, Deepa Mankikar, and Ronald D. Ross, "A Case Study of Environmental Injustice: The Failure in Flint," *International Journal of Environmental Research and Public Health* 13, no. 10 (October 2016): 951.

was able to give the residents a cause and a name for their foul water: "lead." But lead as he tested for it, if not in his personal understanding, was simply an element on the periodic chart with a specific atomic weight, valence, and so on. To the members of the community, in contrast, lead was a threatening invader and a symptom of racial discrimination.

The same object, "lead," crossed the boundary between science and everyday understanding. It had two different lives: a scientific life as an element and an experiential life in which it played the role of threat to "normal" human development, that is, to the realization of human potential—specifically the potential of the growing brains of the city's children.[77] It is in this sense that, as Marcuse writes, there are not only "mathematical truths" but also "existential truths" of nature.

Bridges can be built between the two truths around concepts such as "health" and "security"—substantive universals to which the formal universals of science correspond.[78] Such concepts enable communication between different discourses. Their effect is to translate values into facts, discursively formulated demands into new technical specifications. In turn, the public translates scientific and technical concepts into everyday language in order to articulate a discontent, and bridging concepts make that discontent comprehensible to technical experts, who then translate it into specifications of a modified technical system or artifact. These are incomplete halves of a dialogue between the public and the experts who represent its interests in technical fields. The complete circuit drives scientific-technical development forward toward normative goals.

The notion of dialogue suggests a peaceful colloquy around a seminar table, but in reality, the dialogue between science and society is often conflictual. Neither science nor society is a unified subject, and their disagreements may cross the boundaries within and between them. In some cases, reconciliation is possible through innovations

---

77 This is an extension of the concept of "boundary object" developed in science and technology studies, according to which objects can be shared in certain cases between lay and scientific personnel in the course of research. Susan Leigh Star and James R. Griesemer, "Institutional Ecology, 'Translations,' and Boundary Objects: Amateurs and Professionals in Berkeley's Museum of Vertebrate Zoology, 1907–39," *Social Studies of Science* 19, no. 3 (1989): 387–420.

78 David Hess calls these interactions "object conflicts." David J. Hess, "Technology- and Product-Oriented Movements: Approximating Social Movement Studies and Science and Technology Studies," *Science, Technology, and Human Values* 30, no. 4 (2005): 515–35.

that concretize functions and ally corresponding actors—as with the outcome of the struggle over AIDS research. In other cases, one or another actor prevails and orients the development of technology toward its exclusive goals—as was the case with nuclear power in the United States. I will illustrate these two cases in what follows.

In the 1980s, infection with the virus that causes AIDS was almost universally fatal. Patients' only hope was participation in clinical research, but opportunities to participate were strictly limited. Paternalistic concern for dying patients excluded them from access on the grounds that they could not freely consent to participate.

AIDS patients entered the medical arena at the height of a major political organizing drive in the gay community. Given the mobilization of energies around social and political rights during the preceding decade, they were better equipped to resist paternalism than any previous group of patients. These energies were turned on the medical system, and networks of protest, patient education, and support arose on a scale never before seen in connection with any other disease.

This led to conflicts between patients, treated as mere research subjects, and the scientists involved in research on their disease. In addition to vociferous protests orchestrated by the AIDS Coalition to Unleash Power (ACT UP), some patients in the studies refused to serve as controls, taking their pills to a lab to uncover their status. Noncompliance thus became a serious problem.

Fortunately, an accommodation was found. The US Food and Drug Administration responded to the pressure by offering patients with incurable disease wider access to experimental therapies. The patients thus succeeded in changing both the procedures and the concept of the object of clinical research, namely, people like themselves. The experimental "subject" was no longer simply an object of scientific manipulation and observation but was to be treated also as a patient and an informant. This was a "revolution" in clinical research that has effects to this day.[79] It should be emphasized that research continues successfully under the new system.

---

79 Steven Epstein, *Impure Science* (Berkeley: University of California Press, 1996). Andrew Feenberg, "On Being a Human Subject: AIDS and the Crisis of Experimental Medicine," in *Alternative Modernity: The Technical Turn in Philosophy and Social Theory* (Los Angeles: University of California Press, 1995), 96–120.

In this case, differing concepts of universal validity were at stake. The pursuit of truth as science conceived it violated patients' expectations. Different epistemologies and values engaged in conflict and compromise.[80] Each party to the conflict perceived the other as merely "particular," biased by interests or prejudices. Yet each could claim a portion of the whole, that is, what we finite humans use for truth. The situation is similar in some respects to competing gender struggles in which conflicting claims must find a resolution. As Judith Butler writes,

> The question for such movements will not be how to relate a particular claim to one that is universal, where the universal is figured as anterior to the particular, and where the presumption is that a logical incommensurability governs the relation between the two terms. It may be, rather, one of establishing *practices of translation* among competing notions of universality which, despite any apparent logical incompatibility, may nevertheless belong to an overlapping set of social and political aims.[81]

Where this logic operates, co-construction becomes the basis for reconciliation around new and improved policies.

However, reconciliation is not always possible. The struggle between actors with different priorities, differently situated in the lifeworld, may be reflected in fundamentally incompatible design choices. Capitalists imposed their priorities on industrial technology with little interference from the public until fairly recently. Their achievements were once celebrated, and often rightly so. But many of those very same achievements now appear as threats. Such cases call for fundamental change in technological trajectories. Scientific-technical experts have to revise their approach, and in doing so they become key allies in the struggle to transform the technologies they created.

Take the case of nuclear power, a spectacular achievement of modern science whose meaning has changed over the years. At first, it signified the transcendence of natural constraints and promised to enrich the

---

80 For an example, see Feenberg, *Technosystem*, 60–1.

81 Judith Butler, Ernesto Laclau, and Slavoj Žižek, *Contingency, Hegemony, Universality: Contemporary Dialogues on the Left* (London: Verso, 2000), 167.

world with "unmetered power." The nuclear industry declared, "The atom is your friend!"[82] This was Progress with a capital *P*. But, after several serious accidents garnered mass publicity, nuclear power came to be seen as a source of terrifying and insidious dangers. Nature no longer threatened us with wolves and landslides but with invisible radiation emanating from human activity. The value of Security canceled the value of Progress. In the United States, this change in meaning has led to the decline of the technology.

These examples show that public actors have begun to play a role in forcing changes in the inherited technology—a proposition that the climate change movement further illustrates.

The Logos of the Environment

In 1896, the chemist Svante Arrhenius explained the mechanism and consequences of the greenhouse effect. "Ecology," a term introduced in 1866 by the famed zoologist Ernst Haeckel, took off in the 1930s when botanist Arthur Tansley developed the concept of the ecosystem. It is startling to realize how long ago the theoretical concepts were available to predict and forestall the climate crisis we are living today. Yet, even now, when the evidence is clear and compelling and the practical implications of environmental disaster apparent, the necessary measures are taken only grudgingly where they are taken at all. What is the reason for this signal failure of a civilization that prides itself on its rationality?

The obstacle is the disjunction between economic rationality and ecological rationality. Corporations make most of the investments in technology in accordance with the former, while nature operates in accordance with the latter, indifferent to corporate balance sheets. After much resistance and hesitation, business has conceded that something must be done to address the crisis, but corporations are bound by the long-term momentum of their tradition, and by the short-term logic of depreciation and the discount rate. Past investments in environmentally unsustainable technologies and the associated skills still

---

82 In high school, I received an award as the best chemistry student in my town. Included in my award was a textbook of nuclear engineering. I was destined for that exciting new field but, fortunately, took the other path.

have a ways to go and new investments must pay off in the future at their present discounted value. Unfortunately, climate change is moving a lot faster than business and is already disrupting whole regions of the earth. The worst is yet to come.

From a constructivist point of view, "climate" has very different meanings, and is a very different object, at different times in history. For thousands of years, it was the preserve of the gods who visited good and bad weather alike on helpless humans. Later, Greek science begins to explain the natural causes of events in the heavens. This naturalized climate is a fundamentally different object from the one suffered or enjoyed according to the moods of the gods. Modern science improved on premodern ideas of causes, making possible more or less accurate predictions. Again, a new object emerges, this one entwined with scientific foresight.

For the most part, business appears to operate still with this purely contemplative concept of climate. But today, "climate" has become an object not only of science but of politics and technical control. This is the version of "climate" that provokes the intervention of the public in science and technology, not directly as researchers, but through the translation of concerns into objects of research and design. As Paul Edwards writes of climate science,

> This knowledge-production system delivers not only specifics about the past and the likely future of Earth's climate, but also the very idea of a planetary climate as something that can be observed, understood, affected by human wastes, debated in political processes, cared about by the general public, and conceivably managed by deliberate interventions.[83]

The everyday experience of climate change increasingly forms the background of scientific research and the technological changes it mandates. That research is independent of everyday experience but

---

83 Paul N. Edwards, *A Vast Machine: Computer Models, Climate Data, and the Politics of Global Warming* (Cambridge, MA: MIT Press, 2013), 8. Writing in 2009, Edwards shows the emergence of the global climate as object of knowledge in the context of the Cold War. Today, it has also become an object of technical intervention under public pressure to mitigate global warming.

correlated with it through the construction of the objects of the science. What we experience as "weather" is represented scientifically by measurements that are more precise, and extended geographically and temporally far beyond our reach.

The methods of physics, chemistry, and biology used to construct the scientific equivalent of weather constitute a fund of skills and techniques that enable scientists to achieve consensually validated results.[84] As Marcuse argues, the methods are based on "calculable, predictable relationships among exactly identifiable units." Quantification and formalization lie at their core, no less than in the case of physics. However, where the object is defined by concern for the "aesthetic" experience of the "violation of nature" by fire and flood, science is no longer entangled with the capitalist project of domination; on the contrary, it undoes some of the consequences of that project. Scientific rationality in this case is animated by a logos.

Harmony

The ideal of harmony between human beings and nature increasingly replaces the conquest of nature as an ideal. Marcuse's late reflections on nature anticipate this now-widespread change in attitude. He argues that there is no natural condition to be restored; the way lies forward, not back to the past. The harmony to which we can aspire is based not on nostalgia but on the imagination of a livable world that a revolutionary science and technology can help to create.

There is no need to defend the ideal of harmony on metaphysical grounds, and such a defense will not save the planet, yet a good deal of the philosophical conversation around environmentalism is busy seeking just such a metaphysical sanction. Much environmental philosophy works to reunite humanity with nature theoretically as the condition for addressing the crisis.[85] This leads to an underestimation of the institutional complexity of a modern society in which the

---

84 For the role of consensus, see Naomi Oreskes, *Why Trust Science?* (Princeton: Princeton University Press, 2019).

85 For a critique of this tendency, see Andreas Malm, *The Progress of This Storm: Nature and Society in a Warming World* (London: Verso, 2018).

coordination of science and experience is obstructed by capitalism. The confusion is compounded when the problem is identified with the capitalist *idea* of nature rather than with the actual imperatives of business enterprise. This gives rise to the illusion that the environmental crisis is due to something called "Enlightenment rationality," or "modernity," when in fact these caricatured categories only describe the way in which capitalism conceptualizes its world, not the economic laws it sets in motion which have an actual effect on that world.

For example, Bruno Latour's refutation of the "modern constitution" attempts to convince us that the environmental crisis results from the Cartesian "great divide" that separates humanity from nature. A new "non-modern" constitution can deliver us from the consequences of this error. Latour believes he has overcome the opposition of humanity and nature by attributing agency "symmetrically" to both. Or rather, he denies the pertinence of the distinction, since humans and "nonhumans" are always combined, "assembled," in configurations that are prior to and more fundamental than the distinction we subsequently make between them.[86]

As we saw in chapter 2, Uexküll anticipated Latour's rejection of dualism, and it found a place in Heidegger's concept of world. Marcuse traced it back to Hegel's concept of life in the *Science of Logic*. Yet all these earlier ways of breaking with Cartesian dualism distinguish between human agency, which is intentional, and natural causality. They do so not by separating the human and the nonhuman as separate substances but by distinguishing the lived world, in which intentionality plays a role, from factual objectivity. Experiential nature is organized around meanings disclosed to a living subject. It consists in both humanity *and* nature as they appear in experience, while the sciences abstract from the subject of experience to focus on the primary qualities of their objects. In the scientific context the human appears as just another object, human *things* interacting causally with nonhuman *things*.

In the wake of Latour, the metaphysical defense of the "wider" experiential nature confounds it with scientific nature by attributing to science

---

86 Bruno Latour, *Politiques de la nature: Comment faire entrer la science en démocratie* (Paris: La Découverte, 1999). For an attempt to make this conception compatible with Marxism, see Jason W. Moore, *Capitalism in the Web of Life Ecology and the Accumulation of Capital* (London: Verso, 2015).

what are in reality aspects of a very different disclosure. Some philosophers attempt to re-enchant science, to animate it on the terms of experiential nature, but this has very little to do with actual research which goes on as before, still focused on the primary qualities it knows how to measure. Other philosophers actually resuscitate animism and attribute consciousness to natural objects in order to escape the clutches of dualism.[87]

Such metaphysical claims articulate the experience of threatened nature, but they also confuse the environmental issues. To have a political effect, the truth of experience must enter science and technology through translations that constitute objects and designs corresponding in form to experiential content. The operational significance of harmony with nature is revealed as it is de-ontologized and reformulated in scientific-technical terms, for example, the notion that humankind should limit the increase in temperature to 1.5 degrees Celsius. With environmentalism, the two natures are in communication.

Unifying humanity and nature is a practical project that cannot be achieved at the theoretical level. This is the significance of the multiplication of natures, the "narrower" and the "wider" nature, the one constructed in theory by science, the other lived practically in experience. In this context, the unity of humanity and nature is an experiential norm that has scientific-technical correlates.

The "new sensibility" of the New Left disclosed the "wider nature" in which the facts are "entwined" with "historical human existence."[88] This same disclosure persists today as recognition of the forces in nature that favor life, both the life of natural systems and the human life they sustain. The "narrow," stripped-down nature of the capitalist project, which shaped science and technology up to now, recognizes only short-term human purposes and ignores the developmental dimension of nature, its intrinsic potentialities, which are known to the "sensuous" human subject. This is the "existential truth" of nature Marcuse postulates *at work*.

Whether, as Marcuse supposed, the realization of the potentialities of nature is incompatible with capitalism only time will tell. He writes,

---

87 Arianne Conty, "How to Differentiate a Macintosh from a Mongoose: Technological and Political Agency in the Age of the Anthropocene," *Techné: Research in Philosophy and Technology* 21, no. 2–3 (2017): 295–318.

88 Herbert Marcuse, "On Concrete Philosophy," in *Heideggerian Marxism*, 38–9.

"To drive ecology to the point where it is no longer containable within the capitalist framework means first extending the drive *within* the capitalist framework."[89] Insofar as the environmental movement and the environmental sciences function in a capitalist society, they are necessarily ambiguous. Even the most radical movements cannot escape this fate. Marcuse writes, *"Objective ambivalence* characterizes every movement of the radical opposition—an ambivalence which reflects at one and the same time the power of the Establishment over the whole, and the limits of this power."[90]

Co-optation is the normal outcome of social movements as capitalism "metabolizes" its changing environment. But that environment can be more or less humane, more or less destructive, and, most importantly, more or less open to further change. The ambivalence of struggle is not a reason to abandon it.

Abstract and Concrete

This experiment with Marcuse's concepts has shown their relevance to our contemporary situation while dropping Marcuse's most daring conclusion—the notion that a new concept of reason would someday incorporate the data of aesthetic experience in natural science. That notion presupposes a certain nostalgia for the concrete, which, under socialism, transcends the inhuman abstractions of capitalism. However, the focus on science and technology reveals a tension within the Marxian dialectic of abstract and concrete. By pursuing that dialectic to its logical conclusion, even at the risk of failure, Marcuse's work marks a significant turning point in the history of Marxism. Marcuse's new concept of reason recapitulates the logic of Marxian socialism for advanced industrial society and reveals its limits.

I understand Marcuse's innovation in terms of the tension between two different relations of abstract and concrete in Marxism. The dominant relation treats abstraction as a problem overcome through a return to the concrete. But there is another dialectical understanding of the

---

89 Marcuse, "Nature and Revolution," 61.

90 Marcuse, "The Left under the Counterrevolution," in Marcuse, *Counterrevolution and Revolt*, 49.

relation that I have applied in the preceding considerations on scientific
-technical change.

Marx's critique of capitalism contrasts the abstract laws of the
market with the living labor that produces the goods. The argument for
socialism consists in the claim that the market does a poor job of
reflecting concrete social needs, and economic crises and vast inequalities of wealth validate this complaint.

In the "Critique of the Gotha Program," Marx imagined a first phase
of socialism that would reduce inequality by rewarding the producers
in accordance with their labor. But this solution to the problem of
inequality was still abstract, because labor reflects only a single aspect
of the totality of human existence. The full flowering of human potential would require a further advance. A second phase of socialism
would overcome abstraction altogether by rewarding each according to
his or her needs. This would be the final stage in the descent from
abstract to concrete.

An implicit metanarrative underlies this concept of socialism:
namely, that humanity has been dominated by abstractions throughout
the history of class society. The gods are the first form in which abstraction rules the world. In the notebooks for his doctoral thesis, Marx
criticizes Kant's refutation of the ontological proof of the existence of
God, writing, "Didn't the Moloch of the Ancients hold sway? Wasn't the
Delphic Apollo a real power in the life of the Greeks?"[91]

In Marx's *Capital*, the gods and state are replaced by the laws of the
market. The abstract universal has lost its religious and moral disguises
and now appears as a second nature dominating the society. There is an
important difference between these various forms of alienation, and it
is this which makes possible a solution to what Marx called the "riddle"
of history. The gods are eternal. They belong to the world of nature, like
the mountains, seas, and weather from which they are initially
abstracted. Like the gods, the market is beyond human control, but it is
abstracted from social practices, not from nature. Control of those
practices is at least conceivable. Unlike the gods, with their strange
preferences and unpredictable moods, the economy has a rational
order. A society based on the scientific understanding of that order can

---

91 Quoted in Georg Lukács, *History and Class Consciousness*, trans. Rodney
Livingstone (Cambridge, MA: MIT Press, 1971), 127.

join the claims of community with the needs of the individuals, reconciling universal and particular. Alienation begins in religion and ends up in economics. Accordingly, rational administration working to a plan becomes the form of the first socialist society.

However, the results did not conform to the original intention. By the time Marcuse takes up the theme, administration appears as just another form of abstraction. This is reification as Lukács described it: the imposition of abstract forms on social content, as in Marx's reference to Moloch, which Lukács cites in support of his own critique of reification. The principal locus of abstraction is no longer the market but now reflects the logic of modern science as applied to the social world. Alienation no longer ends up in economics, but in science. Might the recovery of the concrete require a scientific revolution?

Where for Marx the ultimate purpose of the revolution was recognition of human potential in all its forms, Marcuse now casts an even wider net that encompasses potentiality as such, in both humanity and nature. This is a consequence of the move from a critique of the market to a critique of natural science. The reified scientific reason of advanced capitalism would be overcome by a new science that would acknowledge the potentialities canceled by the existing concept of reason. According to Marcuse, this advance is required by the ambiguous role of science in advanced capitalism, as both the apparatus of domination and the promise of liberation.

For Marcuse, the issue is complicated by the generalization of reification and the success of capitalist technology. Indeed, the lifeworld is no longer a refuge of unspoiled concreteness that can be contrasted with economic or scientific abstraction. While Marx believed that the proletarian condition offered sufficient reason to revolt, Marcuse argues that his confidence was invalidated by the effects of the higher levels of security and consumption made possible by advanced capitalism. No significant class suffers enough on the terms of the dominant culture to revolt. Therefore, only radical cultural change can motivate the rejection of the existing society. A new culture based on the aesthetic dimension would have to spread the need for a more peaceful and fulfilling way of life. Eventually, the lifeworld constituted by such a society would affect the perceptions and conceptions of scientists and lead to a revolution in science corresponding to the social revolution. In other words, a new way of life would bring a new science.

I have argued in this chapter that the abstraction of modern science cannot be overcome in this way. Marcuse's brief discussion of translation offers an alternative to the dominant Marxist account, but he did not develop that discussion. I have done so in my "experiment" with his concepts and drawn out the implications of this alternative. In sum, a technified society cannot return directly to the concrete social relations underlying its abstract form. This is a rather different "abstract" than the commodity form that Marx analyzed and requires a different kind of concretization.

On this account, science and technology can achieve "concreteness" in something like a Hegelian-Marxist sense, if not through a recovery of the immediate. Recall Marx's gloss on the dialectical concept of the concrete: "The concrete is concrete, because it is the sum of many determinations, [and] therefore a unity of diversity."[92] That diversity is registered in the lifeworld as potentialities from which science has abstracted in the constitution of its object. Social movements such as the environmental movement have shown that those potentialities can be recovered by science through translations that modify the object and render it more "concrete" in this dialectical sense. This is an alternative to Marxism's dominant approach based on Marcuse's conceptual framework in a new historical situation.

This alternative has political implications for the idea of socialism, which has gone through drastic revisions after the failure of planning to yield the emancipatory results it promised. Democratic socialists have argued for a return to local communities or factory councils to eliminate and replace abstract mediations such as the market and the bureaucratic planning apparatus. This notion of socialist democracy made sense during the reign of the commodity, but it must be qualified in a world organized by science and technology. In this new world the abstract mediations cannot be eliminated. What is required is a fluid relation between the reified systems that constitute the infrastructure of social life, and the participants in that social life. Democracy is essential to any such relation, but it must take a variety of forms that

---

92 Karl Marx, "'Introduction' to the 'Grundrisse,'" in *Texts on Method*, ed. Terrell Carver (London: Basil Blackwell, 1975), 72.

involve modifying those systems rather than their elimination. The discovery of those forms is beginning today in the many social movements contesting the technified world through interaction with its scientific-technical representatives.

Conclusion

Marcuse responded to a rather different historical situation from ours, amid the initial emergence of new attitudes, social realities, and protests among the youth in the United States and Western Europe. Many of those who participated called this phenomenon a "cultural revolution"—a term that originated in China but in the American context had nothing to do with Maoism. Denouncing success within the system, the cultural movement proclaimed the higher values of love, beauty, personal fulfillment, and, for many, peace and social justice as well. Despite the many failings of the movement, Marcuse was fascinated by this surprising combination of values, and especially the somatic force with which they were lived by participants.

It is easy now to dismiss this odd conflation between Marcuse's Marxism and '60s youth culture, but that would be to miss the significant point: namely, that Marcuse identified the obsolescence of many traditional Marxist assumptions and the emergence of new sources of social change. Still, today, existential issues and concerns for quality of life motivate resistance to the dominant culture in a variety of domains. Marcuse's category of the aesthetic and the related concept of life affirmation offer a normative basis for a progressive critique of the technosystem even where it is successful on its own terms.

The dystopian prospect that worried Marcuse and many other social critics in the 1960s and '70s recedes today as expertise loses its absolute authority. Progressive movements challenging the socially embedded disciplines have weakened the identification of the object of physics with being as such. The bias of the disciplines appears clearly in the light of the needs they fail to fulfill. As a result, a larger role for the public in science policy and technical decision making has emerged, supporting progressive changes in the social world.

However, there are also signs of danger that became clear with the rise of climate skepticism and the antivaccine movement, culminating in the election of Donald Trump, an avowed enemy of science. Marcuse's worries about democracy are verified once again. Social networking now supplements television as a new means of propaganda.[93] Irrational movements that defy science while stirring up race and gender prejudice unwittingly reinforce the status quo they claim to fight. Critical consciousness and a concern for the flourishing of life are more important than ever. However, while such perils are real, they do not justify despair; so far, the overall impact of the new cognitive regime has been positive. Still, there is no guarantee for the future.

Contestation of science and technology has exposed reason to the public in new ways that are both promising and fraught with danger. The politics of technoscience makes sense of Marcuse's call for a life-affirming concept of reason under conditions he did not anticipate. The technoscientific revolution is not just for the distant socialist future but is on the agenda of contemporary struggles against the rapaciousness of capitalism—struggles that intervene to redefine the social world in terms of humane purposes. New technoscientific objects support the realization of the telos of the lived nature of everyday experience. Extrapolated to the limit, this would mean, in Marcuse's words,

> perfection of the new mutilated and distorted science and technology in the formation of the object world in accordance with "the laws of beauty." And "beauty" here defines an ontological condition—not of an oeuvre d'art isolated from real existence . . . but that harmony between man and his world which would shape the form of society.[94]

---

93 There is a vast literature on the exploitation of social networking by nefarious actors of one sort or another. See, for example, Shoshana Zuboff, *The Age of Surveillance Capitalism: The Fight for a Human Future at the New Frontier of Power* (New York: PublicAffairs, 2019). I have also written on this subject as it relates to the politics of technology. See Andrew Feenberg, "The Internet as Network, World, Co-construction, and Mode of Governance," *Information Society* 35, no. 4 (2019): 229–43.

94 Marcuse, "Cultural Revolution," 138–9.

Conclusion: A Look Back

In this book, I have followed Marcuse through five major episodes in the development of his thought: his encounter with the *Manuscripts* of 1844, his appropriations of Hegel and Freud, the critique of technology, and the new aesthetic concept of reason. As we have seen, Marcuse started out as a Marxist, and he remained true to that early commitment to the end. What made his Marxism so unusual was its roots in phenomenology. Marcuse valorized the world of lived experience, granting it ontological status. Subject and object were united in the lifeworld in different ways throughout his career, but the necessary relation between them always took precedence over the reduction of reality to the nature of natural science.

Marcuse's most enigmatic claims concern the relation of human action to the nature of being—as we saw play out in his interpretation of Marx's concept of objectification and revolution in the *Manuscripts* of 1844, in his interpretation of Freud's concept of eros, and in his argument for a successor science. In these cases, human action is ontological action. Need is the force that drives the relation and "is not to be understood only in the sense of physical neediness: man needs a 'totality of human manifestations of life.'"[1] Need, in this sense, is not blind but belongs to the "unmutilated experience" of the lifeworld. It reveals a correlated reality, the potentialities awaiting realization through labor and revolutionary action. For Marcuse, the realization of those

---

1 Herbert Marcuse, "New Sources on the Foundation of Historical Materialism," in *Heideggerian Marxism*, ed. Richard Wolin and John Abromeit (Lincoln and London: University of Nebraska Press, 2005), 101.

potentialities is at once contingent on the success of the action and necessary, as the need and its means of satisfaction are enacted by the subject.

The role of beauty in Marcuse's critique of natural science is a particularly significant example of ontological action. The need for beauty, the rational understanding of that need, and the revolutionary action that eventually realizes the potential it signifies yield a new dispensation of being reflected in a new natural science. The redemptive significance of beauty in this sense follows Marcuse through most of his work, for nearly fifty years.

Marcuse's implicit ontology is not strictly Husserlian or Heideggerian, but it owes something to both of these early influences, as well as to the distinction between factual existence and meaning they share with neo-Kantianism. During the early twentieth century, German philosophy sought an alternative to both naturalism and metaphysics. It accepted the preeminence of science in the study of the facts. No longer would philosophers posit metaphysical beings unknown to science. God, the soul, and the various spiritual entities that interested earlier philosophy were all but abandoned, at least as objects of speculation. After metaphysics, philosophy was to become an ontology of meaning, considered as a fundamental reality irreducible to psychological or sociological causes. It was on the basis of this philosophical consensus of his youth that Marcuse developed an original version of Marxism, and it remained implicit in his work to the end of his life.

Because Marcuse's ontology remains implicit, it is possible to ignore it and interpret his thought in more conventional naturalistic terms. In fact, this was how he sometimes presented his views in the period between his abandonment of Heidegger and the publication of *Eros and Civilization*. His writings from then on revive themes from his early work that depend on and reference his ontology. It was this turn that prepared his identification with the New Left and distinguishes his politics from that of his Frankfurt School colleagues. His later writings cannot be explained without registering the return of ontology.

Although Marcuse's interpretation of the *Manuscripts* marked his break with Heidegger, I argue in chapter 2 that his version of the Heideggerian concept of "world" is deployed implicitly in the explanation of Marx's concepts of sensuousness, need, objectification, and labor. Heidegger's interpretation of practice as a first-person relation to worldly meanings makes sense of the more puzzling features of the *Manuscripts*, such as the claim that needs are ontological affirmations of being and that nature is the inorganic body of man. This approach is reflected in Marx's first thesis on Feuerbach, which insists that sensation be understood "subjectively," as a form of "praxis."

Marcuse extends something like this notion to the transformative interaction of the collective subject of labor with nature. For him, nature belongs to history through the meanings it acquires as it is "objectified." Those meanings are not arbitrary impositions but fulfill nature's potentialities in the context of the human world. It is in this sense that Marx, and following him Marcuse, call these interactions "ontological."

Under capitalism, external nature appears as a technological resource and a threat. Marcuse, however, presupposed a very different concept of nature he believed would prevail in a socialist society. That concept, once again, has the unity of "world." In his early Hegel interpretation, life depends on a world that is also its essential adversary, an environment of people and things with which it is in tensionful relations leading to overcoming and reconciliation. Those relations challenge it, enabling growth and development, the passage from one stage to the next in a sequence that affirms the powers and fulfillment of the living being.

Marcuse's category of "potentiality" is the link between the concept of life and the critique of capitalist society. Chapter 3 argues that the potentialities for the flourishing of life are real aspects of existence, "real possibilities" in Hegel's sense. The early essays apply this concept to society. Society is not the stable substance of Aristotelian metaphysics, nor is it an accumulation of scientific facts; rather, it is a reified structure fraught with potentialities reflecting unresolved contradictions that can be taken up by a revolutionary subject.

According to Marcuse, the imagination brings these traces of the future within the scope of perception. But it can only do so when urged forward by the erotic projection of the fulfillment of life. Life is the value that orients the subject toward the future in a constructive mood. "Constructive" here is meant in two senses: on the one hand, constructive because it is positive, affirmative; on the other hand, constructive because the projection enables the subject to "construct" or "objectify" the objects of science and technology in accordance with the requirements of life.

As we have seen, Marcuse explains his constructivist concept of science and technology in terms of the ancient concept of technē. Every technē stands under a logos which guides it toward its proper end. The logos is no merely external value but is immanent in technical practice. It determines the object, the means and the purpose of the practice. The inseparability of means and ends in antiquity has been lost in modern times as capitalism has impoverished experience. It must be restored in a socialist reconstruction of science and technology.

Is this idealism? It is not easy to answer this question. On the one hand, Marcuse affirms his roots in Kant and German idealism. On the other hand, he claims that Marxism reconciles idealism with materialism by discovering "the material, historical ground for the reconciliation of human freedom and natural necessity."[2] The idea of potentiality is not reducible to the given facts, and so stems from idealism, but Marcuse assigns it to the senses, which have a role in intuiting the "hidden" dimension of their objects. Praxis and sensation, understood "subjectively" as Marx demands, address nature in its material reality, not as a concept; but they do so in terms of its lived meaning, which Marcuse relates to the "critical, transcendent element of idealism."[3]

In 1960 Marcuse added a "Note on Dialectic" to his book *Reason and Revolution*. An extremely condensed exposition of what he took to be the core of his philosophical position, it is perhaps the closest he comes to explaining his relation to materialism and idealism. The essential point has to do with the difference between science and philosophy. Marcuse writes, "While the scientific method leads from the immediate experience of *things* to their mathematical-logical structure, philosophical thought leads from the immediate experience of *existence* to its historical structure: the principle of freedom."[4]

What is the meaning of this contrast between "existence" and "things?" Ever since Kierkegaard, "existence" has referred to the human subjects of the "unpurged, unmutilated experience" of the world, as contrasted with the objective facts, the "things" studied by science.

---

2 Herbert Marcuse, "Nature and Revolution," in *Counterrevolution and Revolt* (Boston: Beacon Press, 1972), 74.

3 Ibid., 73.

4 Herbert Marcuse, *Reason and Revolution: Hegel and the Rise of Social Theory* (Boston: Beacon Press, 1960), ix, xiv.

There is a complementarity here: existence includes things as they appear in the lifeworld *and* their potentialities, the basis of historical change. Science eliminates potentiality in order to gain better insight into the causal interactions of things as they are.

Marcuse concludes that "no method can claim a monopoly of cognition," thus rejecting positivism. However, he also insists that subjectivity is involved in all forms of knowledge, science included.[5] "All facts embody the knower as well as the doer . . . The objects thus 'contain' subjectivity in their very structure."[6] This subjectivity is in the world but it is not itself a "thing," a "fact." I argue in chapter 2 that it is plausible to identify it with the collective subject of the lifeworld.

Marcuse's relation to idealism and materialism is not the most interesting question. The real issue is political: for it is in politics that the choice of materialism or idealism correlates with an emphasis on either determinism or human will. That has always been a problematic divide within Marxism, reconciled in one way or another at different stages in the development of the socialist movement. Marcuse was able to renew the "contract" between these two heterogeneous aspects of Marxism— its objective analysis of political economy on one hand, and the historical role it assigns to rebellious subjectivity on the other.

Chapter 4 addresses Marcuse's turn to Freud. Psychoanalysis enables him to concretize the concept of world in terms of a more complex understanding of subjectivity. Unlike scientific nature, the lived world is not indifferent to humanity but marked by qualities that stem from what Marcuse, following Freud, called the "instincts." Marcuse took Freud seriously, but as he interprets psychoanalytic theory, these so-called instincts are historically malleable expressions of constructive and destructive potentialities rather than a fixed human nature. As historical, they are socially mediated. Their present configuration is structured by the exigencies of capitalism and its long history of alienation and exploitation of labor.

Marcuse's ontology enters into his study of Freud. While Freud's eros and thanatos are psychological dispositions, in Marcuse's work they transcend the psyche and describe aspects of reality itself. This ontological interpretation of Freud's concepts makes sense only in the

---

5 Ibid., xiv.
6 Ibid., viii.

lived world, which must once again be distinguished from the nature of natural science. Now another nature appears, which exhibits both benign and menacing aspects. This lived nature is not subjective, although its qualities are implicated in subjectivity. This is the nature we encounter in everyday experience, the nature of the Freudian "reality principle." According to Marcuse, this nature is not fixed once and for all as a reified fact but is historically relative, evolving in relation to human technological powers and psychic dispositions.

Freud's pessimism appealed to Marcuse in the 1960s, although he refused to give it the last word. Utopia, he argued, was now possible on the basis of the achievements of modern technology, but the forces in society stoking the destructive instinct threatened to perpetuate the old inequalities and suffering indefinitely. Progress depended on recognition of potentialities, an existential decision motivated by a critical sense of the absurdity of a way of life based on competition and violence in a society that has conquered scarcity. The emergence of a "new sensibility" in the New Left validated utopian hope, but it did not refute the worry about the corruption of democracy through manipulation and propaganda. Not much has changed in the years since Marcuse's death.

Running throughout Marcuse's work is a concept of reason that gives a direction to the sequence of historical developments. Reason is not merely cleverness in manipulating the environment but something more basic that makes cleverness possible, and much else besides. Reason is the capacity to know the universal, to find meaning in the world. It is a liberating power that creates the distance from immediate experience of a free being. For him, meanings are more than labels we attach to things; they support practical projects we can elaborate, revise, and fulfill as circumstances and our own evolving will allows.

As I show in chapter 5, *One-Dimensional Man* explains science and technology as material crystallizations of social meanings. The instruments of production are not simply means; they are the realization in a technical design of a previously lived practical relation to nature. Technology objectifies that relation and stabilizes both its human and the material side. Design plays a normative role, shaping users' identity and their understanding and behavior in terms of a definite notion of what is at issue practically. Insofar as science is a historically situated enterprise, its objects are not fundamentally different; their meaning is relative to the research procedures that engage them, and those procedures themselves reflect an original practical agenda Marcuse identifies with the capitalist lifeworld.

In chapter 6, I explain the relationship between science and lifeworld in terms of the construction of the objects of science.[7] The early Marx argued that the objectified meanings embodied by science and technology take on a life of their own and come to dominate their creators. The transcendence of alienation is possible on the basis of the achievements of capitalism, but it also requires a radical change in the relation of the individuals to their world. As we have seen, Marcuse conceptualized this change in terms of aesthetics, arguing that only an aesthetic relation to nature would make possible a socialist transformation.

Aesthetics involves idealizations oriented by life-affirming values. Where the idealizations belong to a possible developmental trajectory of the social world, Marcuse calls them "potentialities." The concept of aesthetics must be taken in the broadest sense to signify an engagement with such potentialities. Reason can transcend empirical particulars and functional prescriptions toward a new world adumbrated by these potentialities. The New Left was so important to Marcuse's late conception of revolution because it prefigured on a mass scale an aesthetic relation to nature.

The last two chapters of this book focus on Marcuse's critique of science and technology. In *One-Dimensional Man* he invokes Husserl's phenomenological concept of the lifeworld to explain the dependence of modern science on the prevailing practices of capitalism. Following Husserl and Heidegger, he rejects the identification of reality as defined

---

7 In chapter 5, I show that *One-Dimensional Man* explains the ideological function of technology under capitalism on these terms. Herbert Marcuse, *One-Dimensional Man: Studies in the Ideology of Advanced Industrial Society* (Boston: Beacon Press, 1964), 164. A similar relation between the social and the technical is the basis of the critical constructivist philosophy of technology I have developed. I argue that the two standpoints, historical and factual, coexist. The factual standpoint is no mistake, but a founded perspective. It successfully adjudicates factual disagreements and is the basis for scientific truth claims that can be referenced by later research without worrying about the process of discovery. Technology is codified in technical disciplines useful for further work and repair, again abstracted from the social background that instituted them. In the case of technology, what is lost in the abstraction is often of immediate social and political significance. See Andrew Feenberg, *Technosystem: The Social Life of Reason* (Cambridge, MA: Harvard University Press, 2017).

by physics with reality as such—an identification that, for him, is not just a philosophical error but invades common sense in a technified society. On this view, perception of potentiality recedes before a scientistic fetishism of the facts. Marcuse believed that overcoming this one-dimensional outlook would require a radical transformation of the natural sciences to take into account the evidence of art that a better world is possible.

I do not find this plausible, but there are resources in Marcuse's theory that can be repurposed in a critique of the technosciences I think he would have endorsed. In chapter 6, I have followed Marcuse in relating beauty to what is life enhancing at the expense of his own attempt to join natural science with art. This leads to a theory of the co-construction of the lifeworld and the socially embedded disciplines through translations determining shared objects.

There are many scientific-technical disciplines other than physics that interact practically with society. They depend on the conceptual articulation of practical experiences and attitudes born in the lifeworld, and there is a constant translation back and forth between these sciences and social experience. This shows up in the uptake of scientific concepts in the vernacular and in the effects of public concerns on the construction of the objects of the disciplines. Where public purposes enter the disciplines through such translations, they exemplify Marcuse's demand for a life-affirming science and technology.

I have reduced Marcuse's ambitious argument for general ontological transformation to a more modest argument for the transformation of regional ontologies, which involve nature in its various forms relevant to human life. Thus, the revised theory responds to Marcuse's most important intuition: his conviction that human being and nature are mutually implicated in each other's being, and that, as he puts it, "nature, too, awaits the revolution."

In recent years, political demands and social struggles to protect nature and human values have been unprecedented in range and intensity. They encompass movements for access to medical services, lawsuits aimed at abuses in the pharmaceutical industry, protests over the siting of pipelines, toxic waste dumps and other polluting technologies, struggles around water quality, urban renewal schemes, surveillance on the internet, and many other technical issues.

Demands for new energy systems to combat climate change have mobilized youth in movements that recall the New Left both by their tactics and by the cultural attitudes that motivate them. Indeed, Marcuse would have felt right at home with the school strike and Extinction Rebellion. While these may not be the most visible and dramatic protests, collectively they promise to improve life and have already done so, notably in the case of the environment. It is with regard to this genre of technical politics that I have shown the relevance of Marcuse's critique of science and technology.

This revision of Marcuse's critique echoes the concept of revolution through change in meaning that he proposes in his essay on the *Manuscripts*. Revolution is only possible when social objects acquire new meanings in general consciousness that correspond to the objective potentialities of the society at a certain historical stage. Similarly, the transformation of science and technology can only take place where their objects acquire new meanings through public protest compatible with objectively valid trajectories of research and development. This is precisely what has occurred in the years since Marcuse's death, foreshadowing a new dimension of democratic life in modern societies, whether capitalist or socialist.[8]

Marcuse's work validates the rebellious subjectivity of the participants in the many technical systems of advanced capitalist societies. That subjectivity inspires demands and protests that influence the evolution of the technosystem. We enjoy the fruits of those struggles, which compensate for the harms that have accompanied technological development. Marcuse's vision of socialism is still beyond reach, but to the extent that the established powers are vulnerable to these pressures from below, the system is propelled forward by a humane dynamic. Meanwhile, the contest continues between these progressive forces and the capitalist project of total prediction and control of human beings, reduced to mere relays between its gigantic systems.

As seen throughout the preceding chapters, these concepts add up to an original political theory with roots in Marx but transformed by the failure of the revolution he foresaw, and the emergence of new forces he could not have imagined. Today, we are distanced from the already-fading revolutionary hopes of Marcuse's generation. Nevertheless,

---

8 Ibid., 35–7.

struggles for a just and peaceful world continue and have intensified in recent years. The dystopian "end of history" no longer threatens. The dangers now are far cruder, and the hope that a benign version of capitalism would gradually achieve goals formerly identified with socialism has been sorely disappointed. If anything, the total triumph of capitalism has authorized painful regression. It is as though now that nobody is watching—that is, now that the communist world no longer offers an alternative—capitalism has dropped its inhibitions. Will the multiplying abuses lead to a revival of the socialist alternative? Only time will tell.

In any case, Marcuse's expressions of solidarity with struggles for racial and gender equality and against imperialist aggression could not be more relevant today. Crucially, climate change has validated his demand for a reconstruction of the material base of our society in terms of life-affirming values—a demand that seemed quixotic when he first formulated it, but that today appears as his most original contribution.

Toward the end of his life, Marcuse supported environmental struggles as part of what he called the "long march through the institutions."[9] Resistance reveals potentialities of the society masked by the dominant ideology and transforms the agenda of public discussion. In so doing, it orients the sciences toward new problems, new objects of concern. The politics of science is not a substitute for the revolution Marcuse advocated, but it challenges the technological domination he opposed. His thought offers precious resources for understanding these unprecedented struggles.

---

9 Herbert Marcuse, "Counterrevolution and Revolt," in *Counterrevolution and Revolt*, 55.

Index

A

Abromeit, John, 27
abstract, vs. concrete, 138, 210–14
Adorno, Theodor, x, xv, 4, 6, 12–13, 34–5, 67, 73, 83–4, 88, 95, 128, 132, 149, 174, 185
The Aesthetic Dimension (Marcuse), 175, 178
aesthetic potentialities, 178–9
aesthetics
    aesthetic potentialities, 178–9
    aesthetic reduction, 174
    laws of beauty, 172–5
    Marcuse's focus on, 191, 222
    as utopian consequence of Marcuse's concept of revolution, 118–19
AIDS, 203
AIDS Coalition to Unleash Power (ACT UP), 203
alienation
    according to Marcuse, 68–9
    as distinguished from objectification, 45
The Alternative in Eastern Europe (Bahro), 105
Anderson, Perry, 26
Angus, Ian, 29, 32, 184
anti-Cartesian ontology, 57
anti-utopianism, 78, 79
antivaccine movement, 214
Aristotle, 85, 86, 87, 94, 125, 149, 150, 151, 180

Aronowitz, Stanley, 95
Arrhenius, Svante, 205
art
    and the concept of reason, 175–9
    merger with technology, 182
    rationality of, 174, 176–7
"Art and Revolution" (Marcuse), 173, 175
Auden, W. H., 13
Aufhebung, 29, 112
authenticity, 75, 77–8
avant-gardism, 178

B

Bachelard, Gaston, 170
Bachelard, Suzanne, 159
Bacon, Francies, 170
Bahro, Rudolf, 105
beauty
    laws of, 172–5
    role of in Marcuse's critique of natural science, 217
Beaux-Arts, 168
Beckett, Samuel, 14
Befindlichkeit, 123
being
    Heidegger's history of, 156
    as utopian consequence of Marcuse's concept of revolution, 121–4
Being and Nothingness (Sartre), 116

Being and Time (Heidegger), 1, 22, 48, 49, 56, 158
"being-in-the-world" (*In-der-Welt-sein*), 48, 51, 52, 56, 66, 107, 123
Benjamin, Walter, x, 5, 8, 12, 73, 167, 191
Bergmann, Joachim, 134, 147
Bergson, Henri, 16
Bestand (raw material), 151
Bewegtheit (motility), 85
Black Notebooks (Heidegger), 49
Bloch, Ernst, 73, 83
boundary object, 202n77
Brandom, Robert, 50n69
Brown, Wendy, 96, 97
Brueghel, Pieter, 13
Brunkhorst, Hauke, 42
Butler, Judith, 204

C

Callon, Michel, 189
Camus, Albert, 15
Capital (Marx), 16, 74, 78, 79, 197, 211
capitalism
    advanced capitalism, x, xvii, 4, 5, 9, 91, 96, 114, 131, 137, 157, 186, 212
    coordination of science and experience as obstructed by, 208
    as having dropped its inhibitions, 225
    as ontological condition, 46
    potentialities of nature as incompatible with, 209–10
    reification as ultimate form of objectivity under, 23–4
    socialism as potentiality of, xvi
    technology under, xvi
Cartesian dualism, 208
Cassirer, Ernst, 19
Civilization and Its Discontents (Freud), 128, 129–30
class consciousness, 10, 17, 84
class struggle, 11, 155
climate change, 11, 185, 206–7, 224, 225
climate crisis, 205–6
climate movement, 191–2
climate science, 193, 206

climate skepticism, 214
cogito, 18, 31, 35, 52, 61
commodities, fetishism of, 16–17, 157
communes, 9
communism, 8, 15, 103, 112, 113
"The Concept of Essen" (Marcuse), 84, 89, 90
concrete, abstract vs., 138, 210–14
consciousness, according to Lukács, 71
Considerations on Western Marxism (Anderson), 26
continental philosophy, xii
counterculture, 7, 10, 35
Counterrevolution and Revolt (Marcuse), 178
COVID-19 pandemic, and technology, xi
The Crisis of the European Sciences (Husserl), 30
critical reason, 30, 160
critical theory, xi, 14, 147. *See also* Frankfurt School
Critique of Pure Reason (Kant), 44, 81, 120, 192
"Critique of the Gotha Program" (Marx), 211
Crowell, Steven, 22

D

Dasein, 22, 24, 29, 47, 48, 49, 51, 52, 55, 75
Davis, Angela, 3
death instinct (thanatos), 111, 121, 191, 220
De Man, Henri, 42
democracy, as pursuit of happiness, 100–8
dereification, 26, 70
Descartes, René, 37
determinism, 39, 76, 77, 178, 220
Dialectic of Enlightenment (Horkheimer and Adorno), xv, 128, 132, 149, 174
dialectics, according to Marcuse, 88–9, 96
Dialectics of Liberation conference (1967), 79–80

Dilthey, Wilhelm, 18–19, 39
discrimination, 188
dystopian fears, x, 9, 109, 191, 214
dystopian visions, 7, 12

E

Eclipse of Reason (Horkheimer), 174
ecology, use of term, 205
Economic and Philosophical Manuscripts (Manuscripts) (Marx)
    ambiguity in, 37, 55
    on demands of reason, 93
    on distinction between human beings and animals, 172
    emphasis on ontological status of beauty, 174
    on human existence not being transcendable, 39
    on human's special role as beings that bring meaning to nature, 56
    as incomplete sketch of philosophy of praxis, 35
    as inspiring notion of new science, 168–9
    Marcuse's discovery of, 28
    Marcuse's interpretation of, 17, 24, 26, 29, 31, 32, 37, 41, 42–7, 48, 51, 54–5, 61, 64, 66, 67, 70, 73, 74, 75, 87, 93, 118, 172, 187, 216, 217
    Marcuse's review of, 27, 28
    Marx's abandonment of early critique of science in, 156
    as overcoming opposition of materialism and idealism, 68
    and philosophy of praxis, 123
    priority of practice in, 59
economism, 76
Edwards, Paul, 206
Einbildungskraft (imagination), 120
Ellul, Jacques, 135
Engels, Frederick, 79, 156
Enlightenment, 78, 96, 103, 106, 111
environmental crisis, and technology, xi
environmentalism, 11–12, 126, 129, 147, 167, 170, 191, 199, 200, 205–6, 225

epistemological rupture, theory of, 170
epistemology, 65
Erfahrung, 8
Erlebnis, 8
eros (life instinct), 111, 115, 121, 122, 124, 125, 126, 129, 175, 191, 216, 220
Eros and Civilization (Marcuse), x, xv, 103, 109, 115, 116, 118, 123, 125, 127, 172, 217
An Essay on Liberation (Marcuse), 5, 10, 93, 118, 125, 173–4, 175, 177
essence, 86–7, 90, 151
ethics, 76–7
existentialism, 15–16, 77

F

Fanon, Frantz, 16
Farrell, Katharine, 189, 190
feminism, 126, 188
fetishism, of commodities, 16–17, 157
Feuerbach, Ludwig, 36, 39, 46, 57, 59, 218
Fichte, Johann, 31
first-person materialism, 68
formal bias, 139, 140, 161, 163
formal possibility, 81
formal rationality, 143–4, 145, 157
formal universals, 160–1, 162, 163, 202
Foucault, Michel, 6, 19, 96–7, 156, 198–9
Frankfurt School, x, xi, xv, xvi, 4, 6, 8, 12–14, 23, 88, 96, 97, 123, 148, 217
French May Events (1968), 3, 5, 177
Freud, Sigmund, xv, 99, 102, 106, 109–14, 116, 121, 122, 125–6, 129–30, 158, 216, 220–1. See also *Civilization and Its Discontents* (Freud)
Freudo-Marxism, 114, 127, 128, 129
Fromm, Erich, 109
Funtowicz, Silvio, 189

G

Galileo, Galilei, 31, 74, 150, 159, 190, 195
German idealism, 219
The German Ideology (Marx), 39, 59
Gestell (enframing), 151, 154
God, 18, 20, 144, 154, 211, 217

Goethe, Johann Wolfgang von, 166
Goldmann, Lucien, 5, 15
Gorgias (Plato), 94–5
Gramsci, Antonio, 23, 39, 46, 67, 73
"Great Refusal," 5, 154
Greeks
  on nature, 150–1
  on potentialities, 152
  on science, 206

H

Habermas, Jürgen, xi, xvi, 27, 32–5,
  105–7, 122–3, 125, 134, 141, 147, 148
Haeckel, Ernst, 205
happiness, democracy as pursuit of,
  100–8
harmony, between human beings and
  nature, 207–10
hasard objectif, 178
Hegel, G. W. F., 2, 39, 44, 45, 52, 62–3,
  76–88, 125, 128, 138, 149, 162, 174,
  208, 218
*Hegel's Ontology and the Theory of
  Historicity* (Marcuse), 76, 84, 85, 88
Heidegger, Martin
  Being and Time, 1, 22, 48, 49, 56, 158
  Black Notebooks, 49
  concept of world according to, 47–56,
    75, 86
  as cultural conservative, 148
  Dasein. See Dasein
  discussion of Greek techne by, 63
  on emergence of values, 154
  history of being, 156
  on identification of reality, 222
  Lask's influence on, 20
  Marcuse's break with, xvii, 27, 76,
    217–18
  Marcuse's distancing from, 28
  Marcuse's study with, 10, 17, 30
  ontology of, 122
  phenomenology of, xiii, 2, 29
  practice according to, 56–61
  "The Question Concerning Technology,"
    149, 152, 166

  on science and technology, 135, 149,
    150, 151, 152, 153, 166, 194–5
  version of lifeworld, 32
Heidegger-Marxismus (Marcuse), 53
Hess, David, 202n78
historical materialism, 60, 68, 172
historical memory, 90
historicism, 46
History and Class Consciousness
  (Lukács), 23, 26, 71, 76–7, 123, 132,
  156
Holman, Christopher, 104
Honneth, Axel, xi, 97–8
Horkheimer, Max, x, xv, 4, 73, 95, 128,
  132, 149, 174–5
humanism, 38, 42, 46
human nature, 42, 59, 78, 97, 99, 100, 106,
  127, 129, 178, 220
Husserl, Edmund, 2, 20–2, 27, 30–2, 121,
  149, 150, 158, 184, 187, 194–5,
  199–200, 217, 222
Huxley, Aldous, 7

I

idealism, xvi, 26, 35–37, 39, 40, 46, 56, 57,
  61, 68, 74, 77, 219, 220
imagination
  according to Kant, 120
  Marcuse's defense of, 119, 218
In-der-Welt-sein ("being-in-the-world"),
  48, 51, 52, 56, 66, 107, 123
instinct theory, xv, xvii, 106, 110, 122,
  124
irrational reason, 95

J

Jameson, Fredric, 110
Jasanoff, Sheila, 189

K

Kangussu, Imaculada, 119–20
Kant, Immanuel, 18, 19–20, 31, 38, 44, 64,
  65, 76–8, 81, 120, 170, 173–4, 192,
  194, 211, 219
Kellner, Douglas, 93–4, 108

Kierkegaard, Søren, 108, 219
Koch, Gertrud, 42
Korsch, Karl, 73
Kuhn, Thomas, 156, 182, 189, 200

L

labor
  according to Marx, 38, 59
  alienated labor, 27, 29, 36, 96, 117, 131,
    164, 220
  becoming human through, 44–5
  correlation of human being and nature
    as produced by, 87
  discipline of, 142–3
  division of private property and, 69
  human faculties as objectified in
    nature through, 19, 54
  Marx's concept of world-constitution
    through, xvii, 37
  nature as reduced to human product
    through, 36
  as ontic and ontological, 37, 48, 64
  role of in constructing the "world," 55
  tout court, 62
labor movement, 9
labor unions, 7
La Dolce Vita (film), 192n64
Lask, Emil, 20, 22
Latour, Bruno, 19, 208
Laudani, Raffael, x
Lebenswelt, 2, 27, 30, 31, 35, 93, 118, 121,
    150, 159, 177, 184. See also lifeworld
Leiss, William, 148
Levi-Strauss, Claude, 196
liberation, dialectics of, 78–84
libidinal morality, 129
libidinal rationality, 119
life instinct (eros), 111, 121, 122, 124, 125,
    126, 129, 175, 191, 216, 220
lifeworld, 17, 23, 31–5, 57, 66, 72, 84, 88,
    120, 122–3, 126, 147, 150, 158, 166,
    169–71, 183–4, 186–7, 189, 195, 197,
    201, 204, 212–13, 216, 220, 222, 223
The Limits to Growth, 185n47
logical possibility, 81

logos, 94–5, 99–100, 168, 175, 180, 183,
    187, 193, 207, 219
Lukács, György, 10, 15, 16, 20, 23, 24, 26,
    27, 39, 45, 46, 68–73, 76–7, 84, 123,
    132, 138, 154–7, 212

M

Mallarmé, Stéphane, 23
Manuscripts (Marx). See Economic and
    Philosophical Manuscripts
    (Manuscripts) (Marx)
Marcel, Gabriel, 15
Marcuse, Herbert
  academic career in Germany as
    doomed by rise of Nazism, 76
  The Aesthetic Dimension, 175, 178
  "Art and Revolution," 173, 175
  author as student of, xii, xvi, 1
  break with Heidegger, xvii, 27, 76,
    217–18
  charisma of, 7–8
  "The Concept of Essen," 84, 89, 90
  Counterrevolution and Revolt, 178
  on critical theory, xi
  dialectics according to, 88–9, 96
  dilemma of, 179–82
  dystopian fears of, 9, 109, 191, 214
  Eros and Civilization. See Eros and
    Civilization (Marcuse)
  An Essay on Liberation. See An Essay
    on Liberation (Marcuse)
  fame of, x
  Hegel's Ontology and the Theory of
    Historicity, 76, 84, 85, 88
  Heidegger-Marxismus, 53
  intervention of in social movements,
    131
  as media celebrity, 3–4, 5
  "Nature and Revolution," 64, 169, 172
  objectification according to, 19, 42, 44,
    54–5, 62–3
  One-Dimensional Man. See One-Di-
    mensional Man (Marcuse)
  as open to progressive movements,
    34–5

Marcuse, Herbert (*continued*)
  phenomenological themes in work of,
    xiv
  from philosophy to social theory,
    88–91
  potentiality according to, 97, 222
  puzzling àmbiguity of career of, 16
  Reason and Revolution, 84, 88, 89, 90, 219
  "Re-Examination of the Concept of
    Revolution," 4
  "Repressive Tolerance," 104
  revolution according to, 9–10, 68–73
  as revolutionary theorist, 108
  sensuousness according to, 42, 43–4,
    58–9, 65, 93, 169
  on sexuality, 6–7
  sexuality according to, 6–7
  socialism's vision of, 224
  "Some Implications of Technology,"
    160
  at University of California, San Diego
    (UCSD), 1, 2–3, 29, 43, 92
Marx, Karl
  adoption of anti-Cartesian ontology
    by, 57
  Capital, 16, 74, 78, 79, 197, 211
  "Critique of the Gotha Program," 211
  *Economic and Philosophical Manu-
    scripts. See Economic and
    Philosophical Manuscripts
    (Manuscripts)* (Marx)
  on feelings and passions, 123
  Freudo-Marxism, 127
  The German Ideology, 39, 59
  as interested in technology, xi
  interpretation of Hegel's anti-utopianism
    by, 78
  on man as objective natural being, 44
  objectification according to, 36, 37,
    178, 187, 222
  philosophy of praxis of, 35–9, 123
  practice according to, 56–61
  quoted, vi
  on "real subsumption" of means of
    production, 143

  on reason, 92–3
  on science, 143, 179
  synthesis of Marx and Freud, 111–14
Marxism
  according to Marcuse, 4
  Freudo-Marxism, 109–10, 114, 128,
    129
  Marcuse's contributions to, 10
  Marcuse's original version of, 216, 217
  Marcuse's principal loyalty to, 17
  Marcuse's work as marking significant
    turning point in history of, 210
  normative deficit of, 76
  ontological foundation for, 46
  quasi-phenomenological reconstruc-
    tion of, 59–60
materialism
  first-person materialism, 68
  and idealism, 26, 35, 37, 38, 39, 40, 68,
    74, 219, 220
Matuštík, Martin, 106n79
May Events (1968), 3, 5, 177
media manipulation, xi
medicine, object construction in, 196
Megarians, 85
metaphysics, 18, 20, 23, 26, 37–9, 63, 64,
    75, 110, 162, 170, 174, 176, 183,
    208–9, 217
Metaphysics (Aristotle), 150
Morawski, Stefan, 172–5
Mouffe, Chantal, 106
Mumford, Lewis, 140
Münchhausen, 31

N

Narcissus, 118
naturalism, 2, 17–18, 22, 25, 30, 32, 35, 38,
    39, 46, 69, 74, 75, 95, 110, 111, 184, 217
natural science
  according to Marcuse, 41
  bias of, 198
  nature of, 46–7
  role of beauty in Marcuse's critique of,
    217
  triple life of, 183

nature
  independence of, 74
  liberation of, 176, 177
  Marcuse's concept of, 218
  multiplication of, 209
  potentialities of as incompatible with
    capitalism, 209–10
  the two natures, 166–72
  unity of humanity and, 126
"Nature and Revolution" (Marcuse), 64,
    169, 172
Nazism, 48, 49, 76
needs, according to Marx, 100–1
negation, role of, 89–90
neo-Kantians, 18, 19–20, 23, 39, 73, 183,
    194, 217
neutrality, as bias, 164–5
New Left, 7, 9, 10, 12, 35, 91, 118–19, 129,
    168, 177, 191, 193, 209, 217, 221, 222
new sensibility, 2, 10–11, 91, 93, 125, 126,
    168, 177, 209, 221
Nietzsche, Frederick, 108
Nixon, Richard, 107–8
normative rationality, 141
nuclear power, 204–5

O
object conflicts, 202n78
object construction, 19, 183, 193–7, 198,
    200
objectification
  according to Marcuse, 19, 42, 44, 54–5,
    62–3
  according to Marx, 36, 37, 178, 187,
    222
  alienation as distinguished from, 45
objective reason, 174
Olafson, Frederick, 28, 30
One-Dimensional Man (Marcuse), x, xi,
    xv, 16, 27, 84, 90, 93, 95, 101–2, 109,
    116, 117, 131, 132, 140–1, 146, 149,
    151, 152, 154, 155, 157–8, 160,
    166–8, 174, 175, 190, 195, 221, 222
ontological moments, in Marcuse's
    critique of technology, 140, 147–53

Oppenheimer, J. Robert, 199
Orpheus, 118

P
performance principle, 114, 118, 119
Petrucciani, Stefano, 102
phenomenology
  according to Marcuse, 27–32
  as alternative to naturalism, 17–18
  conception of first-person experience,
    21
  Marcuse's draw on in social critique of
    science, 155–6
  Marcuse's Marxism as rooted in, 216
  as most persuasive critique of
    naturalism, 22
  as separating philosophical and factual
    inquiry, 183
Phenomenology (Hegel), 45
philosophy
  continental philosophy, xii
  difference of science with, 219
  German philosophy, 17, 20, 39, 124, 217
  from philosophy to social theory,
    88–91
  of praxis, 35–9, 123
Philosophy of Right (Hegel), 78–84
physics, transformation of, 192
Pippin, Robert, 88
Plato, xiv, 94–5, 193, 194, 196, 197
politics
  as life-and-death struggle, 107
  as matter of identity, 107
pollution, 200–1
populism, 107
positivism, 2, 220
potential energy, 201
potentiality
  according to Aristotle, 85, 87
  according to Marcuse, 97, 222
  aesthetic potentialities, 178–9
  defined, xiv
  double structure of, 98–100
  of nature as incompatible with
    capitalism, 209–10

potentiality (*continued*)
  role of in new science, 169
  socialism as potentiality of capitalism,
    xv
  social potentialities, xiv, 115, 120
  teleological idea of, 160
  transcending potentialities, 163
practice
  according to Heidegger, 56–61
  according to Marx, 56–61
praxis
  philosophy of, 35–9, 123
  quasi-phenomenological approach to
    role of meaning in, 74
pre-Kantians, 37, 62
primary narcissism, Freud's theory of, 122
private property
  according to Freud, 128
  according to Marx, 45
  division of labor and, 69
production
  divorce of workers from means of, 142,
    145
  real subsumption of means of, 143
  as type of praxis, 55–6
proletariat, 16, 68, 70–3, 76, 84, 105, 112,
    113, 164. *See also* working class

Q
"The Question Concerning Technology"
    (Heidegger), 149, 152, 166

R
Rachlis, Charles, 10–11
Rantis, Konstantinos, 58
rationality
  of art, 174, 176–7
  communicating of, 200–5
  ecological rationality, 205
  economic rationality, 145, 205
  existential meaning of, xiv
  formal rationality, 143–4, 157
  importance of, 98–9
  libidinal rationality, 119
  normative rationality, 141

source of, 106
substantive rationality, 144
technological rationality. *See*
    technological rationality
  as utopian consequence of Marcuse's
    concept of revolution, 119–20
rationalization
  theory of, 135, 142, 144, 165, 197, 198
  use of term, 144
Raulet, Gérard, 48
Ravetz, Jerome, 189
Reagan, Ronald, 107–8
reality
  according to Marxist theory, 113–14
  as contradicting metaphysical and
    artistic truth, 162
  as indifferent to humanity, 121
reality principle, 113–6, 122, 158, 177, 221
real possibility, concept of, 81–4, 86, 89
real subsumption, 143, 146
reason. *See also* rationality
  according to Marcuse, 221
  art and the concept of reason, 175–9
  critical reason, 30, 160
  defined, xiv
  demands of, 91–8
  Marcuse's call for new concept of, 167,
    179, 186–7, 200
  objective reason, 174
  self-critique of, 174–5
  subjective reason, 174
  technical reason. *See* technical reason
Reason and Revolution (Marcuse), 84, 88,
    89, 90, 219
"Re-Examination of the Concept of
    Revolution" (Marcuse), 4
Reich, Wilhelm, 109
Reichenbach, Hans, 19
reification
  according to Lukács, 39, 45–6, 138,
    154, 156–7, 212
  technologies of advanced industrial
    societies as exhibiting, 138–9
Reitz, Charles, 175
relativism, 33, 101

repression
  consequences of reduction of, 119
  necessary repression, 114
  requirement for by civilization, 114
  surplus repression, 114
"Repressive Tolerance" (Marcuse), 104
The Republic (Plato), 197
revolution
  according to Lukács, 68–73
  according to Marcuse, 9–10, 68–73
  cultural revolution, 9, 177, 214
  failure of one foreseen by Marx, 105,
    109, 224
  necessity of, 46
  as philosophical method, 37
  structure of technoscientific
    revolutions, 197–200
  ultimate purpose according to Marx,
    212
  utopian consequences of Marcuse's
    concept of, 115–24
revolutionary political theory, 13
Ricoeur, Paul, 15
romanticism, 148
Rousseau, Jean-Jacques, 78, 103

S
sadomasochistic sexual play, 116
Saint-Simon, Henri de, 176
Sartre, Jean-Paul, x, 15, 16, 116, 117, 158
Schiller, Friedrich, 172
Schmidt, Alfred, 37
science. *See also* natural science;
    technoscience
  according to Heidegger, 135, 149, 150,
    151, 152, 153, 166, 194–5
  according to Husserl, 150
  climate science, 193, 206
  complementarity between science and
    lifeworld, 201
  dialogue with society, 202–3
  difference of with philosophy, 219
  *Economic and Philosophical
    Manuscripts* (Marx) as inspiring
    new notion of, 168–9

evolution of focus of, 185
  gender and racial bias of, 188
  interaction of public with, 199
  Marcuse's critique of, 131–65
  Marcuse's demand that it become
    political, 176, 190
  new science, 38, 41, 168–9, 175, 176,
    179, 212, 213
  normal science, 182, 189
  as not fundamentally different from
    technology, 152
  physics as paradigmatic science, 192
  postnormal science, 189, 190
  pros and cons of, 148
  successor science, 180, 181, 182–6, 187,
    193, 197, 216
  transformation of, 224
Science of Logic (Hegel), 81, 82, 208
scientific revolution, 182, 183
sensibility, according to Kant, 64
sensory experience, according to Kant,
    65
sensuousness
  according to Marcuse, 42, 43–4, 58–9,
    65, 93, 169
  according to Marx, 58, 64
sexuality
  according to Marcuse, 6–7
  genital sexuality, 113, 115, 117
  polymorphous sexuality, 115, 116
  as utopian consequence of Marcuse's
    concept of revolution, 115–18
Simondon, Gilbert, 181
socialism
  argument for, 211
  aspirations of, 90
  Marcuse's vision of, 224
  as potentiality of capitalism, xv
social networking, xi, 215
social potentialities, xv, 115, 120
social theory
  according to Marx, 121
  from philosophy to, 88–91
sociological moments, in Marcuse's
    critique of technology, 140–7

"Some Implications of Technology"
    (Marcuse), 160
species-being, 42, 43, 44, 54, 65, 92
Stengers, Isabelle, 199
subjective reason, 174
subject-object unity, xvi
substantive rationality, 144
substantive universals, 161, 162, 163, 202
surveillance, growing fear of, xi

T

Tansley, Arthur, 205
technē, 63, 95, 160, 176, 193, 219
technical reason, 135, 145, 146, 147, 160,
    165, 176, 177
technological rationality, xv, 133–5, 141,
    142, 145, 149, 155, 163, 164, 174
technology
    according to Heidegger, 135, 149, 150,
        151, 152, 153, 166, 194–5
    according to Marcuse, 11, 125–6
    as biased toward domination, 136–7
    bias of, 137–40
    under capitalism, xvi
    as disclosing nature in two forms, 169
    gender and racial bias of, 188
    Marcuse's critique of, 131–65
    merger of with art, 182
    neutrality of, 135–7
    as not fundamentally different from
        science, 152
    technological aggression and violence,
        125
    transformation of, 224
technoscience, 188, 190, 197–200, 215
technosystem, foundations of, 186
teleology, 62, 170
thanatos (death instinct), 111, 121, 191, 220
thing-in-itself, 19, 38
Thompson, Michael J., xi
transcending potentialities, 164
translation, successor science and, 182–6,
    187

Trump, Donald, 107, 215
two-dimensional ontology, 84–7

U

Uexküll, Jakob von, 52, 208
Umgebung, 52
Umwelt, 52, 54
underground press, 9
UNESCO, 3, 4, 5
University of California, San Diego
    (UCSD), Marcuse at, 1, 2–3, 29, 43,
    92
US Food and Drug Administration, 203
utopian aspirations/visions, x, xvi, 7, 13,
    78, 109, 127, 128, 149, 174, 221
utopian consequences of Marcuse's
    concept of revolution, 115–24
utopian realization, xv, 83

V

values, according to Marcuse, 100–1
"Values in Computing" (seminar),
    199n72
Veblen, Thorstein, 140
Vietnam, war in, 1, 2, 4, 7, 131n1
Vorhaben (having in advance), 158

W

water crisis (2014), 201–2
Weber, Max, 135, 142, 143, 144, 145, 146,
    157, 165, 197, 198
Wesen (being or essence), 28
Whitebook, Joel, 127
working class, 4, 29, 79, 112, 113, 143. *See
    also* proletariat
world, concept of according to Heidegger,
    47–56, 75, 86, 208
world-constitution, xvii, 42, 61–8, 75
worldhood, xiii, 23, 48, 52, 55, 123

Z

Žižek, Slavoj, 87
Zu-Seins, 42